Praise for Elayne Bennett and *Daughters in Danger*

In her widely admired Best Friends and Best Men programs, Elayne Bennett has achieved remarkable success in helping inner-city boys and girls support each other in avoiding sex, drugs, and drinking and in building a strong character and positive future. In *Daughters in Danger*, a personal and passionate call to action, she lays bare the cultural roots of our current scourge of dating violence and sexual assault and spells out what all of us—parents, schools, universities, and young people themselves—must do to become part of the solution instead of part of the problem.

—THOMAS LICKONA, PROFESSOR OF EDUCATION
EMERITUS, STATE UNIVERSITY OF NEW YORK AT
CORTLAND; AUTHOR, *CHARACTER MATTERS*

There is no higher calling than protecting America's children. In *Daughter's in Danger* Elayne Bennett does just that in a vivid way.

—BILL O'REILLY, ANCHOR, FOX NEWS CHANNEL

Elayne Bennett has done more to improve the lives of young girls and boys in America—particularly those from poor neighborhoods—than anyone in America. Best Friends and Best Men have provided practical guidance about avoiding pitfalls like early sexuality, drug use, and alcohol abuse. Both programs go far beyond abstinence education, offering life coaching, a caring community, and college scholarships. These programs don't just warn, they inspire. The light Bennett kindles illuminates whole communities.

—MONA CHAREN, SYNDICATED COLUMNIST

daughters in danger

helping our girls thrive in today's culture

daughters in danger

ELAYNE BENNETT

NELSON
BOOKS

An Imprint of Thomas Nelson

To all the Best Friends and Diamond Girls everywhere.
You enriched my life immeasurably.

Published in Nashville, Tennessee, by Nelson Books, an imprint of Thomas Nelson. Nelson Books and Thomas Nelson are registered trademarks of HarperCollins Christian Publishing, Inc.

Thomas Nelson, Inc., titles may be purchased in bulk for educational, business, fund-raising, or sales promotional use. For information, please e-mail SpecialMarkets@ThomasNelson.com.

Scripture quotations are taken from the Holy Bible, New International Version®, NIV®. Copyright © 1973, 1978, 1984, 2011 by Biblica, Inc.™ Used by permission of Zondervan. All rights reserved worldwide. www.zondervan.com

Library of Congress Control Number: 2013930492

Printed in the United States of America

13 14 15 16 RRD 6 5 4 3 2 1

Contents

Foreword

America has a brilliantly kept secret: our teenage daughters (and sons) are living in the midst of an *epidemic* which threatens their physical, sexual, emotional, and mental health every day. No one can see it because it hides behind smiles and clothing. Even many who are infected don't know it because the majority of the time it has no symptoms. What is this epidemic? It is the epidemic of sexually transmitted infections among our youth. According to the Centers for Disease Control and Prevention, over 20 million Americans contract a *new* infection every year and almost half of those infections are in our young people. The fact that most Americans don't know about it poses a serious problem, because we can't fix a problem we don't see.

The great irony, however, is the fact that while we live with this epidemic, we allow the aggressive and unparalleled use of sex in the marketing of products to our children. Every day our daughters are barraged with sexual messages through music, clothing stores, computers, in movie theaters, and on television. Our daughters learn through the constant stream of these messages that their identities and values stem from being sexy to boys (and other girls) from the time they are in elementary school through college. As adults, we see the same sexual messages and are bothered, but dismiss our discomfort. We rationalize that free speech is important, and furthermore, we convince ourselves that sexually charged messages aren't going to change our daughters' behaviors. How wrong we are.

In *Daughters in Danger,* Elayne Bennett brilliantly traces the roots of this sexualization of our daughters. She describes how well-intentioned feminism paved the way for the degradation of women (particularly young girls) and then meticulously elucidates the fallout. With unnerving clarity, she educates us about the price that our daughters are paying and substantiates her teaching with solid research. She exposes the disturbingly high rates of sexual and physical assaults young women endure on even the most prestigious college campuses. She discusses the disintegration of morality and teaches us why our girls suffer from unacceptably high rates of low self-esteem. As you read *Daughters in Danger,* prepare yourself to be disturbed. The hard part in knowing the truths that Bennett outlines is that they hurt. But this is a time when parents, educators, and physicians must hurt; because our daughters need our help and the only way we are motivated to act is to be shaken by the real dangers they face.

Physicians and medical organizations have not adequately educated our young girls because many believe that the answers for those who may be sexually active is to give them birth control and condoms. They know that this is not the best answer, but physicians live with a bias. Many feel that they are dealing with a runaway train. They perceive that all teens will be sexually active because of the highly charged sexual culture impacting teens. And while physicians *know* that their teen patients face serious health dangers if they have sex, they feel that they have little influence over helping their patients. So, many physicians, like sex educators, simply opt for damage control. That is, they teach our daughters to make sure they insist their boyfriends use condoms.

Politicians don't let the secret out because having a platform promoting abstinence from sex, drugs, and alcohol garners very few votes. Furthermore, companies earn billions of dollars using sex to sell their products and any politician who stood up to these giants—the movie industry, clothing companies, and the magazine industry—and told them to stop using sex to entice our kids to use their products would lose the support of those companies. Besides, supporting abstinence makes politicians appear prudish, outdated, and fanatical. The irony is that if a politician spoke out to companies who sexualize our daughters they would be anything but those things. It is the politicians who support Planned Parenthood, who push condom use on kids, who are *really* medically outdated. According to the NIH, condoms don't do a good enough job against preventing STIs in kids. (You can read about this online under NIH condom report.) But politicians don't know that.

Parents, unfortunately, remain in the dark as well. We are busy raising our kids and trying to figure out which schools our kids should attend, what age they must be to have a cell phone, and how to get them motivated to study. We are so overwhelmed with the choices we face in parenting that paying attention to the very real, but ugly dangers our daughters face is easy to overlook. We don't want to know how tough the world can be for our daughters, so we subconsciously avoid looking. And many parents erroneously believe that we have little influence over our daughters' behaviors. Many believe that when our daughters hit their teen years, we lose them. We are taught that since peers influence their decisions more than we do, we must simply hover in the background and wait until the teen years pass. When they are older, we are taught, our daughters might want to listen to what we have to say. So we stay silent on the important issues our daughters face because we believe what we hear. The truth is, however, that parents (or parent surrogates) hold all of the power in our daughters' lives.

It's time to let this secret out because it holds hands with other dangerous influences such as drinking and drug use. Girls who drink alcohol are more likely to have sex and vice versa. And daughters who use drugs are more likely to be out of control and make bad decisions. And the decisions they make during the tender teen years could affect them for the rest of their lives. The time for us to teach our daughters that they *do* have a choice over whether or not to be sexually active, take drugs or drink alcohol is far overdue. We must realize that while many of us thought that we had a choice about these things when we were teens, our daughters don't believe they have a choice. As one of my young patients recently told me after she went to prom, "Sex is just one of those things that you have to get over with before you finish high school."

How sad that many bright young women like my patient feel they have no choice regarding whether or not to have sex, drink or take drugs. It's time that we give them back those choices.

And here's the great news: we know how to do this successfully. Bennett has shown us the way with her highly successful Best Friends program. If you think you can't have influence over your daughter and the decisions she makes, think again. In the pages that follow, you will learn things you never knew about your daughter's well being. You will learn where the real influence over your daughter's decisions lie—in you. Best of all, you will learn everything you need to know to use your influence to change the course of your daughter's life.

Elayne Bennett's book may be one of the most important in the twenty-first century because most adults, even those who have dedicated their lives to helping young women, simply don't know the research. As one who has worked to champion young women for twenty-five years, I can attest to this truth. The data on the effect of sex in media on our daughters, the epidemic of sexually transmitted infections among them, and how the disintegration of morality harms our daughters is present but hidden because it is truth that no one wants to see.

The impact of *Daughters in Danger*, however, does not end with the elucidation of good research. Most important, it provides answers. Because Bennett has so successfully helped young women avoid high risk behaviors through her Best Friends program, she has the experience and credibility to teach others how to do the same. She knows how to help young women from all socioeconomic and racial backgrounds succeed in life.

Whether you are a mother, father, politician, physician, educator or invested friend of a young woman, *Daughters in Danger* is a book that you must not only read, but put into action. It will help you understand what our daughters face and then give you the tools to help them. I am personally grateful for this book because it is long overdue. Our daughters face dangers which threaten to crush their very souls and we cannot stand on the sidelines and shake our heads in wonder any longer. The daughter or young girl you care about needs your help and mine and she is waiting. So let's get to it.

Meg Meeker, MD

Preface

Many years back, while on staff at the Georgetown University Child Development Center, I had a startling reality check when a twelve-year-old girl brought her baby in for evaluation. This little girl had absolutely no sense of what motherhood entailed. Her own mother had cheated her out of a childhood, so she had never been mothered herself. Now, this new baby daughter had as little hope as the adolescent mother did. She seemed destined to be still another victim of the sad cycle of young, unwed motherhood.

It dawned on me then that we all have a responsibility not just to our own daughters but to all daughters everywhere. As you will see in the pages ahead, some girls enter this world with only a sliver of hope, and others with an abundance, but they all run risks that people of my generation scarcely knew. To neglect to care for our young girls and to neglect to teach them how to avoid risks, I believe, is to be an unwitting participant in a preventable societal tragedy.

Twenty-five years ago, I developed a model for a program that came to be called "Best Friends." Not everyone was appreciative or supportive. When I presented the program model to a group of experts at the US Department of Education, it was met with skepticism. These experts had no hesitation about telling the wife of the secretary of education that I should stay in my "own zip code."

An imposing female PhD tried particularly hard to burst my bubble. "Do not try to take this program to the inner city," she told me. "Those girls are not going to listen to you. They will not relate to you." I was initially taken aback. I presumed the experts must know what they were talking about. After all, they had completed their doctorates, and I had not.

In the back of the room, however, Pauline Hamlette, the statuesque and commanding principal of Amidon Elementary School in Washington, DC, stood up and said, "Mrs. Bennett has volunteered in my classrooms and taught poetry. I have seen her with my students. I want to say that children don't care what color you are; they just want to know if you really care about them. Mrs. Bennett really cares about these students. I want this program next year for my sixth grade class."

With those words, Pauline effectively silenced the naysayers and opened the door to the DC Public Schools. Little did I know then that the Best Friends program, in the words of one hopeful grandmother, would "spread like the measles"! Over the next twenty-five years, nearly thirty thousand girls in fifteen cities in our school-based character education program would embrace the message of self-respect through self-control.

As a strong believer in the need to validate the effectiveness of programs within our schools, I designed a pre- and post-program measurement to determine our impact on participants. The data, first processed by the highly regarded Nick Zill at Westat Inc. and later by Bruno Anthony at Georgetown University, demonstrated what I dared to hope: adolescent girls would listen to, agree with, and share with their friends the message of self-control in the risky behaviors of sex, drugs, and alcohol when that message was presented by a trained instructor in the Best Friends program model and curriculum.

In fact, Dr. Anthony reported that the Georgetown analysis of our data validated our name, Best Friends. Students in our program were significantly more likely to help their friends make a decision regarding sex, and that decision was to wait. The Best Friends model also included a well-designed fitness and nutrition program, a feature scarcely heard of in the 1990s. This component, which involved aerobic dance workouts and our lively theme song and dance, would have made Michelle Obama proud.

Building on our success with adolescent girls, we launched the Best Men program in 2000 with equally gratifying results. Among students who were sexually active prior to program entry, a significant number of male students chose to cease that behavior by the end of the year. The data showed equally dramatic results with drug and alcohol use.

Unfortunately, politics intervened after the 2008 election. The Obama administration threw the proverbial baby out with the bathwater when it instructed the US Department of Health and Human Services to end the Community-Based Abstinence Education Program and denied the Best Friends Foundation, and others like it, the remaining three years of its grant. In doing so, HHS officials had to ignore some powerful evidence, including an article in the peer-reviewed journal *Adolescent & Family Health*, titled "Can Abstinence Work? An Analysis of the Best Friends Program," by Robert Lerner, a University of Chicago PhD.[1] His wife, Althea Nagai, also a PhD from Chicago, worked diligently with me to carry on Lerner's research after his untimely death.

These same officials also had to ignore an eye-opening study by Dr. John B. Jemmott, a brilliant African American Harvard PhD and the Kenneth B. Clark Professor of Communications at the Annenberg School for Communications and professor of communication in psychiatry at the University of Pennsylvania. His wife, Loretta S. Jemmott, PhD, RN, coauthored the journal article accepted by the *Archives of Pediatrics and Adolescent Medicine*.[2] This methodologically sound study demonstrated the significant effectiveness of abstinence-only education in comparison to abstinence-plus and contraception-only education in delaying sexual activity among middle school, inner-city students. Nevertheless, even though it was funded by the National Institute of Mental Health, the study ran afoul of proponents of public school health clinics who advocate dispensing contraception for middle school students. These advocates had regained power after the 2008 election: the Sexuality Information and Education Council in the United States (SIECUS), Planned Parenthood, the National Abortion Rights Action League (NARAL), and the National Organization for Women (NOW). They were determined to defund all risk-avoidance (abstinence education) programs for schoolchildren and to ridicule any study that proved their value.

This all seemed very strange to me. The government never set aside more than $150 million for abstinence programs, compared to the $4 billion-plus for contraception services. Why, I wondered, did the contraception lobby want to eliminate abstinence education for those students whose parents gave their permission? It seemed to me there could have been a peaceful coexistence for parents and students who wanted options. Instead, we faced a hateful and subversive campaign by the extremists who had the new president's ear.

Sadly, the extremists prevailed even though national polls showed that parents wanted their children to receive the message that sex is not appropriate for school-age children. A recently released survey by the National Campaign to Prevent Teen and Unplanned Pregnancy stated that nearly nine in ten young people surveyed said it would be much easier for teens to delay sexual activity and avoid pregnancy if they were able to have more open, honest conversations about these topics with their parents. What is more, our own internal polls showed support among students for the parents' position. Some 87 percent of Best Friends Diamond Girl and 72 percent of Best Men Leadership students stated they wanted to wait until marriage to have sex. In a recent publication, *With One Voice 2012*, of the National Campaign to Prevent Teen and Unplanned Pregnancy, a significant number of sexually active teens—67 percent of girls and 53 percent of boys—wished they had waited to have sex.[3]

What they are waiting for, ideally, is marriage. In our internal survey, 92 percent of female students volunteered that they hoped to be married someday. For our male students, the figure was 95 percent. These numbers, especially for the boys, shock educators and parents, who typically expect them to be much lower. One has to wonder how contraceptive-only sex education programs support youth who would like to postpone sex.

Programs like these may actually put our daughters in danger. By presenting contraception only in sex education for adolescents, they open a Pandora's box of problems—pregnancy, STDs, sexual abuse, dating violence, and traumatizing heartbreak among them. When the assumption is that all students are engaging in sex and when the focus is on protecting students from pregnancy or disease, who is there to protect our daughters from the physical trauma and emotional turmoil of unwanted sex? Who is there to support the young boy or girl who wishes not to engage in sexual activity?

In fact in 2011 David Brown of the *Washington Post* wrote that the National Survey of Family Growth found that among 15- to 24- year-olds, 29 percent of females and 27 percent of males reported no sexual contact with another person ever—up from the 22 percent of both sexes when the survey was last conducted in 2002. The uptick in abstinence, Brown wrote, "is one of many revealing facts arising from structured interviews with a random sample of 13,495 Americans, ages 15 to 44, that were done from 2006 to 2008."[4] Brown also quotes Bill Albert, chief program officer of the National Campaign to Prevent Teen and Unplanned Pregnancy, "Many, many young people have been very receptive to the message of delaying sexual activity. There's no doubt about it."[5] Why has most all federal funding for abstinence programs in middle and high school been eliminated?

The young people in our program who have not completely succumbed to today's culture overwhelmingly want to do the right thing. Why would these students—almost all from single-parent households—see marriage as something they wanted in their future? I have to believe that hope springs eternal. Despite media messages to the contrary, young people see marriage as a positive and good thing and have not become as jaded as the rest of our society. It is for them and their parents and educators that I have written this book. If the media refuse to tell the true story of the dreams our daughters and sons harbor and the danger they face if they stifle those dreams in an effort to fit in today's culture, someone has to. This is my humble attempt to do that.

Life in the Fast Lane

On Saturday, May 3, 2010, having made many wrong turns, I got lost in the morass of Washington, DC's one-way streets, finally arriving breathless at a public school. This was an important day, as I knew John Arnold, a talented producer working pro bono, would be waiting for me. We were to make a video that would highlight the benefits of the Best Friends program I had founded a quarter century ago.

On this day I was to teach a class to our teenage leadership group on dating-violence prevention. I was anxious that we get the very best shots so we could send the right message. As the videographer adjusted the lighting and the backdrop, I began to position students and ask questions.

It was a lively session that made me aware just how real the problem of dating violence is for inner-city students. When the students began to name names, it became clear that they were not talking theoretically, but in fact were speaking about couples in their school who were locked in abusive relationships.

The next morning, Sunday, I got a literal wake-up call from my son. What he told me made me realize as I never had before that the problem I had addressed on Saturday was not just an inner-city problem. It was a national problem. Local lacrosse star George Huguely had just been arrested for the suspected killing of his girlfriend, Yeardley Love. Later in the day, as the details started tumbling out from all sides, I had to ask myself the same questions I had asked the teenagers the day before: *What did anyone do to try to stop this? What did the victim's friends and family know? Why did this lovely young woman have to die? Why did this young man, whose family is a productive part of our community, fail to receive the clinical help he so desperately needed?*

The more I read in the popular press, the less I felt I knew. The reading I had done over the years in adolescent psychology also failed to help me find my way to an answer. What I began to see is that no matter how insightful these articles and books were, several of which I will cite in this work, almost all of them accept our culture as a given and ask girls, their parents, and their schools to accommodate themselves to it as best they can.

By "culture" I mean those large external forces—the media, ethos, trends, customs, habits, and history—that shape all of us, some of us more than others. As most authorities in adolescent behavior will concede, this culture has grown more dangerous for our daughters over the years. As I will explain in detail in the coming chapters, girls today are more at risk, from increasingly diverse threats, than their parents or their grandparents were.

Rather than merely ask our daughters and their parents to accept the prevailing culture as it is and adapt to it, I set out to discover what realistic steps we could take collectively to stand up to our culture. What follows is a description of the problems we face and a series of recommendations for how we can address them—on a personal level, a policy level, and even on a protest level. Our daughters are surely worth the fight.

Warning Signs

Yeardley Love was by all accounts a lovely young woman who did not in any way deserve the cruel fate she suffered. But like so many young women, she inhabited an uncertain world—one that undermines girls and damages their souls, and that long ago, in many quarters at least, sacrificed common sense and decency for ideologically driven cultural "change."

Girls today face a dynamic range of threats, some of them physical and many more emotional and spiritual. In our oversexualized culture, our girls are set adrift in a sea of conflicting messages about their worth, their needs and desires, and their present and future. Despite a wealth of new laws and artificial protections, girls are suffering from anxiety, sexually transmitted diseases, eating disorders, bullying, sexual harassment, drug abuse, alcoholism, sexual pressure, dating violence, and a host of other stressors that have caught their parents unaware. For political reasons, school authorities may refuse to even acknowledge some of the risks our girls are running. In Yeardley's case, no one seemed to recognize the risk at all.

The same culture that is victimizing girls has transformed some of our sons from our daughters' protectors to our daughters' predators. A radically feminized educational establishment, a welfare system that punishes responsible fatherhood, and an ongoing sexual revolution that encourages the most primal of male behavior have possibly put our sons at even more long-term risk than our daughters. If radical feminists choose to fault our sons for their very maleness, I would choose to fault these progressive feminists for their very blindness. As shall be seen, these women and their male enablers are part of the problem, not the solution.

....

On the night of October 17, 2009, Morgan Harrington seemed blithely unaware of any risk as she attended a Metallica concert with her friends at an arena on campus of the University of Virginia. For the record, Metallica is one of the "Big Four" of thrash metal bands, along with the aptly named Megadeth, Anthrax, and Slayer.[1]

When Morgan stepped outside, she was barred from reentry, as is the policy at most such concerts. Alone, vulnerable, and away from home, Morgan disappeared into the night. Her bones were discovered three months later in a rural area ten miles from campus. The killer remains at large. The female students quickly rationalized why what happened to Morgan, a Virginia Tech student, could not happen to them and went back about their business.[2]

The students should have paid more attention. Unfortunately, there exists a false sense of security in America's schools and colleges. The horrible crimes are the ones that get attention. But every day, a hundred times a day, young women are being bullied, abused, and humiliated in ways unique to our time and place. Through my own experience with the Best Friends Foundation, I have gained insight into how we can reverse this trend, but to do so we must first acknowledge what the trend is.

Teammates

Yeardley Love's great passion was the challenging, fast-paced game of lacrosse. With an all-American uncle and encouraging father, Yeardley began playing at the age of five. When her deeply loved father died, the heartbroken fifteen-year-old placed a lacrosse ball in his casket.

As a player, Yeardley compensated for her lack of size with an excess of spunk and dedication, virtues recognized by the coaches at the University of Virginia who recruited her to play there. She prophetically described her recruitment as "the happiest and proudest moment that I will probably ever experience."[3]

For all of her athletic skills, however, Yeardley was not a superwoman—nothing like it. She weighed little more than half as much as the man whose violence may have led to her death, George Wesley Huguely V. She was nearly a foot shorter, but she was much more vulnerable in another way that would ultimately spell her demise; that is, the lesser resilience of her head. Comparing the male skull and brain to the female's, says clinical neuropsychologist Dr. Joseph Bleiberg, is "like comparing an SUV and a VW bug. The same level of impact is not going to cause the same level of damage."[4]

Yet, like coeds on just about all American campuses—presumed sanctuaries with no need of fathers, brothers, or other male protectors—she was somehow thought to be physically equal to men. "Yeardley was nothing if not strong," wrote Amber Hunt in her thoughtful book on the subject, *All-American Murder.*[5] Left to her own devices, however, Yeardley was not nearly strong enough.

Emilie Surrusco, who grew up much as Love did and almost died in the same way, observed knowingly in a *Washington Post* editorial,

> As young girls, we were told we could own the world. What we never learned was what to do if, after we'd done everything right, the ability to control our own future was slowly, surely and deliberately taken away.[6]

At the time of this editorial, Yeardley Love's future had already been taken away.

On the surface, Huguely had as much going for him as Love did. He, too, came from a wealthy family. His father was a real estate entrepreneur; his mother, a former model. He was a star quarterback at his prep school and a star lacrosse player. Like Love, he was good-looking, well liked, and a good student. In fact, he majored in anthropology, which is a challenging course of study. Hunt described what her fellow scribes learned in researching his background, "The most they uncovered was an idyllic childhood marred slightly by divorce."[7]

Huguely's parents divorced when he was in the fifth grade. For Hunt and others in the media, that was an incidental detail. But perhaps not. It appears that even though they were close, Huguely and his father had a great deal of tension.

In one telling incident in Florida, a little more than a year before

Love's murder, Huguely and his father got into a shouting match aboard the family boat. The police would later report "lots of yelling and screaming" but no physical violence.[8] Huguely wanted to return to the beach. His father did not. When Huguely jumped overboard, two miles from shore, to swim back his father alerted the authorities.

On the morning of Yeardley's death, Huguely and his father played golf together. Reportedly, once again, all did not go well between them. They argued passionately and were asked to leave the golf course. Huguely was likely drunk before he left the golf course.

Like too many young men his age, Huguely was growing up in a milieu much coarser and more violent than even our nation's seemingly jaded baby boomer parents might suspect. For males his age, many of whom have given up reading books altogether, the only book some have read of their own volition is University of Chicago and Duke Law School grad Tucker Max's nihilistic mega–best seller, *I Hope They Serve Beer in Hell.* This book is worth reading for those who worry about the future. In it, Max writes about his youthful, drunken sexual orgies in mind-numbing detail.

As cruel and perverse as Max may have been—he professes now to have changed his ways (we shall see)—he serves as a highly observant guide to a side of the culture that girls on many college campuses have had to confront on a daily basis. Wrote Max after humiliating one of his sexual conquests, "I was only like 23 when it happened: what did you expect from me? Compassion? Caring?"[9] With good reason, female students have protested his campus appearances, claiming that his writing "promote[s] a culture of rape."[10]

Like Max, who boasts of an encounter with a Charlottesville policeman near the UVA campus, Huguely had at least one drunken confrontation with the police. A year before Love's murder, Huguely got aggressive with a female police officer in Lexington, Virginia. There, he resisted arrest for public intoxication and had to be tasered into submission. "He was by far the most rude, most hateful, and most combative college kid I ever dealt with," the officer would tell reporters after Love's murder.[11] But word of his arrest for public drunkenness and resisting arrest never got back to the authorities at the University of Virginia. And in Tucker Max's universe, this incident would have been a big joke.

A few months later, Huguely punched a sleeping teammate to the point of concussion after seeing him with Love. A year later, at a party, Huguely pulled Love on top of him on a bed at a party and put her in a chokehold. A lacrosse player from another university heard her cry for help and intervened.

Love returned to her apartment shaken and scared. Her roommate, Caitlin Whiteley, had never seen her so disturbed. "She was hysterical," Whiteley would later testify. "She was crying and physically shaking and upset."[12] When Whiteley later confronted Huguely, he expressed his anger that Love had told her roommates. Sadly, neither Whitely nor Love's other roommates ever discussed this attack with their coach or a counselor or sought help for Love or Huguely. One wonders if they were afraid of repercussions for their teams, or perhaps for themselves. They could not see where all this could possibly lead.

No-Man's-Land

Although the campus hookup culture discourages lasting attachments and encourages equal sexual freedom for men and women, human nature rebels against the artificiality of it all. Huguely was no more capable than Othello of controlling his jealousy. Similarly, Love, like almost all young women, was instinctively possessive. As William Congreve reminded us more than three centuries ago, "Heaven has no rage like love to hatred turned / Nor hell a fury like a woman scorned."[13]

Not much has changed in the centuries since. After the choking incident, when Love learned that Huguely had been seeing another woman, she stormed over to his apartment and protested vigorously, hitting him with her purse. She reportedly had been drinking beforehand.

Alexandra Petri, writing for the *Washington Post*, accurately described the college campus as a "no-man's land in which every-one wants to have fun without consequence. Where people are just mature enough to act immaturely."[14] This time, however, the "fun" had consequences.

Days before the murder, Huguely learned that Love was seeing a lacrosse player from another university and e-mailed her, "I should have killed you." Social media, including texting and e-mails in Huguely's case, allowed him to go cyber with his stalking. What some call "textual harassment" is now, according to dating violence authority Jill Murray, "part and parcel of every abusive dating relationship."[15] This harass-ment goes unreported and unaddressed, as "sexting" and texting are a major part of social communication among young people today.

....

In the early morning hours of Monday, May 3, a drunken and despon-dent Huguely entered Love's apartment uninvited. Her roommate had left the front door unlocked, as is a common practice in off campus housing today. An angry Love told him to leave, walked into her bed-room, and locked the door. Enraged, Huguely punched a hole in the door, reached in, and unlocked it. According to Huguely's testimony, video-taped by the police immediately after the incident, Yeardley hit her own head against the wall as she pleaded with him to go away. But he also admitted to shaking her "a little" and grabbing her neck before they "wrestled to the ground." Then, after tossing her back on the bed, he left her bleeding and, in his own words, "flopping like a fish out of water."[16]

As he left the apartment, Huguely had enough wits about him to take Love's laptop, but not enough to understand the consequences of his actions. He went back to his place, texted another girl to meet him, drank some more, and went to bed.

When Whiteley and a male friend returned to the apartment some-time later, they found Yeardley unresponsive. This being a university coed in 2010, they naturally assumed she had suffered an alcohol overdose, and shared that assumption with a 911 dispatcher. In fact, Yeardley was drunk at the time of her death. She had been drinking all day. Her blood alcohol level was nearly twice the legal limit for driving. She also took Adderall, a drug legally prescribed for her ADHD. Adderall is often abused by young people in concert with alcohol, and in the trial to come, Huguely's attorneys would attempt to link Love's death to the drug. However, there was no evidence that Yeardley had taken more than her daily dose.

The 911 dispatcher told Whiteley's friend to pull Yeardley off the bed and administer CPR. He later testified that when he tried, he heard a crack that he thought came from Love's back, though it could have been her neck. He then laid her on the floor but could not understand how to give her CPR because he was intoxicated from a long night of drinking.

········

According to the University of Virginia substance abuse prevention center, 71 percent of UVA students drink on a typical Saturday night, with 20 percent consuming more than six standard drinks—a phenomenon not at all unique to UVA. And worse, wrote Petri, "colleges around the country are playing the part of those parents who host drinking parties. 'Better here,' they tell themselves, watching another car pull onto the lawn. 'Better here where we can see them.'"[17]

University officials long ago abandoned any genuine "in loco parentis" policies, due in part to liability concerns. Get drunk, as Huguely did on a pathological basis, get arrested for public intoxication, resist arrest, abuse a girlfriend, slug teammates, shout obscenities, and no one notices or intervenes. Huguely's lacrosse coaches, for sure, did not notice or were not told.

Among the more lackluster responses by the academic community to the cultural disintegration within their domain is a document known as the "Amethyst Initiative." According to the Initiative's website, the name amethyst was selected because the gem "was thought to be an antidote to the negative effects of intoxication." Thus it seemed an appropriate symbol for a program that "aims to encourage moderation and responsibility as an alternative to the drunkenness and reckless decisions about alcohol that mark the experience of many young Americans."[18]

How to solve the problem? The 136 university administrators who have signed the Initiative support an informed and dispassionate public debate over the effects of the twenty-one-year-old drinking age. That, I am afraid, is the major thrust of the Amethyst Initiative. Say these administrators, presumably with a straight face, "Alcohol education that mandates abstinence as the only legal option has not resulted in significant constructive behavioral change among our students." The administrators further worry that by being compelled to use fake IDs, students "make ethical compromises that erode respect for the law."[19] Therefore, they say, their goal is to lower the drinking age. This kind of change may lower the arrest rate, but let's face it: the issue here is not at what age students drink but rather how much they drink. Lowering the age limit will not affect that in any positive way. What is much more likely to affect how much students drink is character and culture—in particular, students' self-control and the prevailing campus environment regarding binge drinking.

Good Sportsmanship

Although loved and well respected, "absolutely the epitome of the University of Virginia student," as one university official eulogized her,[20] Yeardley Love was not immune to the siren song of her culture, a culture shaped more by the socialization on campus she inhabited than by the faith that nurtured her.

Yeardley had graduated from Notre Dame Preparatory School, a Catholic high school whose mission is to "prepare women of moral integrity to become more loving, just and wise."[21] In the lacrosse culture, however, the mission is to win. The virtues Yeardley learned, as cited in a tribute to her coach, were "good sportsmanship and working together as a team."[22] These are wholesome enough as far as they go, but they had little relevance when it came to making life decisions or choosing romantic partners.

Much has been made of campus lacrosse culture, some of it unfair. The game itself, which was first created by Native Americans, has a noble history. I have seen many a game, as both my sons played in high school and one in college. In addition to keeping young people fit, lacrosse helps them develop tenacity, teamwork, fortitude, and a host of other virtues.

The very notion of team loyalty may have discouraged Huguely's peers, male and female, from talking to his coaches or even reining him in. It may have also discouraged Love from reporting his increasingly aberrant behavior, which had escalated to abusive acts. It has been reported that when Love went home the weekend before her death, she confided in her mother, Sharon Love, that George was becoming more aggressive. Sharon asked her daughter if she wanted her to do something. Yeardley replied that she could "handle it."

She could not. Neither could Huguely control himself. Instead, they both focused on their studies, lacrosse practice, games, and their graduation as the end of the season approached. Nothing further was done until Yeardley's death. In February 2012, a Charlottesville jury convicted Huguely of second-degree murder.

Crash Into Me

In the wake of Yeardley's death, university authorities made all the correctives you would expect them to make. Yeardley's needless death called to mind the famous saying of eighteenth-century Anglo-Irish statesman Edmund Burke, "Society cannot exist unless a controlling power upon will and appetite be placed somewhere, and the less of it there is within, the more there is without."[23] The "controlling power within" that Burke refers to is the power of character, the inner strengths that help guide and govern conduct. The power "without" is the influence of the external environment. When character is weak, environmental controls have to be strong enough to make up for that deficiency. It seems that many universities today have concentrated their efforts on the easy part, the "without."

Yeardley Love could have died the way she did on a hundred other campuses. In fact, UVA is an extraordinary academic institution, among the handful of truly stellar state universities in America. Its campus culture, however, is not extraordinary. It is much too similar to that of most other large universities.

Most universities find it very difficult to look within. This Liz Seccuro learned in the most brutal of ways twenty-five years before Love died. As Liz has related in her powerful memoir, *Crash into Me: A Survivor's Search for Justice,* she overrode the loving cautions of her parents and ventured alone to Charlottesville, 350 miles from her suburban New York City home. A bright, eager, virginal seventeen-year-old freshman in 1984, she loved UVA's beautiful campus—or the "grounds" as they are known locally—from the moment she arrived.

On a Thursday night in October of that first year, she reluctantly accompanied a male friend who needed her for moral support in his rush activities, and a few other friends from her dorm, to a rush party at the Phi Psi fraternity. Downstairs in the massive Georgian house, the gathering seemed as drunkenly routine as any other such fraternity party. After having one beer just to fit in, Liz, along with her friends, agreed to go on a tour of the house.

Once upstairs, the frat brothers offered the group marijuana. Liz declined and was left alone when the others went off to smoke. Some friendly brothers then approached and offered her a "house special," some greenish punch with a lime undertaste. Not wanting to seem like a "loser," Liz drank it and almost immediately began to grow disoriented. "I felt like Alice in Wonderland," recalled Liz. "Everything was in slow motion."[24]

As Liz remembered the incident, a tall, owlish-looking fellow, William Beebe by name, started imploring her to go see something in his room. When Liz resisted, Beebe got physical and yanked her toward the door. Once in the room, he grabbed her, but she managed to break free and run back to the common room, where she had been earlier. There, another frat brother picked her up and carried her back to Beebe, who ripped her clothes off and brutally raped her. She awoke the next morning wrapped in a bloody sheet, disoriented, in pain, and with almost no memory of what had happened. For Liz, the nightmare had just begun.

In the days that followed, she tried desperately to get both help and justice. When she first told a young male adviser, he said sympathetically, "You stupid, stupid girl. Why don't they tell you never ever to go upstairs at one of those houses? Why?"[25] Although he meant well in blaming the authorities for their failure to communicate risk, he also labeled Liz "stupid," as if she were somehow responsible for the horrible assault, and that humiliated her.

Beebe soon discovered that Liz was talking to the authorities. Obviously worried, he scrawled his name and phone number on her dorm room door with the threat "If you know what's good for you, you'll call me." She photographed the warning and took it to the dean of students, Robert Canevari. Although she arrived conspicuously bruised and still bleeding, Canevari discouraged her from calling the Charlottesville police, claiming that the frat house was not within their jurisdiction. He even suggested that she might want to take the issue up with the student judiciary. "We like to handle these things internally and take care of our own," the dean told her. "If it's a university problem, then there's a university solution."[26]

As it turned out, that "solution" was to sweep the crime under the rug and recommend that Liz transfer to another university if she no longer felt comfortable at the University of Virginia. Later Liz wrote,

"When a college or university tells you as they did me, 'We are review-ing our policies,' it sometimes means, 'Please do sit down, be quiet, and eventually go away.' When they say they've updated the policy, it means, 'Look here—we're doing just enough to make you sit down, be quiet, and eventually go away.'"[27]

To her credit, Liz refused to buckle and went ahead and completed her degree, but emotionally she never fully recovered—not even close. Years later, Beebe tried to reconnect with her as a way of meeting his goals in the Alcoholics Anonymous program. The contact tore open old wounds and drove Liz to seek justice in the courts. The Charlottesville police and prosecutors proved seriously helpful. As it turns out, con-trary to what Liz was told by the administration, the frat house *was* in their jurisdiction, and there was no statute of limitation on rape.

What Liz Seccuro learned in the process was more horrifying still. Beebe was the third frat brother to rape her that night. She was fully unconscious for the first two. Although Beebe would plead guilty and serve time for the rape, the fraternal brotherhood and their families protected the other guilty parties. The prosecutor could not gather enough corroborating testimony from the brotherhood, which closed ranks and invoked a "code of silence." This prevented the prosecutor from pressing any additional charges.

The ethos of the Phi Psi house did not change much over time. In February 2006, a month after Beebe was arrested and two months before he was indicted, the brothers of Phi Psi hosted none other than Tucker Max, on tour for *I Hope They Serve Beer in Hell*. Unlike most book signings, this one proved to be a drunken, daylong orgy.

"There was alcohol to be consumed and women to be exploited," said Max of a similar campus party. At this one, amid his signing duties, he managed two random hookups with sorority girls. Some of the frat boys had found their role model. "You are my god, man. I just love you," shouted one at a Tucker Max seminar.[28] The ethos created by such events, the fraternity's code of silence, and the administration's failure to take effective action after what happened to Seccuro, are all examples of how the external environment can enable irresponsible and destructive behavior.

Untold Stories

In October 2003, a Duke University coed was attacked and sexually assaulted in her own bathroom. This incident led the woman and her friends to speak out about sexual assault on campus. As the women quickly learned, most such assaults were perpetrated by fellow students, and many of these by young men known to the women in question.

One response took the form of a now three-volume online publication called *Saturday Night: Untold Stories of Sexual Assault at Duke*.[29] If the sheer number of these first-person accounts by Duke women speaks to the pervasiveness of the problem, the titles speak to the collective trauma:

"I Knew Something Was Wrong"
"I Was No Longer a Woman"
"Brought Back to That Night"
"Sexual Assault Reality"
"Sleepless Nights"
"A Girl I Didn't Know"
"The First Anniversary"
"I Go Through the Motions"
"I Only Remember"
"Slaying My Demons"
"Dear Mom"

Duke is hardly unique. The comprehensive 2007 Campus Sexual Assault Study reported that 19 percent of female undergraduates on America's campuses had experienced an assault, either attempted or completed.[30] In explaining their motives for publication at Duke, *Saturday Night*'s editors made a more serious assessment of the issue than do most administrators, including Duke president Richard Brodhead, whose signing of the Amethyst Initiative seems to be one of the few actions taken to date. "Preventing this type of sexual assault would not mean locks on bathrooms and increased security patrols," they wrote. "Rather, it would require a change in community culture and a difficult, person-by-person reckoning of personal ethics and responsibility."[31] The solution, they understood, must come from within, not without.

What even the editors fail to understand, at least in full, is that the "community culture" is more complex and corrupt than they know. In her insightful new book, *Adam and Eve After the Pill: Paradoxes of the Sexual Revolution*, Mary Eberstadt used the shorthand "Toxic U" to describe the contemporary campus as "a school of experiential learning where parents are never invited."[32]

Eberstadt has traced the toxicity to "the intersection of two trends"—casual hookups and binge drinking. The problem that young women face, Eberstadt reported, is that they are more vulnerable to the damage caused by both. In drinking, the damage is physical. In sex, it is emotional. Despite the tangible evidence, female nature, Eberstadt asserts, "is being ignored at great peril—to [the young women]."[33]

In his book *Girls on the Edge*, Dr. Leonard Sax detailed a disturbing trend line. In the 1960s, only 7 percent of girls reported having their first drink before age fifteen. Today that number approaches 25 percent. Over the last forty years, alcohol abuse among young males has remained fairly constant. Among females the abuse has increased by a factor of four. Female arrests for drunk driving have been increasing, while declining for men. Says Sax wryly, "Statistics like these give the phrase 'gender equity' a whole new meaning."[34]

One reason for the disproportionate increase in drug and alcohol use among young women is that treatment and prevention programs have historically been designed with men in mind. The National Center on Addiction and Substance Abuse (CASA), under then chairman Joseph Califano, did an exhaustive three-year study on the problem and concluded that young women have "different motivations and vulnerabilities" that need to be addressed in any effective treatment program.[35]

The CASA study argues that girls are more likely than boys to suffer from depression, eating disorders, and the aftershocks of sexual or physical abuse, all of which increase the likelihood of substance abuse. Girls are also more apt than boys to use alcohol and drugs to reduce sexual inhibitions and improve their mood. More problematic still, one drink has the effect on girls that two drinks have on boys. Concludes the report, "One-size-fits-all prevention hasn't worked—and it won't—because it doesn't recognize these differences."[36]

Koren Zailckas fit the CASA profile all too well. She was sufficiently appalled at what she had become that she quit drinking altogether at age twenty-three after sloshing her way through an undergraduate degree at Syracuse University. She was not alone. As she observed in her 2005 book, *Smashed: Story of a Drunken Girlhood*, there has been a threefold increase in the number of women who get drunk at least ten times a month. The consequences of drinking as she did include higher risks of suicide, depression, sexual assault, and a rash of liver and brain ailments. Almost as troubling as what girls suffer is what they fail to experience. Wrote Zailckas:

> I might have been forming real friendships. . . . I might have been writing stories or taking pictures. I might have been sleeping a full six hours a night, or eating three square meals a day, or taking multivitamins. I might have been learning the language of affection: how to exchange glances or trace a man's fingertips with mine. I might have been reading the top hundred books of all time.[37]

Instead of all the richness that a campus life offers, Karen spent her four years getting drunk and having cheap, unrewarding sex.

Just how unrewarding sex can be at Toxic U was unwittingly revealed by a Duke coed named Karen Owen, who compiled her on-campus sexual misadventures with thirteen athletes in a lengthy PowerPoint presentation that she e-mailed to her friends. Needless to say, it went wildly viral.[38] Although Owen apparently aspired to be the female Tucker Max, she did not succeed because of the inherent difference between men and women on the issues of sex and love, a difference that universities tend to either ignore or deny. "The overwhelming sense one gets from the thesis is of a young woman who was desperate for human connection, and who had no idea how to obtain it," wrote Caitlin Flanagan in a thoughtful piece in the *Atlantic Monthly*.[39]

I fully agree with Flanagan's assessment, but not all women do. Flanagan cited any number of them who admire what feminist author Penelope Trunk sees as Karen Owen's "self-confidence, pluck, and earning power." Adds Trunk, "[Owen] inspires me to be brave, take risks, and let my creativity get the best of me."[40] I will talk more about Owen soon enough, but the presence of women like her on college campuses and her actual lionization by elements within the feminist establishment complicate life both for young women and young men.

What happened to Yeardley Love, Liz Seccuro, and the women of Duke should never have happened. These were all tragedies and painful, collective reminders that our daughters face dangers untold. Even the most privileged live in a world that devalues them and prioritizes love and sex, needs and desires, in ways that will destroy their very hearts.

Worse, the people who regulate this world have scarcely a clue what their problems are, let alone how to solve them. *Crash into Me* came out just months after Yeardley was killed. Had the book come out earlier, Yeardley may have read it as the cautionary tale it was. "Where were the adults?" asks Petri.[41]

Writing just before Yeardley was murdered, Liz Seccuro told how the university had updated its sexual assault policy. The female dean involved in the change believed the "real" problem to be that female students were drinking too much and losing control. "There was no suggestion," wrote Liz all too prophetically, "that heavy-drinking, potentially violent male students should receive interventions."[42] Huguely and Beebe were perfect candidates for such interventions. If they had occurred earlier in their college careers, neither would have been imprisoned and bright young women would not have been brutalized. As I write this, another young woman, Alexandra Kogut, a freshman at Brockport College in upstate New York, has died at the hands of her boyfriend, a star hockey player at Utica College. The circumstances of her death sound all too familiar.[43]

Unfortunately, as a society, we shy away from intervention in all but the most superficial of instances. This is a relatively recent phenomenon, and one that needs to be addressed at its roots before it can be solved. In the following pages, I will do just that. I caution the reader that this is not a "feel-good" book. The data I present can be pretty grim. So are several of the stories I will tell. That said, we have had great success working with the girls in the Best Friends program. What we have learned can be shared. A lot of it is common sense and traditional wisdom revived, systematized, and applied. I have seen enough to be confident about the future. I think you can be too.

2.

In Loco Parentis

Two years before Yeardley Love's murder, I was equally disturbed to learn of a murder at the University of North Carolina in Chapel Hill, my alma mater. It seems that when colleges decided they would no longer operate in loco parentis, they presumed the oversight of students would somehow take care of itself. This was a terrible mistake. Parents were sending their trusting, nonjudgmental young daughters to these campuses and thinking them safe. The trial of Laurence Alvin "L. L." Lovette began just months after Yeardley Love's murder. He was accused of killing UNC student body president Eve Carson. A Morehead Scholar with a 3.9 GPA, Eve was scheduled to graduate that May with highest distinctions in biology and political science. To get a sense of the loss, I would recommend readers go to YouTube and watch the video titled "Eve Welcome Back to UNC!" In it, the brilliant and charming Phi Beta Kappa greets new and returning students to campus. "I personally invite you to come hang out with me," says the doomed young woman. "I spend a lot of time in this office, and I love spending time and meeting new people. If I can help you, please come by and let's talk."[1] Eve would tell people she had been elected on the campaign slogan "Efficiency. Vision. Everyone." The "Everyone" tag suggested a young woman who was more openhearted than her world could accommodate.

Beyond Prayer

On the final night of her life, Eve Carson attended a Tarheels basketball game at the Dean Dome, the pride of UNC, and then headed back to her off-campus house on "Friendly Lane" to complete a paper due the next day. She had much work to do for the midterm, and she was known to stay up late to do it, as I did back in the day and many coeds do at universities everywhere.

In the early morning hours, Lovette, then just seventeen, and his running mate, Demario "Rio" Atwater, both on parole, headed to the vulnerable quarters of Chapel Hill to "go rob," as Lovette described their intention. There, they walked in the unlocked door of the house Eve shared with three other students, who were not at home, abducted her, and shoved her into her Toyota Highlander. The pair forced Eve to yield her ATM PIN number, pirated several ATMs, and took her to a wooded area near the campus, where Lovette shot her four times with his pistol. Upset that the shots had failed to silence the frantic young girl fighting for her life, Atwater stood over Eve and shot her directly in the face with a shotgun.

"When I think about the voice of the students, I am a voice," Eve had told the *Daily Tarheel* just weeks before her death. "I'm a loud voice and a talkative voice. I talk a lot, and I talk to whoever will listen to me."[2] Tragically, Lovette and Atwater were not listening. According to the testimony of a friend of Lovette's, in the hour or so Eve spent in the car, she asked him to pray with her. "Before [Lovette] even shot her," the friend explained, she was saying, "'Let's pray.' She wanted them to pray together."[3] It did no good. That night at least, the killers were beyond prayers.

System Failings

Six weeks prior to Eve Carson's death, Lovette killed a Duke University graduate student from India named Abhijit Mahato, who had been studying at his off-campus apartment. In the ensuing weeks, Durham police arrested Lovette at least twice, charging him with nine different crimes ranging from breaking and entering to resisting arrest. Incredibly, after each arrest, Lovette was released on bond.

Rio Atwater was actually in violation of his parole, but his parole hearing had been canceled two days prior to Eve's murder due to a clerical error at the Durham County courthouse. The *Duke Chronicle* reported that North Carolina has one of the least appropriately funded criminal justice systems in the country.[4] If proper attention had been paid in the courts, two brilliant students would not have been robbed of their bright futures and their ability to make meaningful contributions to our society.

A jury took three hours to convict Lovette on all counts, including kidnapping and first-degree murder. He has no chance of ever being paroled. Only his age at the time of the murder spared him a death sentence. The twenty-five-year-old Atwater, having no such out, pleaded guilty to avoid the death penalty. Before leaving the courtroom, Lovette turned to his mother and pounded his fist to his heart, as if to say . . . what?[5] "Take heart"? Lovette surely had no heart when it came to taking an innocent life.

If Lovette was quickly forgotten, Eve Carson's memory lives on. More than ten thousand people turned out for her memorial at the Dean Dome. A scholarship was established in her name. Annual remembrances continue in honor of a life of much promise extinguished by unimaginable brutality.

Curiously, though, at the memorial, no mention was made of the murder of a young woman so trusting that she would leave her home unlocked. What lessons her fellow students might have learned about the risks young women face even on a street called Friendly Lane in a town as idyllic as Chapel Hill went undiscussed. Anger and outrage were discouraged.

In the days that followed Eve's murder, as happened after Yeardley Love's, town and campus authorities reviewed any number of external variables—campus lighting, safety boxes, and probation and parole procedures—in an effort to prevent such future tragedies. But in no instance I know of did anyone take a deep look at what we will examine in this book: the failure by educators to understand the difference between men and women, and the larger failure to realize that those differences can be respected only in an environment where values truly matter. Once these details are understood, institutions that have been entrusted with the care of students—most away from home for the first time—can begin to make sense out of their own mission.

The world their students inhabit is not nearly as orderly as it appears. This I learned through my own experience. As a graduate student at the University of North Carolina–Chapel Hill, I was once approached by a young man I thought was a student, as I had seen him in the pharmacy on Franklin Street several times over the course of the month.

Although taller and broader than most guys, he seemed friendly and clean-cut. When he asked if I would drop him off at his house one evening, I hesitated, but I did not want to appear overly cautious or "wimpy." So I agreed. What could possibly be wrong with helping out a fellow Carolina student?

I had left Reilly, my Sealyham Terrier, nestled in the backseat of my little Dodge Dart. We got in the front seats and took off. The fellow directed me out of town to a remote area with tobacco barns, and I soon grew uncomfortable. Still, I knew students who lived in these rustic dwellings. I squelched my qualms and kept driving.

He then directed me down a dark road. "It's right down here," he said. I turned down the road and looked to my left, where the house should have been. There was nothing there. As I looked back to the passenger side, the guy was lunging toward me.

At that very moment, Reilly let out a ferocious growl and sprang between the seats to protect me. Taken by surprise, this would-be predator jumped out of my car and ran off into the darkness. He had steered me into a dead end. So I gunned the accelerator, backed the car around, and sped home with my heart pounding all the way. As I trembled with fear, I realized that my protective dog may have saved my life.

This "graduate student" disappeared from campus. I never saw him again, anywhere. He was probably not a student, but he was definitely a danger to female students. The drugstore clerk later told me that he had asked about me—whether I had a boyfriend, if I lived near campus. Universities have long attracted predators. They sense how nonjudgmental coeds can be, and I had the same friendly, outgoing, trusting nature as Eve and Liz. Young women tend to see the good in everyone and project the safety they felt at home to their college.

I had no one to blame but myself. I regret to this day that I was too embarrassed and afraid to call the police, even at an age when I should have known better, but young women then and now walk into these situations emotionally unprepared. I will be forever grateful to God that I had a protector that night. From my own experience, I would encourage every girl to live on campus and, if not, to get a dog and good locks for her doors, and to use them consistently. Criminals are opportunists. They can sense vulnerability from a mile away.

A generation later, Chapel Hill girls faced much the same dangers I did. In May 2010, twenty-six-year-old Theodore Walker, who could also pass for a grad student, tried to abduct an eighteen-year-old coed as she jogged by a bank parking lot right next to campus in broad daylight. Happily for the young woman, the two Shelton brothers of nearby Pittsboro successfully intervened, though one was hit by Walker's car in the course of the rescue. "It's a blessing that she survived and she's got plenty more birthdays to come," said the injured brother, Joey Shelton.[6]

The Sheltons ran an additional risk here. Racial tensions were running high in Chapel Hill in May 2010. Atwater had just pleaded guilty to the kidnapping of Eve Carson. He was awaiting sentencing. Like Atwater, the Sheltons are African American. Like Eve, the coed was white. So was Walker. It would have been easy for the police or other citizens to misinterpret what was going on, but the Sheltons saw their duty and did it. The coed was grateful beyond words. Although feminists hate to admit this, women sometimes need protectors. Unfortunately, they cannot always count on finding men like the Shelton brothers.

The predator problem is obviously not unique to Chapel Hill. A young friend of mine, a graduate student at the University of South Alabama, survived a harrowing night with a seemingly respectable date gone berserk—through sheer willpower and ingenuity. When the young man, also a graduate student, locked her in his car with him and threatened to kill her, she remembered a lesson her mother, a psychiatric nurse, had taught her: don't anger the man; placate him. She quietly dialed 911 when he stepped out of the car, explained her circumstance, and left the phone on speaker. She then invited him back to her apartment for a would-be night of pleasure. He fell for it. When they got there, the police were waiting, and she rushed right to them. She also had the courage to press charges and to see justice done. In the course of the trial she discovered she was not the first woman he had preyed on. She was determined he would not terrorize another.

Young women cannot live their lives in a state of paranoia, but they should always remain alert. For starters, they cannot assume that because a young man looks respectable, he actually is. They must also mentally prepare themselves for trouble and be willing to ask for help when needed. These may seem like obvious life lessons, but for no good reason, too many educators today shy from the obvious.

Honor Codes

A little more than an hour south of Charlottesville and two hours north of Chapel Hill sits the "city of seven hills," Lynchburg, Virginia, home to Liberty University. Founded just forty years ago, Liberty is now the largest Christian university in the world. Tucker Max did not stop here on his book tour. He would not have been allowed.

At Liberty, students under twenty-one must live in the residence halls. The Code of Conduct proscribes R-rated movies and comparable video games. It prohibits alcoholic beverages, illegal drugs, even tobacco. As to dating, "All students are asked to display mature Christian behavior in social interaction"[7]—in other words, nothing public beyond holding hands. The entire code flows from the doctrinal belief that students are "reasoning moral agents . . . responsible under God for understanding and governing themselves and the world."[8]

Clearly, Liberty University is not for everyone. Many aspiring female college students would object strenuously to these restrictions and would much prefer a more secular education. Yet even institutions like Davidson College and Princeton University recognize that safety and campus cohesiveness are greatly enhanced if all students live on campus.

The University of Virginia has a Code of Honor far more celebrated than Liberty's. On the university's website, 1979 alumna Katie Couric introduces a twenty-minute video on the subject.[9] Apparently, a UVA student shot a professor in 1840, and this caused the students to evaluate their own behavior. Going forward, they vowed to "to act honorably and uphold the ideals of the community of trust." This translated into a refusal to "lie, cheat, or steal" and a willingness to report those who did. As one student in the video insists, "Cheating is unacceptable." Says another, "If someone is caught being dishonorable, they will be asked to leave." This code is one in which students understandably take pride.

It has, however, some serious shortcomings, and these Liz Seccuro learned through experience. When she reported her rape to the dean, he informed her that her rapist was no longer a threat. He had already left the university.

"Was he expelled because this violated the honor code?" Elizabeth asked.

"No," the dean replied, "he didn't violate the honor code—that is only for lying, cheating, and stealing." He had apparently left for personal reasons.

"So, if you cheat on an exam, you can get kicked out of Mr. Jefferson's Academical Village," Liz correctly surmised, "but if you rape a fellow student, you can just quietly slip away?"[10] Many college students today would be quick to mock the severity of the code of conduct at Liberty University, but in turn, Liberty students would have every right to mock the incoherence and inconsistency of the codes of conduct at most secular universities, UVA's included.

The UVA Code of Honor is far more an anachronism than Liberty's. It was created before the university allowed women, in a time and at a place where women were almost universally respected. Administrators have not adapted the code to an era in which the equality granted young women is elusive, but the abuse they suffer is all too real. Even if the university did update the code, the result would surely be politically correct and consequently unclear.

No One Watching

When I reflect on cases like these, I realize that, of course, the responsibility is in the hands of the killer or the attacker, but there are larger questions: What is the cultural milieu of the places these talented young people inhabit? What is their ethos? Where are the safeguards? What are the responsibilities of friends? Of parents? Of coaches? Of administrators?

Sharon Love, Yeardley's mother, is suing the Commonwealth of Virginia, the UVA associate and head lacrosse coaches, and the school athletic director for her daughter's death. "UVA and its employees, officers and agents had a duty to protect and keep the students safe," says the suit. It continues, "It was well known to the coaches and players of the UVA men's and women's lacrosse teams that Huguely's alcohol abuse and aggressive behavior were getting out of control, especially his obsession with Love and his threats to Love."[11]

The suit details previous incidents of reckless alcohol use and aggressive behavior and contends that Dom Starsia and other athletic officials failed to suspend Huguely from the team, refer him for substance abuse or anger management treatment, or follow university protocol for dealing with a potentially dangerous student.

Obviously, though, the university can only do so much. And if students do not report to or confide in the teachers, how are they to know?

"The point of college is to admit high school students and graduate adults," wrote Alexandra Petri. "But it is impossible to grow up in a world where no one is watching. And this is how things go wrong in a world where nothing is supposed to go wrong."[12] As tragic as murder is, each one offers us an opportunity to examine its causes. There are patterns, and we ignore them at our own risk. We all—especially families—bear the responsibility of encouraging and supporting, training and directing, loving and cherishing our daughters.

It was for this reason that I launched Best Friends, a developmentally sound program conducted in a school setting by trusted adults. Our goal is to help our girls become socially competent individuals, able to negotiate the challenges inevitably coming their way. Our training is heavily indebted to Albert Bandura, whose social learning theory contends that people learn from one another through observation, imitation, and modeling.[13] It is my belief that all youth programs should follow a developmental construct as a basis for their curriculum development.

Bandura argues that young people are capable of self-regulation, but only if they are also capable of self-evaluation. That evaluation does not take place in a vacuum. Positive behaviors need to be reinforced, and negative behaviors censured. Recent studies indicate as much. In their treatise *The Adolescent Brain: A Work in Progress*, Dr. Daniel Weinberger et al. make the case that the brain of young people into their early twenties is by no means fully formed and that they "may not always possess the cognitive workspace—the working memory—necessary for solid planning of complex behavior."[14] Parents and educators need to be reminded that young people do not complete their intellectual development until "perhaps the mid-twenties." As Sarah Brown described in the foreword of this important research document, an important reason that so-called executive functions (for example, the ability to make complex judgments, weigh alternatives, control impulses, and take the longer view) are not reliably in full effect in adolescence is that they spring from a particular area of the brain, the prefrontal cortex—which is one of the last areas of the brain to fully mature. Developmentally this age group is still in adolescence. A startling revelation is, this includes just about all college students from freshmen to seniors.[15]

Adolescents seem particularly weak in estimating probabilities and assessing risk. "At a minimum," say the authors, "the data suggest that [adolescents] need to be surrounded by adults and institutions that help them learn specific skills and appropriate adult behavior."[16] In other words, this new research validates what we have been doing for years at Best Friends—surrounding our children with care and teaching them specific skills.

I will explain more about our program and its use of Bandura's theory of providing social interaction through positive role models for youth as we proceed through the book. The cases of Yeardley Love, Eve Carson, Natasha March, and Liz Seccuro must make us question what it was exactly that our children were learning and appropriating. What should trouble us even more is that so many of our institutions, including our universities, have abandoned any serious role in the modeling process. This needs to change. To quote the fictional Linda Loman in *Death of a Salesman*, speaking not just of her salesman husband, Willy, but of all humanity, "attention must be paid."[17] Because our daughters are in danger, we must all pay attention.

The Feminist Misdirection

There is a feminist philosophy that virtually all women honor, and that includes respect for women, whether in the workplace or at home; equal pay for equal work; and an understanding that sexual harassment is intolerable.

This is not the kind of feminism we will be talking about. We use the word *feminism* here the way contemporary feminists do—that is, as an aggressive appeal to women to be independent, self-sufficient, sexually liberated, and "strong," above all other virtues. For two generations now, this progressive brand of feminism has offered a solution to the problems women face, and for two generations now, these solutions have only made women less happy and less fulfilled.

Few people have described the feminist/progressive agenda as clearly as Dr. Miriam Grossman, a psychiatrist whose position at the UCLA Health Center gave her a front-row seat to the lives of the young women this agenda has affected and often wounded. "They hope to destabilize a truth of science and civilization: that the sexes are deeply and essentially different," she wrote in her book *Unprotected*. "Their goal is an androgynous culture, where the differences between male and female are discounted or denied, and the bond between them robbed of singularity."[1]

The problem for modern feminists, as Grossman and others have documented, is that their teaching flies in the face of human nature. Each young girl they educate has to be educated from scratch and weaned away from her natural instincts. As Jennifer Marshall has observed in her book about living single, *Now and Not Yet*, "little girls learn early to love marriage and family." They do not easily abandon that aspiration. Marshall added that nine out of ten female high school seniors continue to say marriage and family life are important, a statistic that has scarcely changed over the generations.[2]

Hanna Rosin, author of the forthcoming book *The End of Men: And the Rise of Women*, champions the changes feminism has wrought. Yet she also concedes that "studies do indeed show that women are no more happy than they were in the 1970s." She traces this dissatisfaction to "the confusing array of identities available to [women] in modern life."[3]

Although fully sympathetic to the aims of the feminist "consciousness-raising movement," therapist Mary Pipher has had to concede that its benefits were not obvious. In her huge best seller, *Reviving Ophelia*, she expressed her surprise that "girls were having more trouble now." Writing in the 1990s, thirty years after the movement emerged, Pipher had counseled a shocking number of girls with eating disorders, alcohol problems, stress reactions to sexual assaults, STDs, self-inflicted injuries, strange phobias, and the aftereffects of attempted suicide.[4]

Dr. JoAnn Deak, a psychologist and well-traveled school consultant, came to many of the same conclusions Pipher did, in her recent book, *Girls Will Be Girls: Raising Confident and Courageous Daughters*. She contended that girls seem at least "to have it all today." Their choices are much more expansive than they were a generation or two ago. They have much greater access to a wider range of opportunities, like sports. And their talents are finding full expression as never before. For all of the bright spots, however, Deak acknowledged a "darker side" in being a girl in the twenty-first century. She listed the very same threats that Pipher did, and concluded, "It is no exaggeration to say that most girls are in touch with these grim realities as part of the context of their everyday lives."[5]

Regardless of their politics, virtually all psychologists who specialize in the problems of adolescent girls acknowledge that darker side. Whether they admit it openly or not, they understand the darkness to be an unresolved part of the feminist/progressive legacy.

No Gods, No Masters

At the heart of the contemporary feminist failure is a radically individualistic approach to morals and values. The popular saying "A woman needs a man like a fish needs a bicycle" nicely captures the delusional, self-defeating spirit of the movement. In fact, Irina Dunn, the Australian educator who coined the phrase, was paraphrasing a philosopher who said with equal, if not greater, indifference to reality, "Man needs God like fish needs a bicycle."[6] By extension, radical feminists have no need for either God or man, or so they say.

Margaret Sanger, the founder of Planned Parenthood, certainly felt that way. In 1914, this pioneering feminist launched her own publication, *The Woman Rebel*. Its slogan: "No Gods, No Masters."[7]

In the way of background, Margaret Higgins Sanger was born in 1879, the sixth of eleven children. Her Irish immigrant father was a socialist and agnostic who taught his daughter that Christianity was a crutch for the weak-minded. He much preferred left-wing politics as a means of action. She followed in his footsteps and established a path for those who followed her. Despite the occasional denial, that path has become well-worn. Many leading feminists today lean strongly to the left.

After dabbling in school teaching, the attractive, young Margaret Higgins married a wealthy architect named Bill Sanger. She quickly had three children and just as quickly lost interest in raising a family. "A religion without a name was spreading over the country," Sanger would write in *The Autobiography of Margaret Sanger*. "The converts were liberals, socialists, anarchists, revolutionists of all shades."[8] Wanting to be part of the action, Sanger joined the Socialist Party but was still not satisfied—not with socialism, not with her family, not with her husband, not with anything.

"The personal is political" has been a feminist rallying cry since the 1960s, but Sanger had made her personal issues political a half century earlier. She yearned for a female self-mastery and found it in a cause whose name she contrived: "birth control." Although Sanger professed to be a champion of those afflicted with too many children, she liked the oppressed more in theory than in reality. "I hated the wretchedness and hopelessness of the poor," she would later admit, "and never experienced that satisfaction in working among them that so many noble women have found."[9]

Margaret Sanger was all about Margaret Sanger. In her 1922 book, *The Pivot of Civilization*, she laid out her game plan. By this time she had left her husband and all but abandoned her children to concentrate on her cause. In the book, she cited two primary reasons birth control was necessary. The first was "the liberation of the spirit of woman and through woman, of the child."[10] This part of her plan continues to resonate in today's feminist movement. The second part is the one Planned Parenthood would rather we forget about, "to prevent the sexual and racial chaos into which the world has drifted."[11]

Like many of those who have followed her, Sanger had a fondness for "modern studies." One study she cited confirmed, for her at least, "that the least intelligent and the thoroughly degenerate classes in every community are the most prolific." She wanted these people to stop reproducing.[12]

Defectives, Delinquents, and Dependents

In the same book, Sanger cited another study claiming that nearly half of all American World War I draftees—47.3 percent—"had the mentality of twelve-year-old children or less—in other words," she wrote coldheartedly, ". . . they are morons."[13] Sanger had no interest in helping these people. "Organized charity," she wrote, "itself is the symptom of a malignant social disease."[14]

By encouraging these "defectives, delinquents, and dependents," Sanger believed that philanthropists had caused a "positive injury to the future of the race."[15] Eugenicists like the Nazis simply wanted "fit" women to outbreed the "unfit," but for Sanger that would trouble women of means, like herself, with having to give birth and raise children. Worse, from her perspective, it would not eliminate the "ever-increasing army of under-sized, stunted, and dehumanized slaves."[16] Sanger called instead for "drastic and Spartan" measures to control the "moron" half of the population.[17] In 1927, she got her way when the eugenics-friendly Supreme Court approved Virginia's policy of forced sterilization of the unfit.[18]

After World War II, Sanger's American Birth Control League quietly changed its name to the Planned Parenthood Federation of America. It is not hard to understand why. With images of the Holocaust haunting the world's conscience, Sanger's radical eugenics had clearly fallen out of fashion. Happily for Sanger, a sympathetic media cleansed her record. The word *eugenics* was absent from the glowing 1966 *New York Times* obituary of this "dynamic, titian-haired woman whose Irish ancestry also endowed her with unfailing charm and persuasive wit."[19] Since then Sanger has been the subject of a stirring TV movie, was welcomed into *Life* magazine's Hall of Heroes, and was named by *Time* magazine as one of the "25 most powerful women of the past century."[20]

The Personal as Political

Unfortunately, many early feminist pioneers had personal lives as troubled as Sanger's and projected them onto a large political canvas as well. Betty Friedan, author of the 1963 best seller *The Feminine*

Mystique, was one such woman. In her memoir, *Life So Far*, she told how her mother "made our life so miserable, my father, us kids, me especially." She attributed all this inflicted misery to the fact that women like her mother "didn't have jobs or careers."[21] Though Friedan's contemporary, Holocaust victim Anne Frank, chose not "to think of all the misery, but of all the beauty that still remains,"[22] Friedan, despite her immensely better circumstances, appears to have chosen to ignore the beauty, and the truth along with it.

In fact, Friedan's mother was the women's page editor at the Peoria newspaper before she married an older, affluent businessman. She could afford not to work outside the home. Unlike the Depression era's 99-percenters, the family had a maid when Friedan was coming of age. Friedan wrote of her mother, "Once my father gave her a watch set in sapphires for Christmas. She pouted and raved because it wasn't a diamond and ruby watch."[23] Yes, Friedan's mother had issues, but they obviously had less to do with the political than the personal.

"I was consumed with dread of her and, I suppose, hate, and even finally a kind of revulsion," Friedan wrote, conceding her lack of a role model.[24] Although Friedan did not make the connection, one suspects that her distaste for her mother's bourgeois inclinations pushed her hard to the Marxist left. Through the first few years of her marriage to Carl Friedan, she continued to write full-time for socialist publications and turned to freelancing only after the birth of her second child.

In 1969, several years into her highly public career, Friedan split from her husband. "Divorcing Carl was very painful for me because of the children," she wrote. "We both really loved our kids and Carl was a good father."[25] Then or now, breaking the family apart seems an unusual way to show one's love.

....

For years, the "woman needs a man like a fish needs a bicycle" metaphor was attributed to feminist icon Gloria Steinem, the original publisher of *Ms.* magazine. It was only after *Time* ran an article in 2000 on what the seventy-one-year-old Steinem described as her "new and happy marital partnership with David Bale" that she gave public attribution to the aforementioned Ms. Dunn.[26] Steinem justified her seeming change of heart on marriage with the kind of falsehoods one has come to expect from a movement based on the false premise that males were unnecessary to female lives.

Said Steinem at the time,

> I didn't change. Marriage changed. We spent 30 years in the United States changing the marriage laws. If I had married when I was supposed to get married, I would have lost my name, my legal residence, my credit rating, many of my civil rights. That's not true anymore. It's possible to make an equal marriage.[27]

Those baby-boomer women who married in the 1970s and kept their maiden names, credit ratings, legal residences, and civil rights would be inclined to disagree. The Steinem apologia reveals an additional feature of the radical feminist movement: its eagerness to take credit for things it did not do and to exaggerate its role in achieving workplace equity.

One thing Steinem did not do, given that she married for the first time at age sixty-six, was give birth. As an active heterosexual—and onetime *Playboy* bunny—she did, as she readily admits, get pregnant at least once and ended her would-be family life through abortion. Her own family life growing up may have discouraged her from starting a family of her own. When Steinem was just a few years old, her mother suffered a nervous breakdown and never fully recovered. Steinem's traveling salesman father abandoned the family for California when she was ten, leaving her and her ailing mother behind in Ohio. The fact that her mother had a hard time holding a job Steinem would attribute not to her emotional instability but to workplace inequality.[28]

In a recent *New York Times* article, Sarah Hepola recounted Steinem's dazzling career and asked, why "has no one emerged to take her place[?]"[29] In answer to her own question, Hepola offered the "diversity of modern feminism" and the breakdown of a monolithic media. A third possibility is that Steinem's brand of feminism was never really focused on women. It was focused on a progressive agenda that would be hard for anyone to track, let alone duplicate.

Despite her growing wealth and flair for fashion, the restless Steinem has not met the left-wing political movement she could not champion. She cofounded the Coalition of Labor Women, joined the Democratic Socialists of America, cofounded Choice USA, took up the banner of animal rights, and defended Mumia Abu-Jamal, the Marxist poet and cabbie caught with a smoking gun in hand after shooting a cop in Philadelphia.[30]

The progressive contempt for traditional wives and mothers flared into public view during the 2012 campaign when Democratic strategist Hilary Rosen claimed that Ann Romney, wife of Republican candidate Mitt Romney, "has actually never worked a day in her life."[31] Rosen apparently forgot where she was. These kinds of comments typically pass unnoticed in feminist and media circles, but not on national TV. In fact, Ann Romney had raised five boys while contending, at least during part of that time, with both breast cancer and multiple sclerosis.

Ann has also spent much time and put a great deal of work in programs for at-risk youth. Before her husband was governor of Massachusetts, she discovered our Best Friends program model in Washington, DC, and contacted me. She was very supportive of our character-education and risk-prevention model for girls and believed in our mission.

Ann's enthusiasm was such that she even made arrangements for a group of our Best Friends girls to address the General Court of the Commonwealth of Massachusetts. This, of course, was a highlight in the girls' lives. Because of Ann, they had an experience they would never forget. She made certain that Susan Weld, the wife of then governor Richard Weld, was there as well.

Ann Romney continued to provide us her support and her expertise in marketing. She set up a meeting with an ad agency in Boston and secured their agreement to design a brochure for us pro bono. This brochure was helpful in outlining our model and program goals. It was distributed widely and directly resulted in the very successful program in Newark, New Jersey. Ann did all this extra work because she wanted the program to succeed. There was no political agenda. I am here to say that Ann Romney works as hard outside the home as she does within.

But from Rosen's perspective, none of this counts as "work." Unfortunately, young women are exposed to her brand of feminism on a routine basis. Many have become unwitting codependents in their relationship with a media and educational establishment that assails them with the feminist progressive agenda.

Lose-Lose

The worst instincts of the radical feminist movement were on full display in early 2012 when the Susan G. Komen Foundation decided to stop giving annual grants to Planned Parenthood. Komen has been fighting breast cancer in a nonideological way since its founding thirty years prior. The grant to Planned Parenthood amounted to only $650,000, less than one-tenth of 1 percent of Planned Parenthood's annual revenue stream of more than $100 million.

Planned Parenthood and its allies could have accepted the decision and thanked Komen for its past support, and the battle against breast cancer would have been reinforced. Many in the pro-life community, who had hesitated to help Komen because of its alliance with Planned Parenthood, were gratified by Komen's initial decision and began to increase its online accounts with fresh donations.

The tide quickly turned to lose-lose for Komen in particular and for women in general. Planned Parenthood's media allies blasted Komen with such ferocity that the organization buckled under the pressure and felt it had no choice but to reverse its decision. This reversal has now alienated many pro-lifers who had been either unaware of Komen's relationship with Planned Parenthood or were willing to overlook it, as well as many in the pro-choice camp who no longer trust the organization.

In the past, Planned Parenthood did not typically offer mammograms to underserved women. As a practice the organization did not do mammograms. They simply made referrals, and as all women know, a mammogram is easy to put off, especially when that means more time and cost. It is still unclear how many, if any, follow-up services are available through Planned Parenthood once breast cancer is detected. (Since the controversy, the Planned Parenthood website now lists mammograms as a service.)

Is there any evidence that referrals were ever followed up? Was a tracking procedure in place? These issues did not surface in the interviews during the controversy. The silence leads me to believe these procedures were not in place. I wonder, too, how much of the $650,000 was actually spent on manual exams. Who gave the exams? A physician? Many of us have friends who had manual breast exams that showed nothing, but a routine mammogram later showed them to have breast cancer.

Attacking Other Women

From the radical feminist perspective, if a woman does not agree with the agenda, she is considered an enemy. No woman has been the target of more vicious abuse than former Alaska governor and vice-presidential candidate Sarah Palin. Among her most hostile critics has been the political comedian Bill Maher. He has called Palin a boob, a bimbo, and several other sexual insults I cannot even repeat here, the most offensive of which begins with the letter *c*. Maher has even made fun of Palin's child with Down syndrome.

David Letterman's obnoxious and offensive remarks about Willow Palin are the most egregious I have ever heard about a child in the political spotlight. Said Letterman, "One awkward moment for Sarah Palin at the Yankee game, during the seventh inning, her daughter was knocked up by Alex Rodriguez."[33] Palin was in New York at the time with fourteen-year-old Willow. Why no outrage from NOW? Or is it NOLWO? (Clearly they are the National Organization for *Liberal Women Only*.)

I can find no logic in why they hate Palin—an effective and successful former governor of a huge state and a self-described "pit bull with lipstick." Do they hate the lipstick or the fact that she is an attractive, youthful, pro-life conservative who fishes, hunts, and loves her husband and children?

In February 2012, Maher very publicly donated $1 million to an Obama political action committee. Steinem and friends had nothing to say about Maher and his insults of a working woman politician and her children. Similarly, Steinem defended Democratic president Bill Clinton after several women had accused him of actual sexual assault, one of whom, Juanita Broaddrick, accused him of rape. "President Clinton took 'no' for an answer," said Steinem famously in reference to his groping of Kathleen Willey and his exposing of himself to Paula Jones, even though there was a good deal of credible evidence that the attacks humiliated and frightened both women.[34]

All of this said, I would rather not politicize this discussion. In fact, I hope to depoliticize it. But it needs to be shown that women like Steinem have not so much used feminism to advance the cause of women as they have used women to advance the cause of progressivism. We all need to be committed to saving our daughters, but we cannot limit ourselves to saving only our liberal daughters from so-called conservative predators.

Subverting Faith

Following on the heels of the Komen controversy was the Obama administration's open attack on the Catholic Church, which considers contraception, sterilization, and abortion pills morally troublesome. This struck observers as the most flagrant subversion of religious freedom in memory.

The White House proceeded on this front, I believe, because they thought contraception as much an unqualified social good as penicillin or the polio vaccine. Mary Eberstadt, author and research fellow at Stanford University's Hoover Institution, thinks otherwise. As she argued recently in the *Wall Street Journal*, the case for the birth control pill—let alone the abortion pill—is by no means open and shut. "In severing sex from procreation," wrote Eberstadt, "humankind set into motion forces that have by now shaped and reshaped almost every aspect of life in the Western world. Families are smaller, birthrates have dropped, divorce and out-of-wedlock births have soared."[35]

More problematic still, the demographic consequences of the sexual revolution are beginning to erode the welfare state that most of the revolutionaries have pined for. Europe is likely lost. America may not be far behind: "In other words," says Eberstadt, "this isn't just a Catholic thing."[36]

The New Sexual Regime

Today, most women, including myself, consider themselves "feminists" to the degree that they believe girls should have roughly the same opportunities as boys, and women should be paid equally for equal work. What many women do not realize today is that their daughters have been dragged, willingly or not, into the underside of the feminist movement, that of sexual liberation.

If this movement had a pioneer, it was the Australian-born Germaine Greer. Her 1970 best seller, *The Female Eunuch*, encouraged women to rebel against the patriarchy that oppressed them and to assert themselves as men's sexual equals. "The first exercise of the free woman," she wrote, "is to devise her own mode of revolt."[1]

It should be noted that Greer's breakthrough book came out two years after she married a British carpenter, a marriage that effectively lasted only three weeks and that ended in divorce a few years later. Greer was not at all keen on the institution. "If women are to effect a significant amelioration in their condition," she wrote, "it seems obvious that they must refuse to marry."[2] Greer saw romance as the first step in the submission of women to the patriarchy. From her perspective, romance merely sanctioned "drudgery, physical incompetence and prostitution."[3] Friedan would go farther than Greer, famously referring to the homemaker's plight as living in a "comfortable concentration camp."[4]

Greer was particularly annoyed by the success of romance advocates, such as British novelist Barbara Cartland, who sold more than 100 million books in her lifetime. "If women's liberation movements are to accomplish anything at all," Greer wrote, "they will have to cope with phenomena like the million-dollar Cartland industry."[5] Here lies the essential misunderstanding of women like Greer and her fellow travelers. Girls will always like romance novels. Romance appeals to young and old women alike.

The now seventysomething Greer must feel terribly frustrated to see girls and young women make a massive best seller out of the Twilight series. This set of four romance novels by the thirtysomething Stephenie Meyer, a happily married Mormon mother of three, has sold more than 120 million copies worldwide just since 2005. Worse, from Greer's perspective, the novels' female protagonist, Bella, never does anything more sexual than kiss her two suitors and rescuers, one a generally heroic vampire and the other a noble werewolf. The Hunger Games trilogy is another popular series with an even more admirable heroine, who is also chaste and actually has a human boyfriend. (The brutal storyline is disturbing, however, especially for younger adolescents. We have come a long way from Nancy Drew, and I am not at all convinced it is the right direction.)

Loose Girls

Their failure to change female nature does not deter some radical feminists. They have had enough success reshaping the rules women must play by to keep them going. Greer, a self-avowed Marxist, was asked a few years ago on ABC TV whether feminism was the only "successful" revolution of the twentieth century. "The difficulty for me is that I believe in permanent revolution," she answered.[6] "Progressives" like

Greer cannot help themselves. It is in their being: they must progress. The fact that their idea of progress flies in the face of human experience and tradition troubles them little, if at all.

Kerry Cohen's observant 2008 memoir, *Loose Girl: A Memoir of Promiscuity*, serves as a useful guide to the "success" that presumably liberated young women have enjoyed. In Cohen's case, that success has included STDs; "pregnancy scares"; abortion; a flirtation with the soon-to-be "Preppy Killer," Robert Chambers; and most relentlessly of all, "desperation and emptiness."[7] Observes Cohen, now a psychotherapist herself, "For all the ways we were told girls had equal opportunities, all the evidence that we wouldn't have to struggle to have what men have, this double standard seemed intractable."[8] Jennifer Marshall has come to much the same conclusion. "Today we are frustrated by obstacles to lasting love," she wrote, "some of which seem to be the result of the feminist movement itself."[9]

Duke coed Karen Owen's notorious PowerPoint presentation adds even more detail to the self-debasement that in some circles passes for "sexual conquest." One typical adventure, this one with a campus tennis star, began with "long looks" and escalated to a single dance at a local bar. The tennis star promptly asked her back to his apartment. On the cab ride back, he was rude. He barely bothered to kiss her. He finished with her sexually in fewer than five minutes, "after which he simply walked out of the room and did not return." When Owen later texted him to ask for her favorite earrings back, he responded, "I will leave them outside the building for you." On the positive side, he had a "good body."[10]

"It is difficult at this point to suggest what a new sexual regime would be like," Greer wrote in the *Female Eunuch*.[11] Caitlin Flanagan, who documents Owen's tale in the *Atlantic*, has a very good answer to that quandary:

If what we are seeing in Karen Owen is the realization of female sexual power, then we must at least admit that the first pancake off the griddle is a bit of a flop. What rotten luck that the first true daughter of sex-positive feminism would have an erotic proclivity for serving every kind of male need, no matter how mundane or humiliating, that she would so eagerly turn herself from sex mate to soccer mom, depending on what was wanted from her.[12]

Eberstadt has come to a very similar conclusion. "Contrary to the liberation it has promised (and still promises) the revolution instead empowers the strong and penalizes the weak."[13]

This revolution corrupts our young men as it seems to empower them and endangers our daughters as it promises them liberation. Yeardley Love, Liz Seccuro, Kerry Cohen, and millions of others have felt more of its aftershocks than any of them would have wished for. If looked at carefully, these cases all speak to the conflicted nature of the contemporary feminist movement. In the way of background, the feminist movement has historically had a lingering internal division between a powerful antipornography faction and the insurgent sex-positive faction.

For years, the antipornography faction dominated the movement. Its dominance has been challenged over the years, however, by radical-feminist libertarians such as Germaine Greer, who have little use for marriage and the family; who have defended abortion, not just "choice"; and who have advocated what would come to be known as "pro-sex feminism." As "sex-positive" leader Ellen Willis has observed, the claim that pornography represents violence against women was merely "code for the neo-Victorian idea that men want sex and women endure it."[14]

These distinctions are not terribly pure. From Margaret Sanger to the present, both factions have advocated for the sexual equality of females. This causes problems, and no one has articulated them better than social theorist George Gilder, author of *Men and Marriage* among other books. As Gilder has observed, it is the woman who uniquely shapes the long-term future of the human race. She alone can bear and nurture children, which inclines her to long-term thinking. The man has no natural link to this process. In regard to sex at least, short-term pleasure drives male behavior more than long-term planning. The male urge, unless restrained by marriage, tends to be impulsive, predatory, and quickly gratified.

"The Women's Movement," Gilder argues, "tragically reduces female sexuality to the terms of male sexuality." When this happens, the woman, like most unmarried men, sees sex as a recreational activity. "Paradoxically," says Gilder, "when that happens the woman loses all her power over men and the reverence and respect toward the procreative potential of woman is lost."[15] As a case in point, one might recall Mark Zuckerberg's first steps in developing Facebook. Zuckerberg began, as he blogged at the time, by putting "some . . . [female] faces next to pictures of farm animals" and then having students "vote on which is more attractive."[16]

Some thirty-five years before Zuckerberg found his crude inspiration on the Harvard campus, a veritable beta site for female sexual liberation, Greer had written, "As long as women consider themselves sexual objects they will continue to writhe under the voiced contempt of men and, worse, to think of themselves with shame and scorn."[17] Only the willfully blind could deceive themselves into thinking that women have grown in men's esteem—or their own—in the last generation.

In the much-mocked papal encyclical *Humanae Vitae,* Pope Paul VI anticipated Zuckerberg and Tucker Max by a generation when he wrote in 1968:

> It is also to be feared that the man, growing used to the employment of anti-conceptive practices, may finally lose respect for the woman and, no longer caring for her physical and psychological equilibrium, may come to the point of considering her as a mere instrument of selfish enjoyment, and no longer as his respected and beloved companion.[18]

It is not my point to question the use of contraception, but rather to acknowledge that when sex is estranged from love and marriage, females are ultimately marginalized. Although radical feminists would recoil at any identification with the pope, the more conservative faction, at least, generally objects to the reduction of the female to a "mere instrument of selfish enjoyment."

Mutating Viruses

One undeniable consequence of the new regime is disease. In 1960, the birth control pill was first approved for widespread use in the United States. At that time, syphilis and gonorrhea were the only major sexually transmitted diseases, and they were relatively easy to treat. One immediate and obvious effect of the pill was reduced condom use. Men who were using condoms to avoid impregnating women no longer felt the need. In the 1970s, discretion fell by the wayside.

In 1976, chlamydia was first recognized, and in 1981, AIDS. These were not instances in which researchers gave new names to old diseases. These were new diseases that typically resulted from sexual activity with multiple partners. Meanwhile, old viruses continued to mutate and multiply and become more resistant to treatment. By the early 1980s herpes was becoming widespread. The early 1990s saw the emergence of PID, pelvic inflammatory disease. Later in the decade, the human papilloma virus (HPV) was recognized as the cause of 90 percent of all cervical cancer. And today, many young women are infected with HPV within a few years of becoming sexually active.[19]

"Forty years ago we had two sexually transmitted infections to worry about," observed Dr. Miriam Grossman. "Now we have twenty-five."[20] What goes unspoken at school and college health clinics is that, for some basic biological reasons, young women are more easily infected than young men. There are now in the range of 1.3 million chlamydia cases each year, most of those in young women. Managing the disease costs more than $2 billion a year.[21]

Worse, the consequences for women often endure beyond the immediate fix, and they can and do include the inability to have children. Chlamydial hsp, for instance, causes miscarriages years after silent infections. HPV can be troublesome down the road as well. Even a "low-risk" type, one that does not lead to cancer, can cause warts on a girl's genitalia and cervix. The treatment of these warts can cause pain, even scarring, and will cost the girl and/or her insurance plan a fair amount of money. Then, too, a carrier can bear the virus and pass it on to a child. Regretfully, "instead of the grim facts," says Grossman, "women are fed oversimplified and whitewashed information."[22]

From her own personal experience at the height of the sexual revolution, Kerry Cohen explained in her book *Loose Girls* how even a well-educated woman with a gynecologist as a mother could end up becoming a statistic. After contracting HPV—she had already had crabs, and scabies were to come—Cohen visited her local Planned Parenthood to be tested for HIV.

During an excruciating interview on her sexual history, Cohen was asked if her partners consistently used condoms. They did not. The interviewer lectured her on the need to use them. "I want to tell her I'm not stupid," Cohen reflected. "I know everything there is to know about protecting myself."[23] Cohen did not share her thoughts with the interviewer, but she knew full well why she did not insist that her partners use condoms: "In the moment, when I'm busy trying to make some guy mine, thoughts about death and disease are furthest from my mind."[24]

In a manner of speaking, it is hard to fault Cohen. To read the soul-chilling mechanics of an official government brochure on condom use is to realize just how thoroughly the sexual revolution has robbed sex of its spontaneity and joy, not to mention its essential purpose, namely procreation. And Cohen's experience was in no way exceptional. "Listen," the interviewer told her reassuringly, "you're not the only one who comes through these doors and tells me about multiple partners without condoms."[25] So saying, the interviewer gave away Planned

Parenthood's game. The organization must know that its own brand of sex education does not work. Research confirms that. A recent study of heterosexual college students showed that fewer than half had used a condom during their last vaginal intercourse, and that number was an all-time high.[26]

Some former Planned Parenthood workers, such as pro-life activist Abby Johnson, believe that the organization uses sex education as a way to stimulate sexual activity among girls in the hopes of profiting its abortion business down the road. Personally, I do not think its leaders are that cynical or that money-driven. Like their founder, Margaret Sanger, they are agenda-driven. As I see it, ideology trumps money, but whatever their motivation, the results are utterly, totally, inarguably disastrous.

According to the Centers for Disease Control, an estimated 65 million people have an incurable sexually transmitted infection (STI) in the United States, and an additional 19 million people become infected each year. As many as 40 percent of sexually active young women have had an STI; the great majority of those women were infected before age twenty-five.[27] None of this had to happen. And disease is just one of the new threats our daughters face.

A Hijacked Profession

A corollary threat is the feminist stranglehold on the psychology profession. In 2006, when Dr. Grossman published her book *Unprotected: A Campus Psychiatrist Reveals How Political Correctness in Her Profession Endangers Every Student,* she felt the need to publish under the moniker "Anonymous." In something of an understatement, Grossman wrote, "Our campuses and mental health organizations do not always celebrate ideological diversity."[28]

In her book, Grossman described the transition on college campus. Not too long ago, she pointed out, a campus psychiatrist might caution a student about random sex, call it mindless or empty, warn about the threat of sexually transmitted diseases or unwanted pregnancy, and urge self-restraint. That same psychiatrist might encourage a girl to think of traditional marriage and parenthood as valued milestones.

Not anymore. Now, psychiatrists push condoms, wink at promiscuity, and recommend merely a "limited number of partners."[29] An STD is simply a "rite of passage" and pregnancy an inconvenience as easily remedied as tonsillitis. As to motherhood, that is something best postponed for some distant future, if even discussed. Traditional marriage, after all, is just one option out of many, all equally valid. "Dangerous behaviors are a personal choice;" added Grossman, "judgments are prohibited—they might offend." In sum, says Grossman, "My profession has been hijacked. I cannot do my job, my patients are suffering, and I am fed up."[30]

Women like Kerry Cohen have paid the price for this professional abdication. Writing of the time she put a CD together for a boyfriend, she cited two of the songs she chose, both entirely indicative of the time and place in which she lived. The first was "Once" by Richard Brucker, the refrain of which concludes, "I was longing to be saved." The second song was Aimee Mann's self-evident "Save Me." In experiencing the world Greer had created and her own place within it, Cohen wanted nothing more than "to be saved from myself, from my hurting."[31]

Saving our daughters, however, will not be easy. So many of them still don't know what they need to be saved from or where to turn for help.

Coming Apart

In 1991, the swordfish boat *Andrea Gail* set out from its port of Gloucester, Massachusetts, and never returned. Sebastian Junger memorialized the boat's unhappy fate in the best seller *The Perfect Storm*. The book was later made into a movie of the same name, which was, in fact, filmed in Gloucester.

Aboard that ship were a half dozen men who, along with their partners and spouses, would qualify to live in a statistical village that social scientist Charles Murray, in his powerful book *Coming Apart*, calls "Fishtown." To get a handle on how America is changing, Murray places people with no academic degree higher than a high school diploma and a blue-collar or low-skill white-collar job into this abstract village. They don't literally have to be fishermen.

For control purposes, to eliminate the effects of age and race on his study, Murray restricts the collective he analyzes to non-Hispanic whites ages thirty to forty-nine. Today, roughly 30 percent of all such Americans live in Fishtown. Meanwhile, about 20 percent of white, non-Hispanics in that same age range live in "Belmont," the statistical home of people who have at least a bachelor's degree and work as managers, physicians, attorneys, engineers, architects, scientists, college professors, or content producers in the media.

In decades past, the residents of Fishtown, like the fishermen of Gloucester, embraced the nation's civic culture. They enrolled their children in public schools, went to church, worked hard, stayed out of trouble, saluted the flag, and subscribed to the American dream. This is what Fishtown was like a century ago or even a half century ago. Many of the children who grew up in Fishtown would move to Belmont. This was an expectation.

Exorcising Fathers

As Murray sees it, things started to go south in Fishtown about fifty years ago. "Changes in social policy during the 1960s," he says, "made it economically more feasible to have a child without having a husband if you were a woman or to get along without a job if you were a man."[1]

It was in 1960 that the federal government changed the Aid to Dependent Children Program to the Aid *to Families* with Dependent Children, or, more realistically, Aid to *Mothers* with Dependent Children. Fathers, especially working fathers, rendered the family ineligible for aid. In 1964 the federal government added food stamps to the potential bounty for the fatherless family and in 1965 added Medicaid. Soon afterward, in the spirit of the times, the government shifted public housing from fixed rents to rents based on ability to pay, a shift that made working fathers all the more a financial liability for a Fishtown family.

Driving these reforms to a large degree was the nation's residual guilt over its historic treatment of African Americans. By targeting black families, however, the government unwittingly reversed the gains blacks had been making in the marketplace. In 1950, for instance, 85 percent of black children were born to married parents. By 1980 that number had plunged to 35 percent and has continued to erode.[2]

"In some neighborhoods," observes Kay Hymowitz, author of *Marriage and Caste in America*, "two-parent families have vanished.

In parts of Newark and Philadelphia, for example, it is common to find children who are not only growing up without their fathers but don't know anyone who is living with his or her biological father."[3]

In Fishtown, the picture is nearly as discouraging. In 1960, as Murray relates, 84 percent of this statistical cohort were married. By 2010, that number had dropped to 48 percent.[4] Unfortunately for the culture, the unmarried women were nonetheless having children. If, in 1960, only 2 percent of all white babies in America were born to unmarried women,[5] by 2010 that number had soared to 44 percent in Fishtown.

Wrote Hanna Rosin, with her Belmont blinders on, "Women these days understand that their sexual freedom—even if it causes them some amount of heartache—is necessary for their future success."[6] No, Hanna, Fishtown women do not have careers. They have jobs, as they have always had. Women may "no longer need men for financial security and social influence" in Belmont,[7] but they do in Fishtown.

In Belmont, despite women's alleged self-sufficiency, marriage has proved more durable. In the last fifty years, the percent of married women in the thirty to forty-nine age group has dropped from a high of 94 percent, but only to 83 percent. As to childbirth, Belmont women continue for the most part to play by the old rules. In 2010, only 6 percent of Belmont births were nonmarital. Although the Belmonters continued to get married and work hard, it has become nearly taboo for them to criticize those who do neither. This is one reason illegitimacy rates continue to soar.

The first person to sound the alarm, a young assistant secretary of labor named Daniel Patrick Moynihan, got his head handed to him for doing so. In 1965, he alerted his boss, President Lyndon Johnson, to the side effects of illegitimacy. These included not only all the problems associated with fatherlessness but also the departure of males from the labor force. Unnerved by the findings, Johnson made a plea for family during a Howard University commencement. "When the family collapses," he said, "it is the children that are usually damaged. When it happens on a massive scale, the community itself is crippled."[8]

Black leaders objected to the message, and they were not alone. As Hymowitz has noted, "Feminists were inclined to look on the 'strong black women' raising their children without men as a symbol of female autonomy."[9] To contradict this narrative was to run the risk of being labeled a racist and a sexist. The Moynihan report was quickly dispatched down an Orwellian memory hole.

Slouching Toward Gomorrah

If any American city deserves the actual moniker "Fishtown," it is surely Gloucester, roughly 92 percent of whose thirty thousand residents are white. In 2008, Gloucester made the news again in ways it would rather not have. In June of that year, *Time* magazine broke the story that seventeen girls at Gloucester High, none older than sixteen, were known to be pregnant. This was four times more than just a year earlier. In investigating the cause, school authorities discovered that some of these girls had made a pact as early as the sixth grade to get pregnant and raise their babies together.[10]

School authorities had grown alarmed when more and more girls started showing up for pregnancy tests. The school would administer some 150 pregnancy tests in just this one year alone. According to the principal, the girls who made the pregnancy pact "reacted to the news that they were expecting with high fives and plans for baby showers."[11]

The girls involved fit something of a profile. Their families tended to be "broken" and the girls themselves "socially isolated," with little parental supervision. "They could stay out all night if they wanted,"[12] said one of their classmates. Indeed, one of the fathers proved to be a twenty-four-year-old homeless man.

As in much of nonjudgmental America, authorities in Gloucester lacked the wherewithal to challenge behavior that all but condemned these girls to a lifetime of poverty and emotional distress. Even *Time* was forced to wonder whether "the high school has done perhaps too good a job of embracing young mothers." Students at Gloucester High take sex education in their freshman year, and young moms push strollers boldly through the hallways to the school's on-site day care center. To solve the growing problem, the nurse practitioner and doctor who run the school's student clinic advocated the provision of contraceptives "regardless of parental consent," and quit their jobs when they did not get their way. In a rare moment of media sanity, the *Time* reporter admitted that contraceptives "won't do much to solve the issue of teens wanting to get pregnant."[13] Said one of the more responsible authority figures at Gloucester High, track coach Jim Munn, to point out the folly of condom education, "Kids drink too. So why not also dispense alcoholic beverages to students and give them a 'safe place' to booze it up."[14]

One friend of the pact-makers told *Time*, "No one's offered them a better option."[15] I write this book in the belief that there *are* better options. In some cases, school administrators may be as ignorant of these options as the students are. For ideological reasons, however, there are people in power who see no problem with pushing birth control pills on girls who have barely reached puberty.

This subject surfaced a year before the Gloucester incident in nearby Portland, Maine. There the school board, at the ACLU's prompting, decided to distribute birth control pills to girls as young as eleven. In November 2007, Bill O'Reilly interviewed me on his popular TV show to discuss the decision. Not surprisingly, the head of the local ACLU chapter declined to appear.[16]

As I explained to O'Reilly, most girls of that age really don't want to have sex. There is any number of reasons for educators to stop encouraging them otherwise. The epidemic of sexually transmitted diseases should be reason enough. More fundamentally, girls in their early adolescence are not physically, let alone emotionally and cognitively, ready to have sex. If the educators don't know this, the girls certainly do. We surveyed teens in the District of Columbia, and 91 percent of them wanted to hear the abstinence message. Sex is not what these children are about. They have a lot of things going on with their lives at this stage, and sex complicates everything. (By the way, although I don't want to embarrass him, Bill O'Reilly has been a steadfast supporter of the Best Friends program.)

Cultural Breakdown

In 2011, the largely black Frayser High School in Memphis showed the people of Gloucester just where their future may lie when some ninety students in the coed, eight-hundred-student school were reported as being pregnant or having babies in just one calendar year.

Local authorities responded by announcing a $4.2 million program that will "focus on identifying pregnant teens and teen mothers and link them to services." The program will not address the fact that pregnancy rates for black girls ages ten to nineteen increased from thirty-eight pregnancies per thousand in 2002 to more than sixty-two in 2010.[17] Here, too, authorities and students alike apparently do not know their options.

As Heather Mac Donald has documented, the illegitimacy rates in the black and Hispanic equivalents of Fishtown have been a cause of concern for years. As of this writing, some 72 percent of black babies are born out of wedlock across all classes. Among Hispanics roughly 53 percent of babies across all the classes are born out of wedlock, a percentage that is increasing rapidly as new immigrants adapt to the feminized American customs. Aggravating the problem is that Hispanic women continue to have twice as many children as the average American woman. Social workers have been overwhelmed by the increasing caseloads, especially in border states such as California. Says Mac Donald, "Not only has illegitimacy become perfectly acceptable, they say, but so has the resort to welfare and social services to cope with it."[18]

In *I Beat the Odds,* his eye-opening account of growing up in Memphis as the son of an unmarried mother, Michael Oher reveals from the inside the stress unmarried motherhood puts on the state and the chaos it can force children to endure. Born in 1986, Oher was one of the few of his mother's twelve children who knew his father. He felt lucky. Oher had at least met him on a couple of occasions. His father would later be murdered in prison.

Oher grew up very nearly homeless. His mother, a crack addict, could not consistently care for her children. She would lock the door to her apartment and disappear for weeks on end, leaving Oher and his siblings to beg for food from the neighbors and to sleep on floors. The state stepped in, but imperfectly. The children, cleverly, would avoid state caseworkers to stay together. Oher spent his childhood moving, often randomly, between his mother's many houses, foster homes, and sheer homelessness. "You're not poor," says Oher, "if you know where your next meal is coming from."[19] I will talk more later about how the admirable Michael Oher survived his environment, but those who have seen the movie *The Blind Side* already have a good idea.

A Revolutionary Process

The left wing of the feminist movement has played a major role both in advocating the policy changes that caused this shift toward single parenthood and in oppressing discussion of its consequences. As Mac Donald has wryly observed, "The cardinal rule for writing about child poverty if you are in the mainstream media is this: Never, ever mention single parenthood."[20] While the evidence of the ill effects of single parenthood becomes more obvious, feminists grow more aggressive in their attack not only on the proponents of marriage but on marriage itself.

The late Andrea Dworkin, a self-professed lesbian who disdained her mother and identified with her socialist father, had this to say on the subject: "Marriage as an institution developed from rape as a practice. Rape, originally defined as abduction, became marriage by capture. Marriage meant the taking was to extend in time, to be not only use of but possession of, or ownership."[21] Dworkin had no great love for children either. "Childbearing is glorified in part," she once said, "because women die from it."[22]

The "rape" metaphor runs through much of feminist literature. In her acclaimed book *Against Our Will* Susan Brownmiller argued that rape "is nothing more or less than a conscious process of intimidation by which *all men* keep *all women* in a state of fear."[23] Brownmiller described herself as "a single woman," one who remained celibate because she was "not willing to compromise."[24]

Linda Gordon, the Florence Kelley professor of history at New York University, takes the insanity a step farther. "The nuclear family must be destroyed," she wrote. "Whatever its ultimate meaning, the break-up of families now is an objectively revolutionary process."[25] In feminist circles, Gordon is not considered an extremist. A two-time winner of the Bancroft Prize for best book of history, she has also been awarded any number of prestigious fellowships. If she has a husband or children, the biography page on her website makes no mention of them.

Activist and former *Ms.* magazine editor Robin Morgan was blunter still. Said she, "We can't destroy the inequities between men and women until we destroy marriage."[26] Morgan, by the way, was born out of wedlock to a father who wanted nothing to do with her. She had her own child with Kenneth Pitchford, a self-described gay and a founding member of the "male feminist Effeminist Movement," whatever that means. Ironically, she first found fame as a child actress playing one of the daughters in the TV version of *I Remember Mama*, a loving account of a nurturing, two-parent "Fishtown" family.

Herself a single mother at twenty-two, writer Bonnie Goldstein is dismayed at the casual way the media and the feminist establishment seem to be celebrating the unmarried-mom phenomenon. Although

Goldstein does not regret keeping her baby some forty years ago, it was not at all easy, and she had the support of an extended family. "Parenting is difficult, expensive, energy-sapping and full of unexpected challenges," she wrote. "To do it right it takes (at least) two." She urges the would-be mother to finish school, find a loving partner, and give herself "a chance to grow up before she has to manage the very complicated development of her own child's tiny existence."[27]

As parents, we need to take Goldstein's message to our daughters and any other girls we influence. They will not likely get this information in schools, they surely won't get it on TV, and they may not even get it in church.

6.

Suffering the Consequences

As much as our feminist friends have isolated themselves from the movement's aftershocks, the more traditional residents of Fishtown, the ones who have to endure their neighbors' behavior, do not. As Charles Murray has acknowledged, children born to unmarried women fare far worse on every measurable variable than children raised in intact families. This disparity persists even after controlling for the income and education of the parents.[1]

Crime is one such variable. From 1960 to 1995, Murray has observed, the violent crime rate in Fishtown increased by a factor of six, while remaining virtually flat in Belmont. Workforce participation is another variable. In 1968, only 3 percent of Fishtown males with no more than a high school education placed themselves "out of the labor force." By 2008, even before the current recession, that number had spiked to 12 percent. In other words, one of every eight men in this class had dropped out of the workforce while fully in his prime.[2]

We are told repeatedly that jobs for men of this category have disappeared or that their wages have shrunk. Neither bit of conventional wisdom is true. Working-class males can continue to make a "family wage" that enables them to marry as long as they work. As Murray has pointed out, "The average male employed in a working-class occupation earned as much in 2010 as he did in 1960."[3]

Murray did not explore all the unfortunate consequences of growing up in a fatherless home, but disparities exist across the board.

- 63 percent of youth suicides are from fatherless homes.
- 90 percent of all homeless and runaway children are from fatherless homes.
- 85 percent of all children who show behavior disorders come from fatherless homes.
- 80 percent of rapists with anger problems come from fatherless homes.
- 71 percent of all high school dropouts come from fatherless homes.
- 75 percent of all adolescent patients in chemical-abuse centers come from fatherless homes.
- 85 percent of all youths in prison come from fatherless homes.[4]

On the 2012 campaign trail, Republican former candidate Rick Santorum uniquely advocated for a focus on marriage. "Do you know if you do two things in your life . . . you're guaranteed never to be in poverty in this country?" he accurately told a crowd in Iowa. "Number one, graduate from high school. Number two, get married before you have children."[5] Not surprisingly, Santorum's plea evoked mostly ridicule and/or outrage in feminist circles.

Amanda Terkel offered an all-too-typical rejoinder in the progressive *Huffington Post*. To her credit, she did acknowledge a 2009 Brookings Institution study, "Five Myths About Our Land of Opportunity" by Ron Haskins and Isabel Sawhill, that backed Santorum's claim. According to the study, Americans who finished high school, got full-time jobs, and got married before having children had a 2 percent chance of winding up in poverty and a 74 percent chance of winding up in the middle class. By contrast, those who ignored all three norms had a 76 percent chance of winding up in poverty and only a 7 percent chance of winding up in the middle class.[6]

This was not evidence enough to placate Terkel. To counter the Brookings' claim, she cited the work of Algernon Austin, the director of the race, ethnicity, and the economy program at the Economic Policy Institute. "Continually high poverty rates among blacks and Latinos are the result of high unemployment and incarceration rates and declining shares of good jobs in the American economy," argued Austin, in full compliance with the party line.[7]

"The decline in marriage among these groups," he added, in willful ignorance of reality, "is a collateral consequence of these negative economic conditions."[8] What Austin and Terkel both ignore is that the white residents of Fishtown are also suffering from the malaise, and they do not have race as an excuse. In truth, Austin and his fellow travelers have the story exactly backward. It is the lack of paternal discipline that leads so many of these young men to joblessness and jail.

By the way, the president of the Economic Policy Institute is Lawrence Mishel, who is a longtime member of the Democratic Socialists of America. If Austin's argument were not reason enough for Terkel to dismiss Santorum, the fact that he opposes same-sex marriage certainly is. As Terkel sees it, same-sex marriage would "theoretically lower the nation's poverty rate."[9]

The Great Divergence

Spurious insights such as these have helped create what Murray calls the "great divergence," namely the increasing cultural divide between the residents of Fishtown and those of Belmont. Fifty years ago, virtually all residents of either community subscribed to "the American way of life." Wrote Murray, "It was a culture encompassing shared experiences of daily life and shared assumptions about central American values involving marriage, honesty, hard work and religiosity."[10]

The gradual rejection of this way of life may put our daughters at risk. In Fishtown, many young girls have never been to a wedding—never been to church, for that matter. Some have never even worn a dress. Emulating their mothers and their older sisters, they can see little beyond a life lived on public assistance, aided infrequently by the males in their lives, who are just as likely to leave them as to love them.

Feminists try to conceal or deny it, but single-parent households more frequently suffer abuse toward the mother and, especially, toward her children. A study by the Office on Child Abuse points out the disparity between children in single-parent homes and those living with both parents. The former experience:

- 77 percent greater risk of being physically abused;
- 87 percent greater risk of being harmed by physical neglect;
- 165 percent greater risk of experiencing notable physical neglect;
- 74 percent greater risk of suffering from emotional neglect;
- 80 percent greater risk of suffering serious injury as a result of abuse;
- 120 percent greater risk of experiencing some type of maltreatment overall.[11]

By all accounts, children who are abused are likelier to become abusers themselves, both of their sexual partners and of their children. Although no class of females is immune, the collapse of a shared culture isolates those females without dependable male stakeholders in their lives—husbands, brothers, fathers, uncles. If the males on which young women lean are transient figures without a real stake in their future happiness, those females render themselves more vulnerable. This could be just the short-term vulnerability of college students like Eve Carson and Yeardley Love or the long-term vulnerability of Fishtown women. The overall numbers are chilling.[12]

- Every 9 seconds in the US a woman is assaulted or beaten.
- Around the world, at least one in every three women has been beaten, coerced into sex, or otherwise abused during her lifetime. Most often, the abuser is a member of her own family.
- Domestic violence is the leading cause of injury to women—more than car accidents, muggings, and rapes combined.
- Studies suggest that up to 10 million children witness some form of domestic violence annually.
- Nearly 1 in 5 teenage girls who have been in a relationship said a boyfriend threatened violence or self-harm if presented with a breakup.
- Every day in the US, at least three women are murdered by their husbands or boyfriends.
- 92 percent of women surveyed listed reducing domestic violence and sexual assault as their top concern.
- Domestic violence victims lose nearly 8 million days of paid work per year in the US alone—the equivalent of 32,000 full-time jobs.
- Based on reports from 10 countries, between 55 percent and 95 percent of women who had been physically abused by their partners had never contacted nongovernmental organizations, shelters, or the police for help.
- The costs of intimate partner violence in the US alone exceed $5.8 billion per year: $4.1 billion are for direct medical and health care services, while productivity losses account for nearly $1.8 billion.
- Men who as children witnessed their parents' domestic violence were twice as likely to abuse their own wives than [were the] sons of nonviolent parents.

In addition to the alarming statistics listed, two that I have addressed within the Best Friends Foundation program in public schools are (1) one out of ten high school students has been a victim of dating violence, and (2) nearly 80 percent of girls who have been physically abused in their intimate relationships continue to date their abuser.[13]

Through the Best Friends program I began an initiative called *Stop the Silence. Prevent the Violence.* During this two-day conference teenage girls and boys learned strategies for recognizing and ending abusive relationships and skills for developing healthy relationships with their boyfriends or girlfriends. We all must work hard to ensure our daughters (and sons) do not become statistics in this escalating social affliction.

7.

Beyond Abuse

There is one element of cultural fragmentation from which Canada, given its demographics, suffers even more than the United States. I refer here to the failure of many Muslim families to come to terms with the basic rules of Western civilization. Throughout this book I encourage parents to resist the culture when necessary, but some accommodation is sometimes appropriate. The following story is an example of a family that violently opposed popular culture—to the point of murder. Unfortunately, there are many more much like it.

Aqsa Parvez, a sixteen-year-old Ontario girl, had been growing restless under her family's restrictions and clashed with them frequently over her desire to wear slim-fitting, Western-style clothing. She had also started attending movies, looking for jobs, and doing a host of little things that enraged her Islamist father, Muhammed. Finally, he reached a tragic breaking point. One morning, Aqsa's brother picked her up at her bus stop and took her home, where he and Muhammed strangled her to death. The father promptly called 911 to turn himself in. The brother, slightly more Westernized than the father, told police that he did not feel his sister deserved death, "but if it was his daughter, he might have broken her legs."[1]

The United States is not immune to the same phenomenon. In one well-circulated photo, Amina Said, then eighteen, and her sister Sarah, then seventeen, were seen smiling, with Amina wearing a sweatshirt emblazoned with the word "American." Their father, Yaser Abdel Said, was not pleased with the girls' eager assimilation into their Texas life. On January 1, 2008, just months after the Parvez murder, Said hunted down the sisters—they had fled home with their mother—and shot them both dead. "This was an honor killing," the girls, aunt told reporters.[2] In what culture, I wonder, is it genuinely honorable to murder your own daughter? Apparently, Said had long abused the girls and became furious when he discovered they had boyfriends.

Although there is much in this book that will help Muslim families struggling with acculturation, nothing I could say would speak to extremists like Yaser Abdel Said or Muhammed Parvez. The people close to Aqsa Parvez and the Said girls, like those close to Yeardley Love, were responsible for intervening. Admittedly, in some Muslim communities, speaking out against abuse is difficult to the point of dangerous, but we are all obligated to save our daughters from danger, no matter what their faith, no matter where they live.

Feminist Complicity

A complicating factor for Muslim girls is the refusal of advocacy groups and the media to acknowledge the distinct problems they face. Shahina Siddiqui, president of the Islamic Social Services Association, obviously absorbed enough of Western culture to know the excuses. "The strangulation death of Ms. Parvez was the result of domestic violence, a problem that cuts across Canadian society and is blind to colour or creed," said she, disingenuously.[3] Sheikh Alaa El-Sayyed, imam of the Islamic Society of North America in Mississauga, Ontario, could not agree more: "The bottom line is, it's a domestic violence issue."[4] The media took them at their word and turned a blind eye to the thousands of other Muslim girls suffering under similar circumstances.

As eagerly as the media have advanced a feminist agenda, they seem equally reluctant to question the aggressive misogyny of radical Muslims.

Nina Shea, director of Hudson Institute's Center for Religious Freedom and an authority on Islamic culture, in a piece she wrote for the *National Review,* recently exposed the daily oppression under which women around the world labor and about which many journalists have been silent. In Saudi Arabia, for instance, women must enshroud themselves in anonymous black robes from head to toe when they appear in public. They are banned from driving, working in most retail stores, and even from mingling with unrelated men.[5]

In Iran, if a woman accuses a man of rape but fails to convince the judge, she is subject to eighty lashes. An Iranian man is allowed to kill an adulterous wife, and women convicted of adultery can be stoned to death. To protest for women's rights in the face of this oppression is to invite disaster. Although Pakistan does not dictate dress codes as severe as those of Saudi Arabia or Iran, its legal system can make life insufferable for Christian women as well as Muslim. In one well-documented case, as reported by the Asian Human Rights Commission and the British Pakistani Christian Association, a twelve-year-old Christian girl was kidnapped, raped, and forcibly converted to Islam. When she managed to escape nearly a year later, the authorities demanded that her parents return her to the kidnappers, as she was now a Muslim bride. Unwilling to do so, the family was forced into hiding.[6]

Young women are profoundly at risk not only in Muslim countries but also in those enclaves in North America where sharia law is imposed and enforced. And yet, asked Kay Hymowitz in the *City Journal,* "as you look at this inventory of brutality, the question bears repeating: Where are the demonstrations, the articles, the petitions, the resolutions, the vindications of the rights of Islamic women by American feminists?"[7] Hymowitz's answer to this question is worth exploring.

Unacceptable Excuses

As Hymowitz sees it, there are several varieties of feminists, and each has its reason for staying largely silent on the issue. For "gender feminists" in the Gloria Steinem vein, all men are more or less brutish. The difference between men who would blow up buildings and men who would forcibly prevent them from blowing up buildings is a distinction without a difference. By contrast, most women—with the notable exception of women such as Margaret Thatcher and Golda Meir—are, by nature, peaceful and antiwar. "They are too intent on hating war," wrote Hymowitz of these feminists, "to ask if unleashing its horrors might be worth it to overturn a brutal tyranny that, among its manifold inhumanities, treats women like animals."[8]

Postcolonial/multicultural feminists have even less interest in saving our Muslim daughters than do the gender feminists. These women believe Westerners to be so corrupted by the legacy of imperialism that they have no right to judge former colonial peoples, especially those whose radical positions are seen as an "authentic expression" of Arab and Middle Eastern identity.

The third category of feminist Hymowitz described as "world-government utopian."[9] The utopians seem less interested in liberating women to make their own choices than in imposing the feminists' own views of how a liberated woman ought to behave. In discussing the lethal riots that greeted a Miss World pageant in Nigeria, columnist Jill Nelson caught the spirit of this movement perfectly when she wrote on the MSNBC website, "It's equally disrespectful and abusive to have women prancing around a stage in bathing suits for cash or walking the streets shrouded in burqas in order to survive."[10] I cannot imagine that she surveyed the women in these two opposing camps.

The distinction among feminist subsets bends and blurs, and their grudges overlap. Still, as Hymowitz acknowledged, many feminists of different stripes have denounced Islamic oppression. More need to do so. "American feminists have a moral responsibility to give up their resentments," said Hymowitz, "and speak up for women who actually need their support."[11] Well said!

Media Complicity

In the Muslim world, the abusers and enablers can at least fall back on entrenched ideologies to justify their tolerance of violence toward women. In the secular world of American pop culture, there are no excuses, but there is still plenty of abuse. In 2009, pop singer Rihanna was violently assaulted by her boyfriend, Chris Brown, also a well-known singer. According to the police report, the two were driving along a Los Angeles street when Rihanna picked up Brown's cell phone and noticed a long text from a former girlfriend of his. Do not believe all the talk of our emerging hookup culture. No one ever likes to be cheated on. When Rihanna protested, Brown tried to throw Rihanna out of the car. Failing that, he punched her bloody, choked her, and left her bleeding in the car in front of her home until Rihanna's screams prompted a neighbor to call 911.[12] Brown eventually pleaded guilty, was put on five years' probation, and was served a restraining order.[13] He was just nineteen at the time. Had he not been a celebrity, he likely would have gone to prison.

Given the youthful nature of her audience and the publicity surrounding the attack, Rihanna had an excellent opportunity to speak out meaningfully against dating violence. To say the least, she did not take advantage of it. Within weeks of the battering, the couple was reportedly seen together. Three years after the assault, Rihanna and Chris Brown began recording together again. The song they recorded on Rihanna's new album, the lyrically inane, sexually explicit "Birthday Cake," includes this disheartening request by Rihanna, "If you still want to kiss it, come and get it."[14] Although some Rihanna fans were appalled—"Ah, so now it's okay to beat up women. I hope my boyfriend doesn't get that memo"[15]—far too many young women read Rihanna's subtext in her reunion with Brown quite as she intended. What follows is a sampling of the scores of tweets on this subject, each more disturbing than the next:[16]

 Call me crazy butttttt I would let Chris Brown Beat me up anyyyy day.

 Not gonna lie ... I think I'd let Chris Brown beat me.

 I'd let Chris Brown punch me in the face

 I'd let Chris Brown beat me up anytime ;)

 Like I've said multiple times before, Chris Brown can beat me all he wants

 Chris Brown you can beat me if you want

 I don't know why Rihanna complained. Chris Brown could beat me anytime he wanted to.

Each of these messages, by the way, identifies the sender by her Twitter handle and photo. To a person, they are young women. White or black, most of these women pose provocatively. I hope they do not mean what they say, but I fear that many of them do.

Among the few editorialists to speak out against Rihanna's failure to separate herself from Brown was Bonnie Fuller in the *Huffington Post*. Wrote Fuller, "Rihanna needs to learn from another beautiful, talented award-winning singer who endured 16 years of an abusive relationship in marriage—that's Tina Turner."[17] For Tina, pulling away held much more risk, as her husband, Ike Turner, was her business and musical partner and a control freak if there ever was one. Broke and homeless, the admirable Tina Turner willed herself to quit Ike and rebuild her life. In so doing, she showed thousands of women across America that it was possible. Rihanna, unfortunately, sent the opposite message. But though Rihanna may have failed to communicate anything helpful to our girls, a song she recorded with rapper Eminem—"Love the Way You Lie"—was actually the catalyst for a valuable lesson on dating violence. I describe how we utilized this song in a positive way in chapter 16.

An All-Too-Natural Failing

San Francisco sheriff Ross Mirkarimi met Eliana Lopez, a Venezuelan soap opera star, at an environmental conference in Brazil. After Lopez became pregnant with Mirkarimi's child, she moved to San Francisco to be with him. They had a son, Theo, in April 2009, and were married either soon before or after the birth, the license having been sealed. On New Year's Eve 2011, Lopez reportedly asked Mirkarimi if she could take Theo to visit her family in Venezuela. According to Lopez, Mirkarimi began to scream obscenities at her and claimed that she was trying to take Theo away from him. He then began "pushing, pulling and grabbing" Lopez and bruised her arm in the process.[18]

A tearful Lopez told all of this to a neighbor the next day, and the neighbor videotaped Lopez's testimony as well as her various bruises. Quick to do the right thing, the neighbor alerted the police. They seized the video and arrested Mirkarimi. At this point, despite her high profile, Lopez did what many domestic violence victims do: she clammed up and stood by her man. This was, of course, high tabloid fodder in a city that may be more sensitive to feminist concerns than any in the country, and the message Lopez sent was exactly the opposite of what domestic violence advocates wanted to hear. It provoked a fair share of honest discussion of why women remain in abusive relationships. This is not a simple issue and merits its own book.

Mirkarimi eventually pleaded guilty to a reduced charge of false imprisonment, a plea that resulted in probation and community service. Were he not so visible, he likely would have suffered less punishment. In San Francisco the previous year, 911 dispatchers took more than 7,000 calls for domestic violence. Nearly 2,000 cases were referred to the district attorney. Of these, 373 cases resulted in a plea bargain like Mirkarimi's, and only 14 resulted in conviction.[19] If this is what justice for women looks like in America's progressive capital, it may be a good time to reevaluate "progress."

Beyond Statistics

Given the cultural breakdown in poor and working-class areas, the risks our daughters face on college campuses are not as immediate as those they face in America's urban high schools. This is something Madilia Marsh-Williams, the mother of Natasha Marsh, learned the hard way.

On a quiet February 2000 evening, while Madilia waited for her daughter Natasha and Natasha's beau, Andre Wallace, to return home with groceries, she heard eight shots ring out in rapid succession. "Oh Lord," she said, "please don't let it be my baby."[20] Tragically, it was. An unknown shooter had gunned down Natasha and Andre right in front of the house, the last bullet for each delivered at extremely close range.

In the days that followed, a sustaining narrative quickly developed in the local media. Natasha was a seventeen-year-old honor student at Wilson High, one of Washington, DC's better schools. She was set to interview for a summer internship at a large accounting firm. She had her sights set on West Virginia University. Andre Wallace, also seventeen, was a standout receiver and defensive back, the cocaptain of the football team. Additionally, he was a member of the jazz and marching bands and a teacher's assistant at a nearby elementary school. He, too, was eyeing West Virginia University. A scuffle had broken out earlier involving Andre and Wilson High dropout Carlton Blount at a basketball game. These things happen. Andre had gotten the best of Blount. In another era, that would have been that. But in 2000, given the ready access to handguns, Blount retaliated.

The mothers outfitted the young couple in their graduation gear and laid their matching powder blue caskets side by side at the funeral. Some four thousand people attended. The day after the funeral, the president of the United States, Bill Clinton, weighed in on the tragedy at a press conference. "Guns in the wrong hands continue to claim too many young lives," he said, "lives like those of Andre Wallace and Natasha Marsh, the fine young DC residents who were gunned down in front of Natasha's home last week and were buried just yesterday."[21] The *Washington Post* editorialized along the same lines.[22]

In the year that followed the killings, when the story moved from the A section of the *Post* to the B, a more revealing narrative emerged for those who cared to know it. A *Post* headline summed it up, "Defense in Wilson Case Alleges Web of Affairs; Jealousy Led to Killings, Attorneys Say." For all of her real virtues, Natasha proved vulnerable to the passions that have stirred young women from time immemorial. For some months, she had apparently been having a secret affair with twenty-four-year-old Jermaine Johnson, a friend of the accused shooter, Blount. "I didn't know anything about this," Natasha's mother would lament. "I had never seen Jermaine Johnson before in my life."[23]

Johnson encouraged Blount to take revenge and drove him to the scene. Johnson would plead guilty to manslaughter. Wallace, meanwhile, had been having an affair with the girlfriend of a fellow named Julian Jones. To complicate matters, Jones's girlfriend and Natasha had had their own fistfight earlier, in a Wilson High bathroom. Any number of people had reason to take the football star and honor student down a peg. Jones would accompany Blount and Johnson on their lethal mission. The scuffle at the basketball game set it off. "I don't know why he's looking at me. I'm not the one [sleeping with] his girl,"[24] Blount had reportedly said within earshot of Wallace. This is the kind of provocation that could have ignited a conflict anywhere.

Here, the story takes an odd misogynistic twist and shows just how uniquely vulnerable young women are. According to trial testimony, Blount showed more fury in shooting Natasha than he did Wallace. Blount felt the need to shoot Natasha close up in the head, perhaps to humiliate Wallace and to resolve his own shame at being beaten. In fact, Blount walked away from Wallace before turning and shooting. Accordingly, the jury convicted him of first-degree murder in Natasha's death, second-degree murder in Andre's.

It was not just the availability of guns that made the killings possible. Romeo did not need a gun to kill Tybalt or Tybalt a gun to kill Mercutio.[25] Besides, the District has the toughest gun control laws in the nation. What was truly missing in this milieu were the internal restraints that fathers have historically imparted to their sons and daughters. In none of the *Washington Post* articles I consulted could I find any reference to a father of anyone involved, victims or killers. What I read instead were heartbreaking accounts like the following:

> After the verdict, the mothers of the victims stopped to embrace Blount's mother. "Inside, I'm hurt that she's losing her child just like I lost my child," said Laura Wallace. "I held her and embraced her and told her I know what she's feeling. . . . But I am satisfied where my son is right now. I wouldn't want to be her, knowing where her son will be."[26]

In a world without fathers, and in a school system that long ago gave up any attempt to impart enduring values, these young people were left to sort out their fates according to their own lights. The media they absorbed could not have helped. From one of the early *Post* articles, for instance, the reader learns that the couple had planned a trip to Jamaica for spring break. "It would have been an exceptional whirlwind adventure for the pair," the reporter wrote much too casually of two seventeen-year-olds obviously being treated like adults long before they had the emotional equipment to deal with adulthood.[27]

I am sure their mothers meant well. They almost got their children over the hump before the morally anarchic environment pulled the two youngsters back in. If children are gone, the pain endures. Said Natasha's mother, "I used to wonder how victims of suicide came to the point where they didn't have any more hope. Well, I no longer wonder. Now I understand. It's not a pain that you can take a pill for or a pain that any doctor can cure. It's a pain that's in the core of your heart. It's in your soul."[28]

Looking for Scapegoats

Instead of addressing violence realistically and identifying genuine aggravating factors, radical feminists have tended to blame men for the very act of being men. There is no clearer illustration of this mindset than the manufacture of the Super Bowl Myth, nicely dissected by author Christina Hoff Sommers in a *National Review* article titled "The New Mythology."[29]

Sommers traces the genesis of the myth back to January 27, 1993. On that fateful day, a coalition of women's groups held a news conference in Pasadena, California, the site of that year's Super Bowl. The organizers informed reporters that Super Bowl Sunday was "the biggest day of the year for violence against women." They confidently predicted that 40 percent more women than usual would be battered on that day. For verification, Sheila Kuehl of the California Women's Law Center, a lesbian and future state senator (and for those of us of a certain age, "Zelda Gilroy" on *The Many Loves of Dobie Gillis*), cited a study done at Virginia's Old Dominion University three years earlier.

Linda Mitchell, of the media "watchdog" group mislabeled "Fairness and Accuracy in Reporting (FAIR)," lent her organization's credibility to the claim.

Simultaneously FAIR's publicists were sending out a large mailing that warned at-risk women, "Don't remain at home with him during the game." On Friday, January 28, Denver psychologist and author of *The Battered Woman*, Lenore Walker, appeared on *Good Morning America* to help propagate this newly created myth. Walker claimed to have been documenting the Super Bowl abuse phenomenon for ten years. Here, too, a representative from FAIR sat in to add credibility. On Saturday, January 29, the *Boston Globe* reported that women's shelters and hotlines were "flooded with more calls from victims [on Super Bowl Sunday] than on any other day of the year." The reporter cited just one study "of women's shelters out West" and extrapolated from there. Most of the media bought in uncritically. Robert Lipsyte of the *New York Times*, for instance, would soon be calling the game "Abuse Bowl."[30]

In a refreshing departure from such groupthink, *Washington Post* staff writer Ken Ringle asked an author of the Old Dominion study about the connection between violence and football games. "That's not what we found at all," the author told him.[31] When Ringle tried to find the real source for the claims these organizations were making, he came up empty.

The *Post* published Ringle's deconstruction of the "myth thing" on the January 31 front page. Two days later, the *Boston Globe* published a retraction of its story.[32] FAIR eventually backed off in its support of the story line. The shelters and hotlines reported no variation in the number of calls for help on that Super Bowl Sunday, not even in Buffalo, whose team lost the game for the third consecutive year, this time in a blow-out.

Still, despite the efforts of Sommers and Ringle, the myth lives on. In 2011, a group called SAVE—Stop Abusive and Violent Environments—felt the need to ask the National Football League to repudiate the myth that Super Bowl Sunday is a "day of dread" for women. "While we appreciate Commissioner [Roger] Goodell's efforts to bring attention to the issue of domestic violence," said a SAVE spokesman, "he should also refuse to allow this persistent lie to stereotype NFL players as abusers or to tarnish the family appeal of the annual Super Bowl event."[33]

SAVE quoted Sommers, who reiterated, seventeen years after first helping to expose the fraud, "Women who are at risk for domestic violence are going to be helped by state of the art research and good information. They are not going to be helped by hyperbole and manufactured data."[34] In the pages ahead, I will share some of that research and good information and discard more of the bad. Only the truth can save our daughters, but there is a shocking number of well-placed people who do not want them to hear it.

8.

Blaming Boys

Although not yet quite obvious, trouble is brewing in Belmont as well as Fishtown. If Eve Carson and Natasha Marsh experienced the vengeance of Fishtown losers, Yeardley Love and Liz Seccuro suffered the wrath of Belmont's alleged best and brightest. To understand the increasing vulnerability of young women like Yeardley Love and Liz Seccuro, we need to know something about what is happening to America's boys and young men. No one in my experience has done a better job of expressing the unhealthy state of affairs than Dr. Leonard Sax, author of, among other books, *Boys Adrift: The Five Factors Driving the Growing Epidemic of Unmotivated Boys and Underachieving Young Men.*

As I mentioned in the opening chapters, boys are not the villains of this book. They are victims as well. They are far more likely to die from violent causes than females of the same age, and fifteen times more apt to be victims of a violent crime. They are four times more likely to commit suicide and to be addicted to drugs and alcohol. In addition, boys greatly outnumber girls in special education programs.

Our sons are subject to the same ideologues that undermine our daughters, the ones who insist boys are hardwired no differently than girls. "Instead," wrote Sax, "they insist that girls and boys behave differently because our society expects them to."[1] Once this unnatural ideology is imposed on our youth, it leads many young males to disengage not only from school and academic achievement, but also from the enduring rituals that shape boys into men.

Highlighting one glaring symptom of the problem is the fact that, nationwide, fifty-eight female students are enrolled for every forty-two males in our colleges. Some males wash out before they even get to college. The ones who find their way there understand quickly that the odds allow them to behave less admirably than they might on a more equal playing field. As Tucker Max crudely summarized his campus days, "I realized that I could be an a_____ and get away with it."[2]

Kindergarten Interrupted

Dr. Sax believes this growing educational disparity begins in kindergarten.[3] Thirty years ago, children *played* in kindergarten, usually a half day, at that. They were introduced to structured activities, but those activities were usually fun—blocks and clay and running about. In a move not without ideological implications, educators began to insist that kindergarteners do the kind of schoolwork children used to do in the first grade. More and more, children were expected to sit quietly in place and learn to read and write.

For little girls, this was not much of an issue. As Sax explained, their cognitive processes at this stage develop more quickly. Plus they are more likely to be comfortable sitting in place. Disregarding inherent gender differences, educators see a boy's failure to adapt to the new model as a sign of a nascent problem. To be fair, many school districts have set aside programs for kindergartners not ready to study. They dress these programs up with all the expected verbal claptrap, but even at age five or so, children know a euphemism when they see one, especially if it is assigned to them. They begin to identify themselves as losers. Some always will.

Self-Respect Through Self-Control

Lacking, too, in many school settings is what Sax calls "a healthy image of what a man should be."[4] He cites a California case in which a male schoolteacher was censured for trying to teach his students in an experimental all-boys public school about strength, self-control, and other masculine virtues. As the evaluators saw it, the teacher was attempting to "reinforce traditional gender stereotypes," and that merited punishment.[5]

A century ago, the Boy Scout organization was created specifically to make men out of little boys. Manhood, Sax makes clear, is not a given. It must be learned. In a thousand different ways, cultures have elevated this transition into ritual, so important is manhood to the health of the community. In a similar spirit, we at Best Friends created a parallel program for boys called Best Men. Our unapologetic goal is to build character. We challenge our boys to abstain from violence, sexual activity, drugs, and alcohol. In today's environment, we have our work cut out for us.

Our message is simple: self-respect through self-control. If conscientiously applied, it works. Missy Howard, a former Best Friends program director in Charlotte, North Carolina, reported to me that boys tell her that even though they were angry and wanted to lash out at a peer, they were able to reflect on the Best Men message of self-control and restrain themselves. She found, too, that "they were proud of themselves for having the tools of discernment."[6] Parents likewise saw places in their own lives where taking time for self-control improved their relationships with their children and within their professional circles. As Missy stated, the unique credo in the Best Friends program, "'Self-respect through self-control,'" is a message that everyone would do well to weave into their life each day."[7]

There is less support for programs like ours than the reader might suspect. In California today, and elsewhere, educators have all but banished the Boy Scouts from public facilities for daring to insist that the young scouts honor God and stay "morally straight"[8] on their path to manhood. As the recipient of public funds, we, too, are fully constrained from entering a spiritual element into our program. Of course, Boy Scouts must monitor their adult leaders' behavior as role models.

Self-Discipline

Sax explores only peripherally the role that churchgoing plays in the culture. On this subject, a friend tells me of his experience in attending a traditional Catholic church. What impressed him from the very beginning was that every child older than two in the church could keep her or, more impressively, *his* mouth shut through ninety-plus minutes of utterly incomprehensible Latin. One week he counted forty-two altar boys on the altar. Although roughly half of them were younger than ten, all of them were able to kneel or sit in respectful silence in full view of the congregation for the entire Mass.

As my friend observed, these boys all had one thing in common: a father who had taken them to church every Sunday, sat beside them, and attended to them as often as needed until they could sit up straight and pay attention on their own. This process, he tells me, takes years.

Unfortunately, many boys do not have a father at home willing to fill this once-traditional role. Not surprisingly, the morally anarchic Tucker Max described a childhood shaped by "parental instability, multiple divorces, remarriages (seven between my two biological parents), stepparents, constant relocation, loneliness, and emotional pain."[9] His parents got divorced when he was a year old, and his father was "essentially a nonentity"[10] in his life until he was about sixteen. It certainly showed in his treatment of women.

Medicating the Problem

To govern improperly socialized boys in a school system designed primarily for girls, teachers and parents turn to doctors. Given their training, doctors are inclined to ascribe the boys' problems to various medical conditions. Among the more popular is ADHD (attention deficit/hyperactivity disorder). Rare just a generation ago, ADHD is nearly as common a diagnosis in schools today as is strep throat. As Sax points out, if Mark Twain's Tom Sawyer were a real boy and alive today, he would meet all the criteria for ADHD "with exuberance."[11]

Boys are diagnosed with ADHD at least three times as much as girls, and affluent children are diagnosed with it more frequently than are low-income children. Lacking time to properly diagnose these children, doctors often recommend the calming palliative of drugs such as Adderall, Ritalin, Concerta, Metadate, Focalin, and Daytrana.

The drugs become to the boys what the magic feather was to Disney's Dumbo—the prop they need to fly. Dumbo thought himself dependent on the feather. His male mentor, Timothy Q. Mouse, showed him otherwise. Once Dumbo learned to trust his own inner resources, he transformed himself from clown to circus star.[12] Lacking male mentors, too many boys dare not proceed through life without their magic feathers. As Sax has noted, boys in 2007 were thirty times more likely to be using these drugs than they were just twenty-five years earlier.[13] The solution often proves worse than the problem it was alleged to solve.

Emasculating Literature

These diagnoses have proved popular in no small part because they relieve parents of the responsibility to turn their boys into men. It does not help the parents at all that the media and educational establishments discourage them from even trying. Teachers, for instance, shy from recommending formerly popular books and stories, like those, say, of Ernest Hemingway or Jack London, ones that introduce boys to the rituals of manhood. They see this material as too violent—too masculine, really. Similar fears have driven sports such as dodgeball and even kickball out of physical education classes. The competition on which boys thrive has become, in too many schools, verboten.

To get a sense of what students are expected to read, I reviewed a past recommended high school reading list from my local library here in Montgomery County, Maryland.[14] The following is a list of the young adult fiction titles, to show the range of choices:

Arakawa, Hiromu. *Fullmetal Alchemist*. Brothers Ed and Al experimented with alchemy to resurrect their dead mother, leaving them with missing body parts which only the Philosopher's Stone can restore.

Carbone, Elisa. *Jump*. P.K. and Critter, two runaways, head away from parents toward rock climbing out West and a better understanding of themselves.

Condie, Ally. *Matched*. Cassia's future is decided by the Society, but then a computer glitch gives her two "matches" or partners.

Dessen, Sarah. *Along for the Ride*. Auden spends the summer with her remarried father and his young baby, and discovers that having fun is a good thing.

Donnelly, Jennifer. *Revolution*. Andi, dealing with death and divorce in her family, discovers a diary that leads her back in time to the French Revolution.

Draper, Sharon. *Copper Sun*. Amari, brutally taken from Africa and sold into slavery in Carolina, is befriended by Polly, an indentured servant.

Elkeles, Simone. *Perfect Chemistry*. Reluctant lab partners, perfect Brittany and gang member Alex become much more.

Green, John and David Levithan. *Will Grayson, Will Grayson*. Two teens named Will Grayson, one gay and one straight, accidentally meet.

Na, An. *The Fold*. Joyce, a Korean American, must decide

whether to agree to the eye surgery her aunt encourages her to have.

McCormick, Patricia. *Sold*. Lakshmi, 13, leaves her mountain village for the city and finds herself sold into sexual slavery.

Pratchett, Terry. *The Wee Free Men*. A young witch, six-inch-high blue men, and the Queen of Fairyland. [*sic*]

Skovron, Jon. *Struts & Frets*. Sammy's band is self-destructing, his grandfather is in failing health, and his love life is very confusing.

Of the twelve books, nine were written by women and eight have female protagonists. The three books written by men offer close to zero guidance for boys struggling with their male identity issues in the twenty-first century.

- *Will Grayson, Will Grayson* tells the story of an insecure boy whose best friend is gay. When he meets another fellow also named Will Grayson, also gay, his life is changed forever. The first book by coauthor David Levithan was called *Boy Meets Boy*.

- *The Wee Free Men* deals with the witches and queens of fairyland. The author is a self-described British "humanist" and honorary associate of the National Secular Society, which was created for those who reject the supernatural.[15]

- *Struts & Frets* is the first book by Jon Skovron. His second book, *Misfit*, may tell us more about this author. Its protagonist is an adolescent girl whose father is "a bitter ex-priest who never lets her date and insists she attend the strictest Catholic school in Seattle."[16] Holly Black, author of the Curse Workers series, describes the book as "a diabolically delightful paranormal about a teen girl discovering her inner strength and power—and her potential for darkness"[17]—in other words, a perfect book for the aspiring Goths at your breakfast table.

If I surmise correctly, all three of the books written by men, and likely some of those on the list written by women, offer something to offend people who take their faith seriously. As Sax, who is Jewish, points out, the Judeo-Christian tradition has helped provide guidelines for young males the world over for the last two millennia. In this tradition, being a man means "using your strength in the service of others." I cannot imagine that the young male reader will find much of this message in any of the twelve books listed. In reviewing this reading list, I can see why boys are failing to connect with a feminized, fantasy-oriented curriculum. Today, young girls are roughly ten times more likely to read a book on their own than boys.[18]

Masters of the Universe

Denied the potentially instructive pages of masculine literature, and offered little in the way of instructive masculine film or TV, boys increasingly express their Nietzschean "will to power" in the hyperviolent, take-no-prisoners world of video games. Sax makes an excellent case that video games, which are far more pervasive and addictive than most adults realize, cause boys to further disengage from the real world. The findings are "unambiguous," says Sax. The more time a child spends playing video games, the more likely he is to experience failure in school, to have a violent self-image, and to lack motivation to succeed beyond the parameters of the game.[19]

Just as problematically, the video gamers see themselves as the masters of their own universe, a false sense of superiority already fed, in many cases, by indulgent parents. "If there is no God," Jean Paul Sartre once said in his famous paraphrase of Dostoevsky's Ivan Karamazov, "everything is permitted." In the minds of so many of these boys, if there is a God, it must surely be they themselves. "I don't think anything I've ever done is wrong," confirms Tucker Max, with little in the way of irony.[20]

Virtual Sex

Perhaps even more disturbing for our daughters, our sons have turned increasingly to their computer screens for sexual fulfillment as well. The culture has borne the brunt of sex removed from marriage for decades. Now it is beginning to experience the effects of sexual satisfaction divorced from women. Pornographic images are replacing the real thing. As Sax has observed, some 70 percent of college-age men now view pornography on a regular basis.[21]

At age twenty-one, after his first year at Harvard Law School, Ben Shapiro wrote the insightful book *The Porn Generation* about the corrosive effect of pornography, hard and soft, on his own peers. Although pornography predates the printing press, the Internet has made it a genuine threat to the sustainability of the culture, not only for its pervasiveness but also for its ease of access. Porn can visit you at your computer station even if you don't ask for it.

The consequences are decidedly unhealthy. As Shapiro relates, child pornography alone generates more than $3 billion in revenue each year, with at least one hundred thousand such websites up and running. To accommodate the appetites of the easily bored, porn producers have moved on to bestiality porn, incest porn, "schoolgirl" porn, "college roommate" porn, "virgin" porn, and lesbian porn between alleged coeds. Says Shapiro, "The idea that the porn industry doesn't push men to look at fifteen-to-eighteen year old girls as sex objects is ridiculous."[22] Many young men have become so jaded by watching pornography that they are asking their doctors for Viagra or Cialis because they no longer find it satisfying to make love to real women. Sax cited one Harvard study of men with sexual problems that showed 50 percent of them needed the help of pornography to achieve erection.[23]

Unfortunately, some of our daughters feel the need to compete with pornographic images to get attention. Sax asked one sixteen-year-old why she was going to a high school Halloween party as a Hooters Girl. Said she, "If you don't dress like this, nobody will even notice you."[24]

Tucker Max confirms the syndrome. Wrote he of one young woman in his sights, "She wore too much makeup and not enough clothes, which is always a sign of despair." Max's response to women this vulnerable, like that of so many young men, was pure exploitation. "I would meet them," he wrote, "sense their insecurity, feed off it, play with it, and before I knew it the girl was in love with me."[25] Here, he exposes the underlying fault line in the contemporary social scene. If undisciplined young men primarily want sex, young women, no matter how they dress, want love. The emotional turmoil that results can be seismic. Too much of it causes even young women to grow calluses on their souls. Kerry Cohen, author of *Loose Girl*, would agree. Speaking of her misguided quest for affirmation she wrote, "I am sick of myself. Sick of my desperation and emptiness."[26]

In a recent CNN article, my husband, Bill Bennett, observed how sexually desensitized men and emotionally abused women seem to be creating their own sexual subcaste. He cited E. L. James's *Fifty Shades of Grey*, a trilogy of sadomasochistic novels that have proved hugely popular among women. Their popularity disturbs the *New York Times*' Maureen Dowd, who wonders how, after years of feminist struggle, her sisters-in-arms can indulge themselves in tales of female submission. "In the act of degrading women," Bill wrote, "men are also degrading themselves. And the voyeurism, inspired by such entertainment, debases men and women even more. This is a parlous, dreadful outcome for both sexes."[27] Knowing the premise, I refuse to read these books, and I would seriously caution mothers of adolescents to keep these books out of their homes. I believe the message of these dangerously popular books to be harmful not only to the children but also to their mothers.

"Teenage boys without strong leadership can easily become barbarians," wrote Sax, and some never grow out of the barbarian phase.[28] Some, in fact, grow dangerous. In 1989 in suburban Glen Ridge, New Jersey, a privileged group of local athletes grew bored just watching porno flicks routinely after school. They thought it would be much more entertaining if they could make their own. Lacking access to any willing starlets, they recruited a special-needs girl from their school, who was desperate for approval and attention. These degenerate boys turned on the video camera and proceeded to violate her sexually with a broom handle and a baseball bat.[29]

Authorities were slow to understand exactly what had gone wrong. In both cases, the media traced the breakdown to the boys' participation in sports, a much easier target than sexual license, absent parents, inadequate discipline, or values-free sex education.

As one teenage boy told therapist Mary Pipher in another circumstance, "The schools pass out condoms and teach us about pregnancy, but they don't teach us any rules."[30] And as one Langley High School student wrote in her evaluation after my Best Friends presentation, "Everyone tells us to protect ourselves, but no one says don't do it."

Gateway Stimulus

Pornography has inspired greater monsters than the boys of Glen Ridge. One was the infamous Ted Bundy, who confessed to killing thirty of our daughters before justice caught up with him. Like Tucker Max, Bundy was charming and good-looking and knew how to exploit female sensibilities. Unlike Max, he did not content himself with sex and humiliation.

On the day before he was executed, Bundy was interviewed by Christian leader Dr. James Dobson.[31] Bundy initiated the conference to talk about one specific subject. "I take full responsibility for all the things that I've done," he said. "That's not the question here. The issue is how this kind of literature contributed and helped mold and shape the kinds of violent behavior." He was talking, of course, about pornography.

As Bundy told the story, he revealed that his trip to the dark side began with soft-core pornography when he was about twelve. It did not end there. "Once you become addicted to it," he observed, "you look for more potent, more explicit, more graphic kinds of material." The most dangerous of all, he insisted, is the kind "that involves violence and sexual violence."

In his years in prison, Bundy had met any number of violent offenders. "Without exception," he said, "every one of them was deeply involved in pornography—deeply consumed by the addiction."

As a final plea, Bundy said, for all who would listen, "You are going to kill me, and that will protect society from me. But out there are many, many more people who are addicted to pornography, and you are doing nothing about that."[32]

Judith A. Reisman, PhD, a visiting professor of law at Liberty University School of Law, is an internationally recognized expert on sex science frauds and pornography. In 1977, following the shocking indifference of trusted adults toward her young daughter's rape by a thirteen-year-old lad guided by his dad's *Playboy* magazines, Dr. Reisman went on a mission to uncover the causes of child sexual abuse. Who was making America so dangerous to all our daughters?

Her journey led her to Hugh Hefner. Until he read zoologist Dr. Alfred Kinsey's 1948 and 1953 books on sex, Hefner, like most college men in the fifties, was still a virgin. These books transformed him into "Kinsey's pamphleteer." He began promoting his guru, Kinsey, the "father of the sexual revolution."[33] As Dr. Reisman researched Hefner, she discovered the long-hidden facts of Kinsey's closet bisexual adulteries; his masturbatory, pornographic and sadomasochistic pathologies; sex science frauds; and barbaric sex abuses of up to 2,034 children and infants—some as young as two months of age—by his Indiana University Kinsey Institute "team."

Reisman told me, "At long last, the British medical journal *The Lancet* confirmed our child sex abuse findings in 1990, when they concluded that 'Dr. Reisman and her colleagues demolished the foundation of the [Kinsey] reports.'"[34] She sighed and added, "In fact, in

1995 we had fifty-one legislators who agreed to a congressional investigation of the Kinsey Institute for child sex crimes before the inquiry was squashed from above."

I asked Reisman about a *Playboy* lawsuit against her in the Netherlands in 1994. She replied that *Playboy* had charged her with libel for saying on television that *Playboy* magazine had systemically sexualized children from the fifties to the mid eighties. However, she said, "After I sent the Dutch judge the evidence from my study of *Playboy*, *Penthouse*, and *Hustler*—for the United States Department of Juvenile Justice—the judge ruled in my favor, citing: 'the uncontested factual findings of Dr. Reisman.'"[35]

Reisman told me that her team had documented 6,004 cartoons and photos of children under age eighteen in these magazines, most of them sexualized. *Playboy*'s highest year was 1971 when it averaged sixteen child images per issue. "They eliminated sexy children after my report was issued in 1986," said Reisman, "but *Playboy* still inserts child sex cartoons once in a while to test the waters."

I asked about the role of pornography today in child sex abuse. Reisman said, "The evidence is, as always, overwhelming."

As Reisman noted, global studies confirm that pornography undermines men's ability to love and mate for life. A more immediate problem is that young men who use pornography will sometimes seek out younger children as subjects. Reisman's own daughter was molested by such a person.

Reisman also cited Michel Heimbach, unit chief for the FBI's Crimes Against Children Unit, who testified in Congress on the relationship between pornography and child molestation. According to Heimbach, "some offenders show pictures of other children engaging in sexual activities to overcome the children's fears, indicating to their intended victims that it is all right to have sex with an adult because lots of other boys and girls do the same thing. They also use pornographic images of other children to arouse victims, particularly those in adolescence."[36]

I truly admire Judith and her tireless crusade to inform the public of the dangers to our children's well-being.[37]

Failure to Launch

Although there are fortunately very few men like Ted Bundy, whom we discussed earlier in this chapter, there are more and more young men who have grown very nearly as estranged from the traditions of their fathers and grandfathers. Referring to a recent movie of the same name, Sax described these fellows as the *Failure to Launch* generation.[38]

In the movie, the protagonist, Tripp, played by Matthew McConaughey, is an employed thirty-five-year-old who still lives with his parents. They want him out. Like too many young men today, he is in no hurry to leave.

In one scene, Tripp's father walks in on him in bed with a young woman. (The bed has the same Superman sheets that have been on it since Tripp was six.) "You live with your parents?" says the girl, in shock.

"Is that a problem?" Tripp answers in all innocence.

"Are you kidding me[?]" she responds.[39]

Although more productive than many real-world, live-at-home sons, Tripp flees commitment as surely as most such young men do. When asked by a buddy if he is afraid of love, Tripp answers:

> No, no, no, no, no, man. I'm not afraid of love. I love love. Look, I've had a lot of girlfriends, right? And sometimes I'm the rebound guy. Other times, when I get lucky, I'm the "explore new areas of your sexuality" guy. But every single time, we have fun. Thank you. I have fun. They have fun. It's good for me. It's good for them. And I would argue that it's damn good for civilization as a whole.[40]

Unfortunately, "civilization as a whole" does not benefit. Men like Tripp used to be an anomaly. Forty years ago, the median age at first marriage for men was twenty-three. Today, it is twenty-eight, and trending north. Furthermore, 40 percent of twentysomethings will move in with their parents at least once during this decade in their lives; some two-thirds will shack up with a romantic partner.[41] Tripp may be having fun along the way, but it is unlikely that the women he loved and left by the wayside enjoyed the experience quite as much as he did. They are more likely to be working and less likely to be living at home than their brothers.

"It's a trend," read a *New York Times* headline from 2006. "Men with no jobs or ambition." Having studied the data, the *Times* reporters concluded that millions of American men between thirty and fifty-five had simply dropped out of regular work, despite the hot job market at the time. "They are turning down jobs that they think are beneath them," the article continued, "or are unable to find work for which they are qualified, even as an expanding economy offers opportunities to work." At the time, 13 percent of American men in that age group were not working, up from 5 percent in the late 1960s.[42]

When Sax went public with his findings on the "failure to launch" phenomenon, the public response overwhelmed him. Many of the respondents were living through the phenomenon either as participants or as codependents. One woman's response I find particularly perceptive:

> I believe that what's happened to boys is directly related to what's happened to girls. Girls today feel that they don't need boys so much anymore. And boys have figured that out. Girls used to give motivation to boys to be successful so that boys could "take care of them." Without that motivation, what is left for boys? Video games, where they can still be the hero? Sleeping around—because, as you succinctly stated, girls still have sexual needs—but we've learned how to satisfy ourselves in that aspect, also. No, it's not the same, but it will do in a pinch.[43]

This respondent makes one salient point that seems to have evaded our feminist friends. The fates of girls and boys, women and men, are forever entwined. What affects one, affects the other. A male respondent expressed this interdependency on a more positive note. After commenting that "these man/boys have it all," he explained why he does not do what they do.

The motivation that keeps him working, keeps him producing well beyond his own needs, "is the love of a good woman and the ambitions we have together for the family we are raising and for the world we want them to inherit." He then asked about our intellectual elite, "Have we violated something that the ancients knew intuitively but which we have arrogantly ignored?"[44] The answer to his question would seem to be yes. I will talk more about the ways to address these violations in the chapters to come.

9.

Why the Home Matters

In one of the most famous scenes in film history, the Tin Man asks a distressed Dorothy what she learned in her journey through Oz. "It's that—if I ever go looking for my heart's desire again," says Dorothy, "I won't look any further than my own backyard. Because if it isn't there, I never really lost it to begin with!" Having answered correctly, Dorothy begins her journey back to Kansas with the mantra, "There's no place like home."

Awakening in her own bed, she finds herself surrounded by the familiar faces of her family—Aunt Em and Uncle Henry—and ranch hands Hunk, Hickory, and Zeke. "Most of it was beautiful," she tells them of Oz. "But just the same, all I kept saying to everybody was, I want to go home."[1]

On watching the *Wizard of Oz* for the first time as a young girl, I remember how desperately scared I was that Dorothy would never get home and how thoroughly relieved I felt when she did. There is no more powerfully universal theme than the individual's yearning for the love and security of home, whether it be a little girl in a Hollywood movie or a powerful warrior like Odysseus in the greatest of Greek epics, *The Odyssey*. Ideally, that home has a mother and father, but even if not, it can still be a home. Dorothy had neither mother nor father, but she never doubted the love and support of Auntie Em and Uncle Henry, who raised her. Whether it has married or single parents, every home can be the haven and shelter in which our daughters are nourished and filled with hope and promise.

If we could shield our daughters from the perils of the outside world, our lives would at least seem simpler. But like Dorothy, young women today have to test themselves in an increasingly strange and sometimes hostile environment to achieve real maturity. "Why didn't you tell her before?" the scarecrow asks the good witch Glinda upon learning that Dorothy herself had always had the power to return home.

"Because she wouldn't have believed me," Glinda responds. "She had to learn it for herself."[2]

No one I know of appreciates the value of home more than Michael Oher. The NFL star spent a childhood wandering through a nightmare Oz, looking for a family to bond with. Even his own deeply dysfunctional family was better than no family at all. It was this quest that led him finally to the strong and caring Tuohys, who would eventually adopt him. In seeing how real families worked, Oher was shocked to feel safe from violence and to see people who worked for a living and came home to take care of their children. This was all magical to him, and he wanted to be part of it. "I wasn't a special project to them," he said of the Tuohys in *I Beat the Odds*. "I was a kid who wanted to feel loved and supported and to know that my dreams and my future were just as important as anyone else's."[3]

Oher was surprised by how many girls and young women identified with his story. One girl who wrote him, "E," had lived an early life nearly as chaotic as his own. While still a student, E had lapsed into addiction and homelessness and may never have recovered had one woman not stepped up to mentor her and a family stepped in to provide her a home. "I finally have what I always wanted," E would write, "a family that loves and cares about each other."[4] Sometimes, that is all it takes. It is just not all that easy to get there.

To assist readers on the journey, I have worked out a series of recommendations, based on the advice of experts I trust and on my own observations in our Best Friends program. I am still learning. Any and all feedback is appreciated.

1. Set the Example

Teenagers are famously cynical creatures, even in Oz. They cannot be told how to behave, at least not successfully. They have to absorb life's lessons from what they experience. There is no better place to learn than at home, and no people more capable of imparting those lessons than a girl's parents.

Beginning in fits and starts in the mid 1990s, a massive, $25 million longitudinal study of adolescents confirmed this very point. Known by the shorthand "Add Health," the study spawned some four thousand journal articles and a host of surprisingly useful conclusions. I say "surprisingly" because academic studies are often skewed to confirm the preconceptions of the researcher. This one was too large and too public to be hijacked. Researchers began by interviewing twenty thousand adolescents from all backgrounds, as well as their parents, and they tracked these youths and others over time. Several of the researchers have translated the data into practical advice that aligns very closely with what I have learned through my own experience with the Best Friends Foundation and what I have gleaned from following traditional, hands-on practitioners, like Dr. Meg Meeker.

2. Keep the Family Intact

For any number of reasons—excitement, acceptance by peers, a need to feel loved—our daughters have sex before they are ready. In her experience, Dr. Meeker sees a continuous theme. "Basically," she wrote, "teens are having sex to find something missing in their lives."[5]

What is usually missing, Meeker believes, is a connection with the adults in their lives, most prominently, their parents. This helps explain why, for instance, divorce is so hard on young girls.

In her breakthrough book *The Unexpected Legacy of Divorce*, Judith Wallerstein found that our daughters never really recover from parental separation. Tellingly, in general, girls from divorced homes start having sex younger than children from stable homes, and with more partners. These same girls tend to marry later, if at all, get divorced more if they do marry, trust their spouses less, and have fewer children. Wallerstein came to these conclusions after a twenty-five-year longitudinal study of her Marin County patients. Her findings caused her to reverse her own thinking on divorce. Even as adults, the children Wallerstein had counseled through divorce nurse a "continuing anger at parents," more often at the dads, whom they regard as "selfish and faithless."[6]

This problem is not limited to Marin County. *A Separation*, which won the 2012 Oscar for best foreign film, details the devastating effect of divorce on an eleven-year-old Iranian girl. At the film's heartbreaking end, she is left standing alone before a judge and being asked which parent she chooses to live with. In some respects, her answer doesn't really matter. Her world as she knew it has already fallen apart.

3. Bond with Her

Michael D. Resnick, a lead Add Health researcher from the University of Minnesota, has argued that, although commissioned by government-supported agencies, the study results have potentially more meaning for parents than for policy makers. Among his general findings was one we will explore in some depth—that teenagers who bond with loving, caring parents are far more likely to avoid high-risk behaviors, sex included, than their peers. I am not sure we needed a $25 million study to confirm this, but all reinforcement is useful.[7]

Many of us in child development call this variable "connected-ness." For Meeker, connectedness begins by getting to know the world your daughter inhabits. "This doesn't mean you have to agree with everything she does or says," she wrote in her book *Your Kids at Risk: How Teen Sex Threatens Our Sons and Daughters*. "Teens can deal with disapproval, so long as they know that you accept and love them despite their flaws."[8]

4. Pay Attention

Add Health researcher Clea McNeely, now at the University of Tennessee, concurs:

> What Add Health does tell us—whether we are politically on the left or the right—is that parents should focus on the appropriate supervision and monitoring of their teens. They should meet boyfriends and girlfriends, get to know their teens' friends, and always know where their children are. They should establish a warm and caring relationship with their children and foster age-appropriate autonomy and independence. Ultimately, good parenting is more important than the specific content of the communication about sex. For me, that's the bottom line.[9]

Resnick, like McNeely and Meeker, believes that effective parenting demands a close attention to how your children are living their lives. "You can look at all sorts of variables related to sex," says Resnick, "but the most powerful predictor is whether teens have been in a romantic relationship for more than 18 months." Resnick draws surprisingly specific conclusions from the data and does not hesitate to share them: "Parents can discourage heavy one-on-one dating and emphasize going out in groups. They should attend to issues like the age at which adolescents start dating and the age difference between partners."[10]

5. Share the Love

Supervision does not work without love. Faith, values, expectations, and discipline are only fruitfully communicated in homes where love is demonstrated. This demonstration begins when the child is old enough to comprehend the world around her, and that comprehension begins when she comes home from the hospital. Girls who feel the love and feel secure in their parents' love will have less need—in the immortal words of Johnny Lee—to go "lookin' for love in all the wrong places."[11]

Along with collaborator Jayne Blanchard, McNeely has extracted from the Add Health data and other research a highly practical book, *The Teen Years Explained: A Guide to Healthy Adolescent Development*.[12] What I like about McNeely's approach is that she helps parents see their children's adolescence less as a time of turmoil than of opportunity. This is the time our daughters will become the women we want them to be.

Or not. Beginning with the bellwether 1955 film *Rebel Without a Cause*, the media have presented adolescence as a problem to be solved, not as a transition to be savored. When we first meet Judy, the character played by Natalie Wood, she is telling a juvenile officer why she has run away from home.

"He hates me," Judy says of her father. When the officer asks why she thinks that, Judy answers, "I don't think. I know. He looks at me like I'm the ugliest thing in the world. He doesn't like my friends—he—he doesn't like anything about me—he calls me—he calls me . . . He calls me a dirty tramp—my own father!"[13]

This formula has been repeated a thousand times since: callous parents, rebellious daughter, high-risk behavior, disaster. The formula clearly works, because we have all seen examples of the same in real life. It is, however, not the norm. As McNeely argues, most kids have more or less successful teen years. They don't end up pregnant, in jail, or dead. And yet, as we have seen in the several tragic cases we have explored, these possibilities loom even for girls who live decent lives.

We improve the chances of saving our daughters from disaster by keeping connected.

Keeping connected today, however, is arguably harder than it has ever been. Our daughters are more mobile than ever, more on the go, and more likely to be electronically walled off even when home. When a parent tries to penetrate that wall, even an attentive parent can be rebuffed, and that is never fun.

6. Maintain Intimacy

A psychologist friend of Dr. Meeker's defines intimacy to mean "INTO-ME-SEE," a useful shorthand if there ever was one.[14] As the child matures, however, she almost inevitably pulls the blinds on what she wants her parents to see. Parents can expect to be rebuffed both in terms of language and of touch.

This is to be the natural course of things. The parent's response will make all the difference. "You must love your child whether or not she returns the favor," says Meeker sagely. "It is the greatest gift you can give, and it will yield great blessings to you and your child."[15]

7. Talk to Her

Once the format is established for conversation, parents need to seize the opportunity to connect with their children. Dr. McNeely and her collaborator, Jayne Blanchard, offer some useful suggestions in that regard.[16]

- Ask questions that encourage real thought beyond a yes-or-no, up-or-down kind of answer.
- Avoid the knee-jerk criticisms of our children's thoughts, of which we are all sometimes guilty.

- Use real facts to encourage a deeper grasp of issues.
- Make teens aware of the way emotions can affect judgment.

I would add to this list, "Give positive reinforcement." During adolescence both boys and girls especially need to be told good things about themselves. I love the phrase, "Catch your child being good."

For better or worse, children learn the art of conversation at home. They need someone to teach them the power of words, the power to soothe, the power to amuse, the power to instruct, the power to hurt. Too many children don't know how to tell a joke or to laugh at one. As much as I respect McNeely, I cannot fully agree with her when she says, "Teasing should be taken seriously and never tolerated at home, in school, or in the community."[17] Remember, laughter is the best medicine. Find good-spirited humor in your world where you can find it.

Children will always tease. They just need to learn to tease within acceptable limits. Sisters, for instance, can tease their brothers about their weight. Brothers can never tease their sisters about *their* weight. Humor only works when no one gets hurt. As writer Gail Parent observed of her own mother, "She knew what all smart women knew: Laughter made you live better and longer."[18] The parents' experience is invaluable here. They have to set the tone.

8. Listen to Her

"If you want to be listened to," said novelist Marge Piercy knowingly, "you should put in time listening."[19] Dr. Meg Meeker adds her professional approval. "Even if you don't like what you hear, listen," she says. "Somewhere in the words and sentences are reflections of what's happening in your child's heart."[20]

Meeker has some practical tips on how to facilitate listening:

- Find a space in your daughter's world in which you can enter unobtrusively.
- Sit down.
- Make eye contact and shut out distractions.
- Don't interrupt.
- Ask personal questions.[21]

If parents start listening to their children when small, it will not seem obtrusive to continue asking questions as the children mature. Even if parents begin this process when their kids are in their teens, it can still be effective if, as Meeker noted, they do so "persistently, gently, and sincerely."[22]

9, Negotiate the Gray

Dr. Joann Deak makes the case, as virtually all professionals do, that young girls today are growing up in a moral climate much more fraught with peril and uncertainty than the one their parents experienced, no matter how young the parents might be. She has observed that "destructive or high risk behaviors that used to play out on the social fringe are part of mainstream culture now, and girls struggle to accommodate them."[23] Today, even strict traditionalists will find themselves and their daughters wading through a lot more gray than they might expect.

Deak believes that the gray should be negotiated with both the parents and the daughter making contributions. She advises the parents not to rush to make a fix, but to "layer" their responses to cover an evolving situation, to discuss viable strategies, and to guide the daughter's decision making throughout.[24]

In the tragic stories we have covered in this book, the young women in question could have used this kind of involved parental help in negotiating the gray areas of their own lives. Without that help, for all their virtues, several of these girls made some unfortunate decisions. Yeardley Love did not seek protective relief from George Huguely. Natasha Marsh thought she could maintain a secretive relationship with an older man, while still being a part of a well-known couple in her high school, without negative consequence. And Morgan Harrington left the security of the concert on university grounds, alone.

In each case, the young woman underestimated the evil in the world and overestimated her own ability to handle whatever evil there was. To a certain degree this failure flows from the "I am woman; hear me roar" drumbeat of the feminist establishment. Yes, we want our daughters to be proud and independent, but we also want them to be safe.

McNeely agrees with Deak that adolescents need to assume responsibility for the decisions that will affect their lives, but parents must instruct them early on that there is an art to decision making. Teaching by example is, of course, the most natural and effective way to instruct. On selected family decisions, children can benefit if they see their parents weighing the plusses and minuses of a given course of action out loud.

Family counselors almost universally agree that parents need what Deak calls a "core value or philosophy" on which to center their decision making.[25] What she does not say, what few in the mainstream do say, is that the firmer and deeper that core, the less gray there will be to negotiate. A family whose daughter has a moral commitment to chastity, for instance, will not have to negotiate birth control, shacking up with a boyfriend, or whether oral sex is really sex.

Whatever their core values, parents do well to instruct their daughters in a risk-benefit analysis of any action of consequence. How much happier will a given course of action make a girl, and at what cost? "Many adolescents live in the now," say McNeely and Blanchard. "Show them the benefits of future thinking by anticipating difficult situations and planning in advance how to handle them."[26] It also helps steer our children toward friends who, on balance, make more wise decisions than not.

10. Set Guidelines

As useful as it is to have our daughters participate in the decisions that affect their lives, they need to know there are limits within which those decisions must be made. In *Reviving Ophelia*, Mary Pipher shares a couple of case studies of loving, supportive, two-parent families in which the parents' liberalism overtakes their good sense.

In encouraging their daughters' autonomy from early on, the parents had no idea how unprepared these girls were for the tsunami of cultural signals that would blow them away as soon as they reached middle school. "Their daughters turned out much as research would have predicted," wrote Pipher—confused, angry, rebellious, overwhelmed by the temptations of adolescence. "The parents' laissez-faire approach didn't work well in a time of AIDS and addictions," she concluded.[27]

In the twenty-first century, love is essential, but it is not enough. Parents cannot treat children, even mature ones, the way they treat adults. Their ability to make sound decisions is not fully developed. Even if they object, especially if they object, children need to be told what they can do and cannot do. They will thank their parents about twenty years later.

11. Eat Together

The earlier the connection is established with a child, the less likely it is that the connection will be severed or strained. One way to make the bond feel natural is through family meals, especially dinner. Those of us who grew up around the family dinner table, where the day's events were narrated and the outside world discussed, treasure those memories. "In the childhood memories of every good cook there is a kitchen, a warm stove, a simmering pot and mom," said writer Barbara Costikyan, and I suspect she is right.[28]

Unfortunately, many of our children will not have these memories. As a society, we have devalued the dinner table, and the breakfast table as well. Kerry Cohen described dining at her childhood home as "eat what you can find when you're hungry."[29] The culprits are many: mothers whose careers take precedence over their families; stay-at-home mothers who resent preparing food on a scheduled basis for their families; fathers whose ambitions overwhelm their good sense; schools that casually schedule practices during dinner hours. I know more than a few women whose social lives take priority over their family time.

We also need to unplug at dinnertime. Shut off the television; put the smart phones away; pull the iPod out of the children's ears. I have had to work on this with my own family, I assure you. It is not easy. The children will resist, but we must insist. Dinner matters. It is never too late to restore a practice so potentially valuable.

12. Restore the Hearth

Parents put a further strain on connectedness when they allow their children's bedrooms to serve as isolated electronic hubs. Too many children now wall themselves in with their own televisions, their own music, their own video games, their own Internet. Parents are much better off not letting this situation develop than trying to reverse it.

A century ago the hearth served as the central focus of a home. In the days before central heating, family members did not need encouragement to congregate there. A half century ago, the family television served a similar function. As much as we liked to gripe about commercials, they encouraged commentary and communication. The limited channel selections minimized arguments. Today, parents have to fight the culture to create a centered family dynamic at the table or in the living room. It is worth the fight.

13. Appreciate Her

The art of appreciating our children is so fundamental that Meeker put it in italics. "At issue," she wrote, *"isn't what they've done; it's who they are."*[30] Our daughters should not have to win something to be appreciated. They should wake up feeling welcome in their world.

If parents want to recognize accomplishment, it is wiser to recognize the virtues our daughters have exhibited in striving for a goal, even if they don't reach it—their patience, their perseverance, their sportsmanship, their modesty. If success comes easily, humility may not. Just as our children keep us humble, so we must them.

Parents should caution their daughters, too, that real accomplishment takes real effort. "I do not know anyone who has got to the top without hard work," said former British prime minister Margaret Thatcher. "That is the recipe. It will not always get you to the top, but should get you pretty near."[31]

14. Teach Empathy

For some girls, empathy—the ability to identify with another person's feelings—seems to come naturally. For others, it is a tough sell. To be certain, empathy starts at home. If parents don't show it, their children will probably not either. As McNeely and Blanchard observe, it is imperative that parents "demonstrate tolerance and generosity in [their] thoughts, words, and actions."[32]

Perhaps the simplest way to teach empathy is to ask how a given action would make a child feel if she were the recipient of it and not, say, a passive bystander, or even the perpetrator. The teaching of empathy sometimes benefits by indirection—that is, talking about an incident that involves people other than our own children.

In teaching empathy, we parents need to recognize that our daughters will be confronting situations where empathy is an unknown commodity. Liz Seccuro discovered this at the Phi Psi house when she went looking for help that she expected to find but did not. (Note: As of August 2012, this fraternity house has been under investigation for hazing. Not only do they not care about their girls; they do not seem to care about future "brothers."[33])

This is the house that years later hosted Tucker Max. "It's not even that I didn't care about other people. It's way beyond that," Max would later confess. "I just didn't even understand that other people even *existed* or mattered."[34] Although Max claims now to see the folly of his ways, far too many seemingly respectable young men have embraced Max as a role model. His books have sold more than 2 million copies. He should buy back the rights to his books, take them off the market, and donate the rest of his ill-gotten profits to helping our daughters.

If he can be taken at his word, Max now has a useful message to impart to his many fans. "There's an emptiness and a loneliness to hooking up so much," he told a *Forbes* interviewer in 2012. "You don't notice it or care, when you're below a certain age, or a narcissist. But once you develop empathy, once you develop a soul, the loneliness and the emptiness become too much."[35]

15. Understand Her Stress

Although the great majority of our daughters will survive their adolescence, and even look back upon those years with a certain fondness, it is a time of seemingly unending stress. The stress results to a large degree from the decisions that teens now have to make for themselves that were once either made for them or beyond the need to be made.

These decisions range from the everyday, like what to wear, to the life changing, like whether to have sex or what to major in.

A veritable library of books exists on stress management. What parents need to know is that they cannot simply talk their daughters out of the stress they may be feeling. Parents need to monitor, to love unconditionally, to connect. And sometimes, when they sense their daughters are in danger, they need to intrude, to impose their own experience. They need to act, and they cannot be afraid to do so. This all begins with an active concern. "I think the one lesson I have learned," said TV news anchor Diane Sawyer, "is that there is no substitute for paying attention."[36]

16. Share Your Faith

Secular psychologists are indifferent to religious faith, if not openly hostile to it. In *Reviving Ophelia*, Mary Pipher does not shy away from saying so. After interviewing a wholesome, happy teen from a fundamentalist family, named "Jody," Pipher observed, "Psychologists would condemn many of the elements in Jody's background—the traditional sex roles of the parents; the lack of lessons, camps and other enrichment experiences; the strict religion and the conformity of family members."[37]

Even Pipher struggles with the issue. "Why would a girl raised in such an authoritarian, even sexist, family be so well liked, outgoing, and self-confident?" she wonders. The answer is not that hard to discern. The faith provides the moral clarity that children need. The family provides the love and reinforcement to help the children honor their faith. Pipher worries that such children will risk "later conformity and blandness," but Pipher likely does not have enough experience with this kind of family to know that her worry is misplaced.[38]

From Pipher's perspective, it is the role of the family "to provide moral clarity without sacrificing too much personal freedom." Yet, as she also acknowledges, the parents have to actively fight a "dysfunctional culture," one that grabs much more of their daughter's attention than they do.[39] This is an unequal fight. A strong, shared faith between parents and children can level the playing field. Not much else can.

17. Express Disapproval

Dr. Meeker does not mince words, and I heartily agree with her. Parents "must" communicate their disapproval of teen sex to their daughters.[40] This is not mere whim on Meeker's part. Dr. Leonard Sax agrees: "Parents have to be willing to assert their authority," he wrote.[41]

Among the findings of the Add Health study is that teenagers in grades eight to eleven "who perceive that their mother disapproves of their engaging in sexual intercourse are more likely than their peers to delay sexual activity." The data also suggests that "when mothers recommend specific methods of birth control, teens are less likely to perceive strong maternal disapproval of premarital sex."[42] Of course, a mother or father who has a strong connection to the daughter in question has a much better chance of being listened to. Says Meeker, "There is perhaps no better or stronger force at their disposal than connectedness."[43]

If the daughter is listening, the parent can explore the other factors that lead young girls to make risky decisions, particularly self-esteem issues and peer pressure. Although it is critical that our daughters know the risks involved, a wholesome, ongoing dialogue on the subject of sex and love generally works better than a scary lecture. As actress Shirley MacLaine cleverly noted, "Sex is hardly ever just about sex."[44]

18. Stress Abstinence

One surprising, and not universally welcome, finding of the Add Health research is that students who took a virginity pledge promising to abstain from sex until marriage were found to delay intercourse by an average of eighteen months.[45]

I say "not universally welcome" because of personal experience. The Bush administration's Health and Human Services department awarded our Best Friends Foundation a five-year, $2.5 million grant to counsel inner-city teenagers on the benefits of marriage and related issues. The original Healthy Marriage grant allowed the discussion of abstinence as well as the risks involved with teen sex. With sexually transmitted diseases and infections at record proportions, most medical and health professionals concur that sex is a high-risk behavior for unmarried people, especially young, uneducated ones.

There is also, of course, the question of teen pregnancy that all but condemns the young mother to a lifetime of poverty. As we learned in the Gloucester pregnancy outbreak discussed earlier, "a lack of birth control played no part."[46] Those were the words of the principal, Joseph Sullivan. These students knew all they needed to about protection and contraception. But since their parents and the surrounding culture did not strongly discourage them from having sex, that knowledge did them no good.

For all the value of teaching abstinence, after the election of president Barack Obama, the word came down from the administration that we were no longer able to discuss the subject or even to talk about the risks inherent in teen sex. Indeed, we were instructed to remove the word "abstinence" from our curriculum materials.

In the way of background, our Best Friends instructors teach that the right choice for young people is to say no to high-risk behaviors of any kind. And certainly, with the very real possibility of STDs and unwanted pregnancies, sex involves great risks for teenagers, with or without the use of contraception. We were not about to present these girls a smorgasbord of sexual options, knowing that some of them could prove harmful.

Today, most parents and many public health practitioners agree that the later a girl becomes sexually active, and the fewer partners she has, the better. Few would disagree that the best and healthiest sexual choice for young people of child-bearing age is and will always be within a monogamous marriage. That much said, the Best Friends curriculum was not "abstinence-only" in the sense that we limited our discussion to sex. From the beginning, our goal has been to give our daughters a holistic sense of who they are and what they could be.

Recent survey data from the Centers for Disease Control (CDC) suggests that programs like Best Friends, especially those with an inner-city focus, have been working. As reported by the CDC, the percent of black high school students who have "ever had sexual intercourse" fell from 82 percent in 1991 to 60 percent in 2011.[47] Although the article tries to make the case for the schools' HIV education as the reason for the decline, the percent of sexually active black youths *not* using condoms increased during the same period.[48]

We are also told that "half of all black men younger than 30 who are gay or bisexual will be infected with HIV within the next decade." Thus, the article's headline, "More Black Teenagers Practicing Safe Sex," makes no sense at all.[49] Those having sex were *less* likely to practice safe sex. If I were the editor, I would have headlined the article, "Significant Decline in Sexual Activity among Black High School Students" and put the article on the front page. In my lead, I would have credited community-based abstinence education programs for the decline and noted that these programs were funded by the government until the Obama administration saw fit to do otherwise.

The reason talk of abstinence education has become verboten would require a book of its own. It has nothing to do with the well-being of our daughters and everything to do with the progressive feminist value system, such as it is. The National Women's Health Network does not shrink from putting its ideology front and center in its allegedly nonideological mission statement: "The NWHN supports access to safe and effective reproductive health technologies, services and information without restrictions driven by ideology," reads the opening sentence on the NWHN "issues" page. "We defend women's sexual and reproductive health and autonomy against anti-choice threats which would undermine access to contraceptive and abortion care."[50]

This is not the kind of thinking that allows for parental involvement in raising healthy, happy, wholesome daughters. This is not the kind of thinking that even encourages the perpetuation of the human race. This *is* the kind of thinking, however, that leaves young women vulnerable to STDs, unwanted pregnancies, and predators even more sexually liberated than the women are.

If educators only talk about how to perform sex "safely," they cannot speak to the moral issues whose absence from the conversation makes sex risky in the first place. Happily married couples don't worry about STDs or HIV. Unfortunately, this is the very philosophy our daughters are exposed to in every public school, all but a few universities, and in a thousand different mass media outlets every day of the year.

Given this silence, I was particularly pleased by the speaker at Princeton University's Class Day in 2011. My younger son, Joe, was graduating, and I was just another proud mom sitting in the back. Addressing the audience that day was Princeton grad Brooke Shields, an actress who had already achieved a level of fame by the time she started classes in 1983. After joking about how the campus's select drama society, the Tiger Lilies, did not extend her an invite, Shields said archly, "By the way, girls, I have the lead in a hit Broadway show, and, oh yes, I was a virgin the entire time I was at Princeton."[51] Instinctively, I let out a whoop. Surprisingly, many of the male students applauded as well.

19. Keep the Home Secure

Today, our daughters face enormous pressure from their peers. This pressure is amplified by the powers of social media. Girls are harassed online to send indecent photos to their boyfriends and bullied by their girlfriends to do all manner of improper things. Boys, even more than girls, are steered by their friends to visit an appalling variety of indecent websites. Parents cannot afford to steer clear of this technological battlefield. Ignorance is no excuse.

Parents should monitor their children's cell phone and Internet activity. One service, called TextGuard, is an application that a parent can install on a child's cell phone. Once installed, a parent can log onto a website and monitor the flow and content of the child's texting, e-mailing, and browsing. The application also allows parents to block suspicious numbers and suspend inappropriate activity.[52]

An application called "My Mobile Watchdog" alerts all relevant parties—including police and school authorities—to messaging that comes to a selected phone from a number on the watchdog list. This is an excellent way to curtail online harassment. A third application, iWonder Surf, allows parents the means to control and monitor the websites the child is visiting. Every time a child goes to a site, the application records the visit and instantly sends traffic reports to the parent.[53]

At some point, a parent must acknowledge his or her child's right to a certain amount of privacy, but that is a right that should be earned, not simply surrendered. Parents would be surprised, I think, at how much their younger children will appreciate the excuse of parental oversight to avoid behavior in which they really would prefer not to participate.

What Mothers and Sisters Can Do

There is much a girl's mother and sisters can do to protect and encourage the young women in their midst. Mothers have a more basic connection with their daughters than fathers ever can. Sisters, especially older sisters, have that same shared experience base. "Mothers and daughters are both female," wrote Dr. JoAnn Deak. "A mother often knows, in the deepest meaning of the word, what it is like to be in the situation her daughter lives through."[1]

Some of my fondest memories as a little girl are the times my mother and I would read books together. Books were my solace and my escape. After my fourth grade year, my father's promotion necessitated a move from Augusta, Georgia, to Charlotte, North Carolina. This meant leaving my best friends and the school I loved, T. Harry Garrett Elementary, where I had the distinction of being Mary in the school Christmas play. Of course, now there *are* no Christmas plays in public schools.

Being the new girl was a very difficult transition for me. And although Northerners could never tell the difference, my Georgia accent struck the Carolinians as backward and comical. When I said "laig" for the first time, the whole class laughed at me. You can believe

I dropped that accent pretty darn fast, but not before I was marked as "the new girl from Georgia." To top it all off, one of the teachers at my school, for some perverse reason, told the class what a backward state Georgia was—pure fodder for the bullies in my class.

I had one resource through it all that every girl should have: a mother who understood and cared. When I went home in tears, my always-resourceful mother immediately went and pulled information from her files as a nursing instructor in Georgia on facts showing where Georgia ranked high in various economic, agricultural, and educational measurements. In fact, in some cases, Georgia outranked North Carolina. She told me to take this information and share it with my fifth grade teacher. To my great dismay, the teacher thought this effort to defend my former state impudent and took an immediate dislike to me, but the point had been made.

I took refuge in my home, where my mother loved for me to read to her. I still remember the wonderful books she got for me: *The Yearling, Black Beauty, Beautiful Joe, Five Little Peppers and How they Grew, The Borrowers, Swiss Family Robinson, Bambi, The Ugly Duckling,* not to mention all the Nancy Drew and Cherry Ames books. These stories inspired me and gave me a lifelong love of literature. I am forever indebted to my mother for providing and promoting this love of reading, which sustained me through a difficult time in my adolescence.

As I reflect back on my transitional years, I realize how important it was that my mother supported me with this difficult teacher and my stressful social life. A mother's loving word or kindness during a tough time can ease the pain and sting of childhood ridicule. By contrast, a sharp word or rebuke from a mother at a sensitive time can cause untold pain to her daughter.

Mothers need to be aware of the incredible impact they have on their daughters, especially between the ages of ten and sixteen. Many mothers today try to be their daughters' best friends. They think that if they buy them hip clothes and share in their gossip, they will endear themselves to their daughters. It doesn't work. What girls this age need, I have discovered, is guidance, direction, and a sense of security. Having a cool mom is not nearly as important as having a warm mom, one who will inspire her daughter intellectually and encourage her to feel compassion for others. A mother who stresses kindness over coolness and integrity over popularity provides lessons that will last a lifetime.

I cannot tell you how many times I read Louisa May Alcott's *Little Women* as a young girl. A best seller when published in 1868, it continues to entrance young readers even to this day. I was heartened to read in a recent *New York Times* article on e-books a comment by Mia Garcia, a twelve-year-old from Touchet, Washington.

After receiving a Sony Reader from her grandparents for Christmas, Mia promptly downloaded *Little Women*. "It made me cry," said Mia.[2] It made me cry, too, when I was Mia's age. The story is timeless, and the twelve-year-old girls today, including those in our Best Friends classrooms, have the same instincts that twelve-year-old girls had 150 years ago. As proof of its timelessness, Hollywood has made three high-end versions of the film, most recently in 1994, all of them successful. In 2004, a musical version debuted on Broadway with the slogan, "Six generations have read the story. This one will sing it." As timeless as *Little Women* are the words of wisdom mothers and sisters can share with a young lady they love.

Explain the Big Picture

The original book tells the story of the March family: the mother, "Marmee"; the father, who is away much of the time with the Union Army in the Civil War as a chaplain; and the four daughters—Meg, Jo, Beth, and Amy. The opening page captures the four March daughters contemplating the challenges young girls have faced from time immemorial. With their father gone, they have very little money. Marmee has recommended that they forgo Christmas presents to aid the Union cause. Young girls being what they are, they are not thrilled. "It's so dreadful to be poor," says Meg. The self-pitying Amy chips in, "I don't think it's fair for some girls to have lots of pretty things, and other girls nothing at all."[3]

Although Steinem or Friedan might tell the girls to think of themselves first, Alcott has a different message. The girls must fight through their own self-involvement to learn how much richer life can be when they transcend self, when they embrace their neighbors, when they sacrifice to support their nation's noble cause, and when they trust in God to see them through.

Marmee shows the girls the way. When Jo asks her how she accepts her husband's absence and the deprivations of war so stoically, Marmee answers,

> I gave my best to the country I love, and kept my tears till he was gone. Why should I complain, when we both have merely done our duty and will surely be the happier for it in the end? If I don't seem to need help, it is because I have a better friend, even than Father, to comfort and sustain me.[4]

Marmee does not hesitate to remind Jo just who that friend is and how much support that friend can lend.

> My child, the troubles and temptations of your life are beginning, and may be many; but you can overcome and outlive them all if you learn to feel the strength and tenderness of your Heavenly Father as you do that of your earthly one. The more you love and trust Him, the nearer you will feel to Him, and the less you will depend on human power and wisdom. His love and care never tire or change, can never be taken from you, but may become the source of lifelong peace, happiness, and strength. Believe this heartily, and go to God with all your little cares, and hopes, and sins, and sorrows, as freely and confidingly as you come to your mother.[5]

For several millennia now, young girls have been turning to God for strength and support much as they have turned to their parents. Over time, society has developed an accumulated body of wisdom about how young women can best enrich their own lives and the lives of the people they love. About a half century ago, a popular movement emerged that would challenge traditional wisdom and seek to replace it with something new and untested. The results have not been pretty.

Encourage Ambition

Implicit in the new feminism is the belief that in the past young women submitted to a patriarchal authority and dared not dream of meaningful work beyond the house. The women who conjured this history have not talked to famed Nobel Prize–winning, African American writer Toni Morrison. "Long before I was a success," says Morrison, who was an adolescent in the 1940s, "my mother made me feel like I could be one."[6]

The great actress Helen Hayes once observed,

> My mother drew a distinction between achievement and success. She said that achievement is the knowledge that you have studied and worked hard and done the best that is in you. Success is being praised by others, and that's nice, too, but not as important or satisfying. Always aim for achievement and forget about success.[7]

And please note that Helen Hayes was an adolescent a century ago.

As a reading of *Little Women* shows, mothers were encouraging their daughters earlier still. When Amy, an aspiring artist, learns that her aunt plans to take her on a trip to Europe, she tells her sisters, "It isn't a mere pleasure trip for me, girls. It will decide my career; for if I have any genius, I shall find it out in Rome, and will do something to prove it." When asked what happens if she finds she lacks the talent to succeed at that level, Amy answers, "Then I shall come home and teach drawing for a living."[8]

The family's real careerist is Jo, the book's authorial voice and an aspiring writer. At one point the girls share their dreams. Both Beth and Meg dream of domestic happiness, Meg's domestic dream a good deal more extravagant than Beth's. At this stage of her life, Jo has little interest in home or family. "I want to do something splendid before I go into my castle—something heroic, or wonderful—that won't be forgotten after I'm dead," she tells her sisters. "I think I shall write books, and get rich and famous; that would suit me, so that is my favorite dream."[9]

In the March household, her father encourages her ambitions. When Jo receives her first acceptance of a story and a one-hundred-dollar check to go with it, she is enormously excited, but Mr. March says, "You can do better than this, Jo. Aim at the highest and never mind the money."[10]

Jo is not at all eager to get married, an institution that she jokes "halves one's rights and doubles one's duties." The domestic future she imagines for herself is a limited one: "An old maid, that's what I'm to be. A literary spinster, with a pen for a spouse, a family of stories for children, and twenty years hence a morsel of fame, perhaps."[11]

It doesn't turn out that way. Jo moves to New York, in part to pursue her career as a writer. There she meets an impoverished German writing instructor. Like her father, Mr. Bhaer insists that she can write better than she has settled for. She takes his advice and does, and eventually they marry. Together they turn entrepreneurial and begin a school for boys, the subject for her next book.

The book ends at Marmee's sixtieth birthday party. Celebrating are her daughters, all blessed with husbands and children and all thankful for their blessings. Says Jo, "The life I wanted then seems selfish, lonely and cold to me now. I haven't given up the hope that I may write a good book yet, but I can wait, and I'm sure it will be all the better for such experiences and illustrations as these."[12]

Although Alcott herself never married, she carved out a successful literary career in an era when today's feminists tell us women could do no such thing. As it happens, she achieved real success only when she began to write about the "experiences and illustrations" of domestic life that Jo imagined for herself at novel's end.

Encourage Marriage

Of course, the best way for a mother to encourage her daughter is to show in her own life the everyday wonder of the institution. Still, occasionally, a little lecturing might help, and no one has done it better than Mrs. March. "To be loved and chosen by a good man is the best and sweetest thing which can happen to a woman," she tells her daughters. "It is natural to think of it, Meg, right to hope and wait for it, and wise to prepare for it, so that when the happy time comes, you may feel ready for the duty and worthy of the joy."

Having said that, Marmee reassures her daughters of her love whether they marry or don't marry. "One thing remember, my girls," she adds. "Mother is always ready to be your confidant, Father to be your friend, and both of us hope and trust that our daughters, whether married or single, will be the pride and comfort of our lives."[13]

Prepare for Backlash

Not surprisingly, there has been something of a feminist backlash against *Little Women*, and especially the character of Jo March. On an NPR piece a few years back, one of the women interviewed expressed the grudges of her time and place.

"Louisa May Alcott was the Jo that I would have liked to see—the one who stayed independent, who supported her family because she was a working woman who was able to earn off the output of her mind," said the woman. She added that Alcott "had to betray a little bit of herself to write Jo in as yet another little woman who marries and looks up adoringly at the man who comes into her life."[14]

Unfortunately, teachers in every school district in America and in every university are sharing this kind of revisionist sentiment with our daughters on a daily basis: marriage and children are secondary, incidental even. Staying "independent" and "able to earn" is the preferred future.

As a case in point, the word *marriage* does not appear anywhere in the spring 2012 list of course offerings for "studies in women and gender" at the University of Virginia. Neither do the words *children* or even *family*. Instead, students learn how "gay rights and women's movements responded to or incorporated the rhetoric of Cold War domestic anxieties" or how "ecofeminist scholars and activists [are] daring to imagine an alternative future" or why "recent work in fields such as queer gothic and phenomenology" is important. One course even endeavors to address "the various ways that men (like women) are gendered, and can be the subject of inquiries into gender, sexuality, inequality, and privilege in their own right."[15]

At some point in the not-too-distant future, state legislators and alumni will wake up one morning and ask themselves, *Why in the world are we subsidizing this nonsense?* In the meantime, our daughters will be exposed to it, and some of them will even believe it.

Be Your Sister's Keeper

It is likely that no one better understood the overflowing impulses of young women than the early nineteenth-century British author Jane Austen. More than even Alcott, Austen's influence endures. Her novels continue to sell well two centuries after they were written, and at least five feature-length films have been made from her books just since 1995. Given the universality of her themes, the books have also spawned popular adaptations, like the hit 1995 film

Clueless, based on the book *Emma* and plausibly set in a Beverly Hills high school.

The Austen book that deals most specifically with a girl's responsibility to her sister is *Sense and Sensibility*, the excellent 1995 film version of which was directed by Taiwanese filmmaker Ang Lee. Upon the death of the family's father, the eldest daughter, Elinor Dashwood, though only nineteen, assumes the father's role, that of the family counselor. What qualifies her is her "strength of understanding" and "coolness of judgment," both virtues that are lacking in her mother and, more problematically, in her beautiful younger sister, Marianne. Today we might use the word *sensitivity* where Austen used *sensibility*. In either case, Marianne has an "excess" of it. She is "eager in everything" and "every thing but prudent."[16]

When Marianne throws herself at the dashing but un-vetted Mr. Willoughby, Elinor tries gently to rein her in. Marianne will hear none of it. "I have been too much at my ease, too happy, too frank," she says sarcastically. "I have erred against every common place notion of decorum; I have been open and sincere where I ought to have been reserved, spiritless, dull, and deceitful."[17] Nothing else matters. Transfixed, Marianne abuses her friendships and ignores her responsibilities in order to focus on her relationship with Willoughby.

Unfortunately for Marianne, Elinor proves to be right. Willoughby turns out to be a scoundrel. He earlier fathered a child out of wedlock and then abandoned Marianne when he saw an opportunity to marry for money. Although Elinor saw a basic decency in the man, she recognized that "too early an independence" had made him "extravagant and vain—extravagance and vanity had made him cold-hearted and selfish."[18]

In recovering from a serious illness, Marianne has the chance to reflect on how deeply she erred. "I cannot express my own abhorrence of myself," she tells Elinor. "Whenever I looked towards the past, I saw some duty neglected, or some failing indulged. Everybody seemed injured by me." When Elinor tries to comfort her, Marianne thanks her for the effort. "I have laid down my plan," she concludes, "and if I am capable of adhering to it, my feelings shall be governed and my temper improved. They shall no longer worry others, nor torture myself."[19]

As it does for many of Jane Austen's characters, all turns out well for both Marianne and Elinor. Each marries a man who loves her and can protect her, although, truth be told, Elinor almost blows her chance by being a bit too sensible. Still, better to err on the side of sense than of sensibility, a bit of wisdom that is all the more relevant today. Older sisters—and brothers, for that matter—would do well to imitate Elinor. Love your sister, counsel her, and don't be afraid to intervene if need be.

Love Your Daughter Unconditionally

Bridget Gove, the beautiful, intelligent, and skilled daughter of my cousin Paul and his wife, Sally, was killed riding on the back of a motorcycle on the Fourth of July, 2012. She had graduated from York College, magna cum laude, with a bachelor of science in nursing. Her colleagues at work so admired her that she was awarded the Excellence in Nursing award, an honor typically given to nurses with much more seniority. I asked Sally, as the mother of two daughters, if she had any words she would like to share with other mothers in this chapter.

In response, Sally said she would urge mothers to remember that when they talk to their daughters, those may be the last words their girls will ever hear. Life is fragile and uncertain, and our loved ones can be taken from us in an instant. Sally is grateful that her last words were, "You look so pretty. I am proud of you." Sally and Paul's strong, abiding faith in God has given them the strength to know that Bridget's years on earth were joyful and fulfilled and that Bridget will be forever young and at peace in heaven.

What Fathers and Brothers Can Do

Comedian Chris Rock is not a man for everyone's tastes. Like too many comedians, he indulges more freely than he might in various profanities, but there is, I think, a method to his coarseness.

One routine Rock has done on at least a few occasions has caught the public's attention. Its nearly two hundred thousand hits on YouTube suggest that it has struck home with a healthy portion of his audience.[1] Rock begins the routine by talking about his then baby daughter. "It's amazing when you have a girl," he says. "You're a man. You have a girl. It's an eye-opener." About this he is absolutely right. Having a daughter can teach a man more about respect for women and his responsibility to protect them than could a college course in the same.

"I realize I am the man in her life," Rock says. "My relationship with my daughter is going to affect her relationships with men for the rest of her life." Here, Rock turns teacher. He begins instructing an audience battered by the worst elements of popular culture and subverted by a government that has for years unwittingly discouraged African American fathers from assuming their natural place in the family. Now, Rock talks of his own daughter and does so in a mounting comedic riff. Still, he never stops teaching. "I'm walking with my daughter," he says. "I'm talking with my daughter. I'm looking at her. I'm pushing her in her stroller, I pick her up and I stare at her."

Assume Responsibility

Rock now gets really serious. Let me paraphrase his message: A father, if he has one absolute obligation, is to keep his daughter out of the sex trade. If he fails to do that, Rock insists in his highly colorful vernacular, he has failed as a father. Here the natural instinct of the father runs smack into the ideology of liberation feminists. As Dr. Leonard Sax has pointed out, it was Germaine Greer who first "provided support to the idea that pole dancers are liberated women,"and that feminine modesty was somehow a symptom of patriarchal oppression.[2] Rock knows better. As industry insiders will tell you, the sex trade depends on girls with what he calls "daddy issues." This includes strippers, pole dancers, prostitutes, and the young women who provide the porn industry with "its product."

"Some of these girls were abused, and some of them just missed a few hugs," says Rock. "Some of them are like, 'Daddy, can we talk?'" Here, Rock imitates the father. "Hey, I'm watching the game." Now Rock's imagined daughter responds by promising to go into the sex trade as a way of punishing her father. Rock exaggerates for effect, but only a little.

A young woman who dated Tucker Max for a year reinforces Rock's thesis in explaining her own attachment to Max. "I mean, why would you throw yourself at a guy who you know is going to treat you poorly, who's always treated women poorly? It doesn't make sense," the woman told a *Forbes* interviewer. "But if you grow up in a house with a dad who's an a_____, it makes a lot of sense."[3]

Be Present in Her Life

Although her word choice is a good deal more refined, Dr. Meg Meeker makes much the same point this woman and Chris Rock do in her definitive book on the subject, *Strong Fathers, Strong Daughters*. "Your daughter needs the best of who you are: your strength, your courage, your intelligence, and your fearlessness," she says to the fathers in her audience. "She needs your empathy, assertiveness, and self-confidence. She needs *you*."[4]

For the last twenty-five years, while raising four children of her own, Meeker has practiced pediatric and adolescent medicine. In the course of her practice, and through her own family life, the good doctor has emerged as arguably one of the nation's leading authorities on parenting and has shared her wisdom in at least half a dozen books. The findings Meeker presents on the benefits of a strong father-daughter relationship are inarguable and entirely worth citing.[5] For young girls:

- Toddlers securely attached to their fathers are better at problem solving.
- Six-month-old babies with active dads score higher on tests of mental development.
- Children with dads present in the home manage stress better.
- Girls whose fathers are warm and protective do better in school.
- Girls who are close to their father are less likely to be anxious or withdrawn.

As our daughters mature, they face more temptations from the culture and more pressure from their peers, but fathers ought never to underestimate their own influence:[6]

- No single factor will discourage drug and alcohol use and

promiscuity more than a girl's connectedness to her father and mother.

- Girls with attentive fathers are more assertive.
- Girls who know their father cares about them are much less likely to commit suicide, to abuse their bodies, or to suffer from depression or low self-esteem.
- A daughter's self-esteem is best predicted by her father's physical affection.
- Girls with involved fathers are twice as likely to stay in high school and much more likely to attempt college.
- Girls with strong fathers in their lives are much less likely to flaunt their bodies to get attention.
- Girls defer sexual activity if they know their parents disapprove of premarital sex and birth control.
- Teen girls who live with both parents are three times less likely to lose their virginity before their sixteenth birthday.
- Girls from middle-class families have a fivefold lower risk of out-of-wedlock birth if their father is present in the home.

Fill the Void

Every man reading this book knows a family that is missing its father either through divorce, death, or abandonment before marriage. There is an opportunity here for those males close to a fatherless family to step up and fill the void. The closer that male is, the more like a responsibility that opportunity looks. Older brothers have a particularly useful role they can play as their sister's protector and teacher if there is no father in the house—or even if there is.

Mothers likewise need to know that their daughters will benefit from having a responsible, loving male in their lives. It could be a grandfather, a godfather, an uncle, or a very steady friend. Among the worst candidates for this role is a mother's current "boyfriend." The rate of sexual and physical abuse of our daughters by boyfriends dwarfs that of married fathers or even stepfathers. Mothers have to be extraordinarily cautious in this regard. The temporary affection of a man cannot begin to compensate for the permanent scarring of a daughter.

Help Her See Clearly

In *Strong Fathers, Strong Daughters*, Meeker creates a vision of female strength that makes one doubt that feminists really understand what the word *strong* means in a female context. One component of strength dear to Meeker is totally alien to today's feminist. Says she, "Genuine humility is the starting point for every other virtue."[7]

My online thesaurus offers as synonyms for *humility* "lowliness," "meekness," and "submissiveness."[8] This is why Meeker is careful to distinguish "genuine" humility from any contemporary misunderstanding of the word. Submissiveness is not a virtue. Neither is lowliness. And although the meek may inherit the earth one day, in the here and now they have their work cut out for them.

In her book, Meeker has elevated humility to the realm of virtue, where it has historically found its home. Yet she also acknowledges that teaching this virtue is "tricky," but no less essential for being that. To elaborate, "Humility means having a proper perspective on ourselves, of seeing ourselves as we really are."[9]

The self-aware young woman avoids the traps that feminism sets for her. She does not delude herself into thinking she can defy her own nature and her own instincts and still be happy. "To fulfill her potential," Meeker wrote, "your daughter needs to understand who she is, where she comes from, and where she's going. And her understanding needs to be accurate."[10]

Help Her Find Her Center

The self-aware young woman also avoids false pride. So many of the messages a young woman receives today, even those from nonideological sources such as TV commercials and fashion magazines, ask her to glorify herself, esteem herself, set herself above and apart from her peers and her family.

Like the March sisters, as Meeker reminds us, "your daughter was created to live in an intricate web of relationships." If the self-aware young woman finds a valued place within that web, "self-centeredness and pride pluck her out of it." The Judeo-Christian ethic, although not the only option, has historically helped ground the faithful. Meeker added, "All we have to do to escape the suffocating quarters of our own lives, to see ourselves with humility, is to recognize that we alone are not the source of all power, intellect, and talent."[11]

In *Little Women*, the mother and father work overtime to prevent their daughters from centering their lives upon themselves. On noting a more generous turn in his daughter Amy's character, her father commends her: "I conclude that she has learned to think of other people more and herself less, and has decided to try and mould her character as carefully as she moulds her little clay figures." Shortly thereafter, Beth March, the best loved of the girls, moves to the piano and sings a hymn that acknowledges the source of all real awareness:

> *He that is down need fear no fall,*
> *He that is low, no pride;*
> *He that is humble*
> *Have God to be his guide.*[12]

Loose Girl's author, Kerry Cohen, has provided a vivid description of what happens when the father is unable or unwilling to help his daughter ground herself. The parents she saw in her circle, Cohen tells us, came of age in the 1960s. And although they are now "bringing in serious cash," they are "still partying and rebelling."[13] Her own parents divorced just as Cohen was reaching puberty, and she never really recovered.

At first, Cohen and her older sister lived with their mom, but the mom decided she had to find herself by going to medical school in the Philippines. When they moved back in with their hipster father, he came across "distant and airy, more like a friend than a parent." Throughout her adolescence, at least when home, the father tried to ingratiate himself with his daughter by buying her whatever she wanted and indulging her increasingly troubled behavior. "I'm thinking sometimes I'd rather have a dad who would kill me for smoking [pot]," Cohen reflected, "who would never smoke with my friends."[14]

Although superficially successful and not abusive, Cohen's dad was close to useless as a father. He "takes pride in being the cool dad," she wrote, but from a daughter's perspective that pride was absurdly misplaced. He provided no center, no stability, no foundation. Said Cohen of her father's fecklessness in a lament with which countless young women must also relate, "It makes me feel like no one will catch me if I fall."[15]

In her insightful book, *From Santa to Sexting*, Brenda Hunter makes the case that if parents don't have warm, supportive friendships of their own, they can become too needy around their own children. They also fail to provide the kind of friendship models that the kids could see and imitate. "If you don't have girlfriends—or, if you're a dad male buddies—then look at your own heart," Hunter wrote, "and ask yourself why not." Regardless of your limitations, Hunter cautioned, "concentrate on your child's needs; don't use him or her to meet yours. Role reversal never works."[16]

Get to Know Her

Like many fathers, Kerry Cohen's wanted no more information about his daughter than was absolutely necessary. Cohen imagined him thinking, "If your grades are fine and you look basically OK, then I don't need to know."[17]

Baron von Trapp, at least as imagined in the 1965 film classic *The Sound of Music*, feels much the same way.[18] After the death of the children's mother, he and his children have lost their balance. In his grief, he has grown increasingly distant and disengaged from his children. He travels often and leaves their care to a series of governesses. The seven von Trapp children whom the new governess Maria meets at the film's beginning have grown rebellious and disruptive in their father's absence and are badly in need of governing. Maria introduces maternal warmth and love back into their lives, and they respond accordingly, but she intuits that they need more, and knows who must provide it.

Initially, the Baron resists the invitation. On one occasion, he expresses his disapproval of the changes Maria has wrought, specifically her creation of user-friendly play clothes for the children. "They have uniforms," he tells her sternly:

MARIA: They can't be children if they worry about clothes.

BARON: They don't complain.

MARIA: They don't dare. They love you too much and fear . . .

BARON: Don't discuss my children.

MARIA: You've got to hear. You're never home.

BARON: I don't want to hear more!

MARIA: I know you don't, but you've got to.

As Maria explains, the oldest daughter, Liesl, is slipping away from him: "Soon she'll be a woman and you won't even know her." The oldest son, Friedrich, "wants to be a man but you're not here to show [him how]." As to the little ones, they "just want love." Adds Maria, "Please love them all." In the space of just a few minutes, Maria has delivered an almost perfect synopsis of what it takes to be a good father: love, patience, discipline, care, and, above all, presence. To make a complete home, of course, takes a father and mother. The

Baron's would-be wife, the Baroness Schraeder, has no gift for the latter role.

"I get a fiendish delight thinking of you as the mother of seven," a friend tells the Baroness. "How do you plan to do it?"

She answers cagily, "Darling, haven't you ever heard of a delightful little thing called boarding school?"

Happily, the Baroness never gets the chance to send the children off. The Baron comes to appreciate Maria's spirit and marries her instead. Now the family unit comes together organically, her softness and goodness balancing his firmness.

Be the Spiritual Head of the Family

Father Michael Sliney, LC, and Matt Williams have put together a useful guide titled "Tips for Men on How to Be Great Dads." High among their recommendations is that a father should live his faith openly in front of his children. "No matter how holy their mother is," say the authors, "it will be to no avail if [the father] is not strong as well." They therefore recommend that the father not just go to church with the children but that he also lead them in daily prayers, read them scriptures that reinforce the role of the father, and help each child set spiritual goals.[19]

Stay in the Picture

Forty years after *The Sound of Music*, with the culture increasingly in disarray, the film *Thirteen* served up an excellent cautionary tale on what can happen to a young girl who lacks a sober, humbling, paternal presence in her home. The first draft of the script was written by thirteen-year-old Nikki Reed, whose parents divorced when she was two. As Reed approached adolescence, she began to act out. To help her cope with the stress, her father's girlfriend, production designer Catherine Hardwicke, suggested that she keep a diary. Reed turned it into a screenplay. Hardwicke helped her shape it, and directed the film as well.

Like Reed, the film's thirteen-year-old protagonist, Tracy, does not have a stable home life. A friend describes Tracy's divorced and distracted mom as looking "like the hot big sister." The father lives elsewhere. Meeker has observed that "when fathers don't teach their daughters humility, advertisers, magazines, and celebrities will teach them otherwise."[20] That rings true in *Thirteen*. Immersed in the overheated celebrity culture of LA, and following the lead of the "hot girls," Tracy throws off one cultural restraint after another. Modesty goes first; then temperance; then, finally, chastity. Tracy and her narcissistic new friends shoplift, drink, do drugs, self-mutilate, and have sex with older boys. Tracy's mom loves her, but she cannot begin to control her.[21]

When brothers are closer to the scene than a father, they have an obligation to translate cultural risks to the parents. They can see them. They can understand them, but they must also assume a protective role and resist them. In the film, Tracy's older brother steps up and alerts the absent father to his sister's increasingly reckless behavior. The father finally comes to the house and demands, "Can someone please tell me what is the problem—in a nutshell?" (A "nutshell" of information is all that he has time for.) "I am trying to kick a___ at this new job," he tells Tracy. "I am trying to get you and your mom more money." As George Huguely's father might have told him, all the money in the world cannot compensate for the absence of a loving father in the home. Wrote Kerry Cohen, "The truth is I go through my life trying to piece together the family I want, the one I didn't get."[22]

Thirteen ends with the mother desperately trying to rein her little girl back in and not having a clue how. Often in reality, as in the film, we ask our daughters to "piece together" a life out of a mass of broken shards, and then express surprise when the final product does not turn out terribly attractive.

Challenge Her Emotions

As Meg Meeker has noted, a young woman's emotions "are overflowing with impulses that, if acted upon, could lead her to self-destruction."[23] The parents' job, particularly the father's, is to challenge her emotions and show her "the power of will" that leads to the triumph of moral reasoning. Parents cannot begin to assume that their daughters, no matter how levelheaded, will always make good choices.

In an unfortunate 2009 story out of suburban Pinellas Park, Florida, we can see that the film *Thirteen* does not exaggerate the perils of contemporary adolescence. In this Florida case, the absence of self-control in the character of two teenage girls destroyed both their lives and those of their families. Rachel Wade and Sarah Ludemann were competing for the attention of one John Camacho, a diminutive slacker with dark eyes, curly hair, and a precocious contempt for women. A pretty blond, Sarah felt secure in her hold on Camacho until she learned of his affection for Rachel, who was just as blond as Sarah, slimmer, and very attractive.[24]

Although both girls were deeply insecure, insecurity is not humility. If their fathers tried to instill this virtue in them—and both girls had fathers in the home—they were overmatched by the culture. Baby boomer fathers often fail to see just how much coarser the culture has become in one generation. They tend to put more trust in their daughters than the girls can endure. In the restricted world of Pinellas Park, John Camacho was the shiniest object that culture had to offer, a hometown American idol. To win his affection, each of the girls tried to elevate herself and tear down her rival. Worse, they competed with their most venal and superficial assets: a better car, an apartment, a better body, blonder hair, more slavish attention, a keener will to fight for one's man.

Camacho encouraged the competition. According to his friends, he would tell the girls, "If you love me, you'll fight for me." Sarah and Rachel would do just that. The fight began in a medium about which the parents knew little, MySpace. Sarah and Rachel were not the first two girls to fight over a boy, nor will they be the last, but by posting their taunts and countertaunts in a public forum, they amplified the feud and put their own reputations on the line.

The feud ended tragically in an all-out brawl. Overmatched and enraged, Rachel pulled out a steak knife and stabbed Sarah in the middle of a suburban street. This was the first time either had been in a fight. Sarah died, and Rachel will spend the next twenty-plus years in prison. Although these girls' fathers surely loved their daughters, to rescue them they would have had to wade right into the culture and pull their daughters out, kicking and screaming if necessary. They did not know enough to do this.

Provide the Balance

Unfortunately, real-life dramas do not always end as happily as a Jane Austen novel. In many ways Joy Keo resembled Marianne Dashwood, the impulsive sister in *Sense and Sensibility*. She was popular, beautiful, and romantic. An honor student and athlete at J. E. B. Stuart High School, Joy fell madly in love with her own "Willoughby," a fellow named Chuck Brewer, who had been voted the school's "most attractive" male student. "It was a really passionate relationship that kind of exploded," said a friend of Joy's. "She became very isolated."[25]

Like Marianne, Joy had no father to provide balance, but she had no big sister either. When Joy was a girl, her parents divorced, and her Thai father returned to Asia in seeming indifference to his children. Joy's American-born mother largely raised her. And although the mom's career involved working with victims of domestic violence, to whom she surely emphasized discipline and emotional restraint, she could provide neither the discipline and emotional restraint nor the masculine love that a father could.

Within months of meeting Brewer, Joy quit school, over her

mother's objections, and ran away with him to Florida. There, his darker side began to emerge. Possessive and insecure, he took his frustrations out on Joy, at one point tying her to a bed and beating her. No masochist, Joy fled home to her mother in Virginia. Brewer followed. A local judge ordered him to stop contacting Joy, but he threatened suicide if she refused to see him. When she continued to avoid him, he tracked her to a friend's house, kicked in the bedroom door much as George Huguely would do years later, and shot her four times.

Brewer served only eight years in prison for his crime. Meanwhile, Joy lived, but she was paralyzed from the neck down. And although she graduated from college and heroically made a life for herself for thirty years, Joy died broke and bedridden. Brewer went on to marry and raise a family. His brother picked up the cost of Joy's condo to settle a lawsuit she had filed against Chuck.

Humanize Your Sons

"You're gonna die, b___," Brewer shouted just before shooting Joy Keo.[26] "Shut up, b___," William Beebe snarled at Liz Seccuro just before raping her.[27] "I would have killed the b___," said Tucker Max of a woman who had done his friend wrong.[28] Upon being booked for the murder of Jennifer Levin, Robert Chambers, the so-called "Preppy Killer," screamed out, "That [profane] b___, why didn't she leave me alone?"[29] Jennifer, by the way, was a veritable clone of Kerry Cohen—a child of divorce, affluent, unmoored, living with an indifferent father, looking desperately for love and attention nightly at Dorrian's Red Hand, a trendy bar on the upper east side of Manhattan. Cohen, who saw Jennifer and Chambers leave the bar that fatal night, envied Jennifer. "Had he ever come to . . . my table," Cohen reflected, "I would have gone with him in a second." The girls all thought "Robert was hot."[30]

Despite the efforts of our feminist friends, or perhaps because of them, young men think nothing today of dehumanizing young women, and the powerful insult "b___" is just a handy way to do it. In each of these cases, the father, either through his absence or his indifference, failed to convey to his son the importance of treating women with respect. If young men get all their messages from the media, they will think of women as objects or animals with no greater purpose than to give them pleasure. Worse, girls have begun to internalize the designation. Indeed, a heading on a recent *Cosmopolitan* magazine cover screamed, "Bad Girl Issue—For Sexy B___es Only."[31]

Speaking of which, recently I came across some prize tweets from one Yuri Wright, an all-star high school football player who had just accepted a scholarship to the University of Colorado. "I can't even trust my mother," wrote Wright in one of his more printable quotes; "what makes you think ill [*sic*] ever be able to trust a b___."[32] The ironic headline of the Denver *Westword*, in which this tweet appears, reads, "[Profane] Tweets and More Help CU Land Top 100 Recruit Yuri Wright." Reporter Michael Roberts argues that if Wright had not sent scores of racist, misogynist tweets—and been thrown out of his high school because of them—some more prestigious football factory would have recruited him.

Wright should well fit in to the campus culture. An investigation into the school's football program in 2005 revealed that at least nine women had reportedly been assaulted by Colorado football players or recruits since 1997. No charges were brought. According to the *New York Times*, "prosecutors cited concerns about evidence and the reluctance of the women to go forward with the cases."[33] As long as the Yuri Wrights of the world know some university out there will take them in and cover for them when they break the law, they will see no reason to change their behavior.

Be the Father She Needs

Given its advanced welfare state, the cultural breakdown in England is even more severe than in the United States. A 2008 British miniseries,

Lost in Austen, imagines what would happen if a contemporary British girl, hardened by this breakdown, magically transposed into a Jane Austen novel.[34]

As the story opens, bank clerk Amanda Price struggles with the everyday crudeness of her own existence. Says Price of her contemporary life, "I do what we all do. I take it on the chin." Amanda's loser boyfriend proposes to her with the ring off the top of a beer bottle. Her divorced mother offers a left-handed endorsement of the proposal, saying of the boyfriend, "He doesn't take drugs. He doesn't knock you about."

Amanda compensates for her charmless present with frequent expeditions into the books of Jane Austen. "I love the manners and the language and the courtesy," reflects Price. But when she finds herself in the everyday life of the Bennett family from Austen's famed *Pride and Prejudice*, that life begins to lose some of its charm.

That said, the miniseries does not attempt to undo the book's spell or make moral judgments about Austen's time and place. Instead, *Lost in Austen* focuses on the comedic divergence between the two eras. Amanda's many little vulgarisms are played for laughs. Yet she finds herself drawn to Mr. Bennett, the father, who emerges as the voice of wise, calming reason, much as he does in the original. Fatherless in her real life, Amanda bonds with him in her fictional world.

Girls have always needed their fathers and always will. Be the father she needs.

Be the Guardian of Her Virtue

Father Michael Sliney and Matt Williams do not hesitate to use the word *virtue* in speaking of a young girl's character and a father's responsibility to protect it. A daughter will respond to a father she loves even if his advice about dress, decorum, dating, and the like runs counter to the imperatives of the culture. The daughter will understand the long-term rewards of virtue, however, only if her mother is actually experiencing them. This puts the burden on the father to provide those rewards in the form of love, devotion, and respect. Girls need to see, through their own fathers, that God the Father is loving, protective, and merciful, and that His unconditional love is enduring.

I am grateful that my father was very loving and supportive. I know I would not have survived the turmoil of the seventies and its changing mores without the confidence that he was always there for me. Unlike Kerry Cohen, who felt as though no one would catch her if she fell, I knew my father would catch me.

In fact, when I was a young professional woman in Chapel Hill, my father came to my rescue. I had a boyfriend then who was moving me to Washington, DC, to be near him. When our relationship was still long-distance, I was unaware of his inability to cope with transition. But under the stress of moving me out of my Chapel Hill apartment, I could see his behavior begin to spiral out of control.

As the day went on, he became more and more aggressive and extremely jealous of friends who came to say good-bye. My gut told me that this guy had some serious psychological problems. I made the decision I could not leave. I called my father and said, "What do I do?" He said, "Get over to your friend's apartment, the one who has that big husband. Go inside and tell them you are afraid, and do not allow this guy to come near you. Have the husband tell him to detach the U-Haul and leave it in the driveway."

My father instantly understood I was in danger and gave me the support I needed. He said, "If he gives you any trouble, call the police immediately." You can imagine what it was like to suddenly realize I was about to give up a very promising job in DC and I had already given up my old job and apartment. My father said not to worry about it, "Stay at your friends' house, and we will talk in the morning."

By the time he called me the next morning, he had already convinced my old landlord to give me another apartment and had contacted an old male friend of mine who was on his way to help me unpack my things and help me move in. I will be forever grateful to my employer who gave me my job back, but most of all to my father, who gave me the courage and strength to trust my instincts. As it turned out, I flourished in the job I almost left and accomplished much more than if I had moved. The greatest thing of all was that one year later I met my wonderful husband-to-be. My father always made me feel that I was smart, capable, and attractive, and that he would protect me. He did the same for my sister. His scrutiny of our boyfriends in high school may have been a source of embarrassment, but now we reflect back on those times with love and pride.

Be Like Atticus

When American women want to conjure up a screen image of a loving, protective father, they can hearken back fifty years to Atticus Finch of Harper Lee's *To Kill a Mockingbird*, a book that remains popular, as does the film of the same name. From that same source, young women can also draw an image of the role a brother—especially an older one— can play in his sister's life.

Throughout the book, the widowed Atticus struggles to teach his tomboy daughter, Scout, how "to behave like the little lady" she is supposed to be.[35] On the surface, this means how to dress and talk and sit, but on a more profound level, it means how to avoid pride, how to deal with anger, how to confront injustice. When Dr. Meeker stresses that our daughters need "direction and authority" from a father capable of showing a daughter how "to live with the outcome of moral reasoning,"[36] she is all but describing Atticus Finch. In the final scene of the movie, when a wiser Scout curls up in her father's lap, the world feels safe once again.

Protect Your Sister

I suspect many girls envy Scout her wise older brother, Jem, almost as much as they do her father, Atticus. It is Jem who keeps a watchful eye on his motherless sister throughout. Although it is clear that he loves Scout, he also accepts his responsibility for helping her control her impulses. On the opening day of school, for instance, when Scout gets into a fight with a hapless poor kid, Jem intervenes and justly scolds his sister for initiating the fight. He then invites the boy home for a meal, over his sister's protests, because he senses the boy has gone hungry. "Our daddy is a friend of your daddy's," Jem tells the boy. "Scout here is crazy. She won't fight you no more."[37]

In the movie's climactic scene, Jem risks his own life to save Scout, and a weird big-brother figure, Boo Radley, finally saves both of their lives. Thanks to the efforts of Jem and Boo, and the protective shield of Atticus, the viewer understands how important the web of family is and how little meaning life has without it.

The responsibility to protect is not limited to film characters, nor to sisters. Jamal Jones, a 2010 graduate of McKinley Technology High School in Washington, DC, had a cousin who was in trouble. Having gone through the Best Men Leadership Healthy Marriage/Healthy Relationship curriculum, he saw the signs of her being in an abusive relationship, even though his cousin was too ashamed to tell him or anyone else. When Jamal Jones approached her, she opened up and shared the circumstances of her abuse.

Jamal made sure his cousin understood that the abuse she was suffering was wrong and that help was available. He then gave her the telephone number for the National Domestic Violence Hotline, 1-800-799-SAFE, which I had compelled all our students to memorize, and urged her to call. She did, and turned her life around. Free from abusive relationships, the cousin now attends a local university. Just in time, she found a protector who cared for her. All young women should be that fortunate.[38]

12.

Why Healthy Relationships Matter

In the final episode of *The Simpsons'* fifth season in 1994, Homer Simpson, conceding his general ignorance—the default condition for a TV father today—ponders the recommendation of wife Marge that he take an adult education course. Instead of taking a class, however, Homer ends up teaching one called "Secrets of a Successful Marriage."[1] He holds the class's attention by sharing Marge's most intimate secrets.

After promising to stop sharing those secrets, but failing, Homer gets booted from the house by Marge. The Simpson children are anxious, as any children would be under those circumstances. "I'll tell you a secret, Bart," Lisa tells her brother. "Every time I'm worried about Mom and Dad"—a sentiment that sounds as if it has been pulled from the memory of a genuinely worried daughter—"I go to the attic and add to my ball of string."

For her part, Marge tries to console her children with something of a standard bromide: "Kids, your father and I are going through a really tough time right now, and I don't know what's going to happen. But just remember that both your mom and your dad love you very, very much."

Homer, meanwhile, is quickly falling apart and desperately hoping for reconciliation. He takes comfort upon seeing the Reverend Lovejoy approach the house. "He has to push the sanctity of marriage," Homer says to Bart, "or his God will punish him."

The good reverend is obviously not concerned about God. "Get a divorce!" he urges Marge.

"But isn't that a sin?" she asks.

A moral relativist to the core—like too many modern clergy—Lovejoy answers, "Marge, just about everything is a sin."

The more traditional Homer will hear none of this. He wants Marge back. "I need you more than anyone else on this entire planet could possibly ever need you!" he implores Marge. "I need you to take care of me, to put up with me, and most of all I need you to love me, 'cause I love you."

Marge looks into his eyes and hugs him. "I must admit," she says, "you certainly do make a gal feel needed."

As dumb as Homer may be, as goofy as this episode was, and as shocking as this may sound, those watching at home that night witnessed—in my case, accidentally—one of the more endearing, even realistic, examples of married love on TV in the last twenty years. Sadly, there are children growing up today who have not witnessed a healthy relationship at home, among their extended family, among their friends' families, or even on television. This is a societal problem that gets shockingly little attention.

As I will explain later in this chapter, the Best Friends program has to fight a variety of cultural influences to convince our girls that marriage is the best choice for the best future, but we get painfully little support from the surrounding culture. True, producers have created a few strong minority father figures over the years—most notably Dr. Clifford Huxtable of *The Cosby Show*—but this show stopped airing in 1992. (We can only hope that teens and adolescents today see the reruns.) I can think of almost no wise, admirable, non-ridiculed fathers in an intact, nonminority TV household since Ward Cleaver in *Leave It to Beaver* and Jim Anderson in *Father Knows Best*, and these shows aired more than fifty years ago.

I will be the first to acknowledge that there are single parents and grandparents who have done wonderful jobs raising their children. Anyone in doubt need only pick up Clarence Thomas's moving memoir, *My Grandfather's Son* or Barack Obama's *Dreams from My Father*. There are wonderful individuals from all social classes who lost a parent as a child and were raised well by the surviving parent. It is interesting in the research, too, that children who lost a parent through death tend to fare better psychologically than those who lost a parent through divorce.[2]

As I mentioned earlier, the crux of social learning theory is that people learn from one another through observation, imitation, and modeling. The absence of viable family shows on which to model their behavior is a problem for youth. Children in the United States watch on average three to four hours of television a day.[3] On subjects such as marriage and family, they reflect what we exhibit. If they do not see a happily functioning marriage at home and do not see any in the media, they may have no real concept of what such a family might look like.

Looking for Models

If nowhere else, American young people over the years have found surprisingly good role models in the White House. The Clintons aside, First Couples from the Fords to the present, despite the enormous stress that comes with such visibility, have done a good job as spouses and parents. Unfortunately, for political reasons discussed elsewhere, President Obama has not often seized the opportunity to publicly promote marriage.

I continue to be impressed by what I have learned about Harry and Bess Truman. To read David McCullough's masterful biography, *Truman*, is to witness one of the century's great and enduring love stories. "I love you as madly as a man can," Harry wrote Bess from France during World War I, when he wanted nothing more than to marry her on return. That he promptly did. Over the next forty-plus years, Truman would write more than thirteen hundred letters to the woman

McCullough described as the "idolized love of his life," and his affection never wavered. "His devotion to Bess appears to have been total," wrote McCullough.[4] Truman was likewise devoted to his daughter, mother, and obviously, to his country, a natural extension. Although these were imperfect human beings, marriage made them all better.

Another great presidential romance was that of Ronald and Nancy Reagan. Though Reagan's second, the marriage was Nancy's first and only. Their relationship so defined their lives that when Reagan died in 2004, the BBC headlined one of its lead accounts "End of a love story." The late Charlton Heston once described the Reagans' relationship as "the greatest love affair in the history of the American presidency." And a former NBC White House correspondent told the BBC of the Reagans' periodic good-bye kisses, "We would turn aside because we felt that there was something very special, private and wonderful going on between them."[5]

Speaking of Charlton Heston, few Hollywood marriages were as enduring or inspiring as his own to Lydia Clarke. They met when both were students at Northwestern University. After their first date, Heston walked Lydia back to the dorm and then ran home along the dark streets, saying to himself over and over, "I love her, I love her." For her part, Lydia says of that same date, "We had a very stimulating conversation and that was it. I was insanely in love with him."[6] The couple married in March 1944 just before Heston had to head overseas as an aerial gunner and radio operator on a B-25 Mitchell.

No matter where in the world Heston was filming in the years to come, the couple would celebrate their anniversary together. Bill and I were fortunate enough to attend their fiftieth anniversary party in 1994, a truly heartwarming evening and evidence of a wonderful, loving marriage. Every guest was provided with the touching chapter "Pursuing Lydia" from his book *In the Arena: An Autobiography*. There were sixty-four such anniversaries before Charlton Heston died, with Lydia at his side, in 2008. Up until the end, Heston referred to Lydia as the "queen of my heart."[7]

Unfortunately, America's young people rarely see stories like these told. If asked about memorable marriages, they would likely cite basketball player Kris Humphries's preposterous seventy-two-day marriage to reality-TV star Kim Kardashian or Britney Spears's fifty-five-hour marriage to childhood friend Jason Allen Alexander, and these couples at least made it to the altar, or the Hollywood equivalent. Magazine features such as *Complex*'s "Hey Ma: The 10 Hottest Celebrity Single Mothers" are more troubling still.[8] Stories like these, unfortunately, compose the news that our daughters see.

Achieving Emotional Security

I agree with my husband, Bill's, statement in the wise and prophetic book *The Broken Hearth: Reversing the Moral Collapse of the American Family*, that there are certain givens in the human condition, among them the need to love and be loved.[9] Most of us have deep longings for emotional attachment. Sexual intimacy can be a means of achieving this. Whether we express it or not, most of us hope to satisfy the yearnings of our souls and become complete human beings. And most of us hope to obtain a safe haven in this world, a home with a spouse to love us, and children to nurture.

These longings can be met, at least to a degree, by close friends and relatives. But it is marriage—the voluntary, lifelong, exclusive commitment to a person of the opposite sex—that comes closest to satisfying our deepest longings. It always has. Having your heart entwined with another human being's is one of life's most affirming experiences. The security of that bond reassures one's children that life is good and that their future can be too.

George Eliot asked,

What greater thing is there for two human souls than to feel that they are joined for life—to strengthen each other in all labor, to rest on each other in all sorrow, to minister to each other in all pain, to be one with each other in silent unspeakable memories at the moment of the last parting?[10]

Bill made another statement I think is especially profound, "Marital love grounded in unconditional commitment is safer, more enduring and more empowering than any sentiment yet discovered, or any human arrangement yet invented."[11] He argued that marriage rests in the complementarity of a man and a woman, the urge that drives two independent people to become "one flesh." This complementarity of the two is based on the "fundamental differences between men and women that are physical and emotional, psychological and sexual."[12] Continuing, he wrote, "Indeed, it is these very differences that help men and women achieve, in marriage, unity and interdependence, completeness and fulfillment."[13]

As Bill has observed, one prominent feature of male-female complementarity is sexual: men and women giving to each other fully, completely, and exclusively. He sees "self-giving" as an essential part of the bond. "Sexual love of this kind," he noted, "is a profoundly moral act, and when and if it leads to [the] occurrence of a man and woman creating a new life it is also an utterly miraculous one."[14] In this kind of environment, that new life can grow up secure and emotionally strong.

Stressing Marriage and Monogamy

At Best Friends, we counter these negative cultural influences by proudly promoting the value of married life. We start by defining marriage as being "the state when a man and woman are formally united for the purpose of living together with certain legal, emotional, and social obligations to each other." Today, it seems, definitions are necessary. We also stress monogamy within marriage and define our terms.

As we tell our girls, this means "being married to one person at a time and not having sexual relations with anyone else."

Through teaching and discussion, our instructors help our girls visualize a successful marriage and prepare themselves for one. We even catalog the positive benefits of saving sex until marriage. I can visualize the smirks as certain people read this sentence. Yes, these are eleven to seventeen-year-old kids. Yes, they live in inner-city Washington, but don't stereotype or underestimate them. At our youth summit of 150 high school Diamond Girls and Best Men, 80 percent said they wanted to wait until marriage to have sex. As I have said many times about our children, "Hope springs eternal." Why replace their hopes and dreams with cynicism?

We work with them on issues of self-respect and self-sufficiency as a preparation for marriage, and we help them see what a good marriage looks like through married role model speakers. Some of the benefits of marriage that we emphasize would have seemed foreign to would-be brides of generations past, like protecting the couple from sexually transmitted disease and HIV/AIDS. Yet these threats make marriage all the more valuable today. We do our girls an injustice by not making them aware of the many emotional and physically healthy advantages of marriage.

Every time I see a couple in their seventies or eighties out for a walk and holding hands, I am reminded of just how wonderful the institution of marriage can be. Watching my own parents embrace or hold hands always made me happy. They were married thirty-seven years before my father died at the young age of sixty-four. Bill and I will celebrate our own thirty-first wedding anniversary this year, and great years they have been.

Nearly two thousand years ago, when faced with an increasingly corrupt culture in Corinth, Saint Paul told the Corinthians just what real love looked like. I was especially moved when my older son John read this passage at the wedding of the only daughter of one of my dearest friends. No one has improved on this description since:

Love is patient, love is kind. It does not envy, it does not boast, it is not proud. It does not dishonor others, it is not self-seeking, it is not easily angered, it keeps no record of wrongs. Love does not delight in evil but rejoices with the truth. It always protects, always trusts, always hopes, always perseveres. Love never fails. . . . And now these three remain: faith, hope and love, but the greatest of these is love. (1 Cor. 13:4–8, 13)

In certain biblical texts, when faith and hope align with love, love flourishes.

Observing the Catholic Model

I have yet to see any confirming data, but I suspect that a couple married with all the beautiful ritual of a church wedding has a better chance at marital success than, say, a couple married at the Little White Wedding Chapel in Las Vegas. This is the site of the famed Drive-Thru Tunnel of Vows and the launching pad of a Britney Spears marriage that lasted all of fifty-five hours. However, successful marriage probably has less to do with the environment than with the preparation for a lifelong commitment by the bride and groom.

The Catholic Church has long set the standard for marital preparation through its Pre-Cana training programs. "Cana" refers to the site of the wedding where Jesus Christ, at his mother's request, performed his first public miracle by famously turning water into wine. By his very presence, Jesus elevated the role of marriage in Christian tradition.

The Respect Life Office for the Archdiocese of New York nicely defines marriage as a "vocation" and a "great adventure," one in which the couple "will establish a new family, grow in love with each other, and encounter Christ."[15] This larger goal orientation, when coupled with serious Pre-Cana training, has helped keep divorce rates among practicing Catholics well below the national norm. The 2004 findings of the General Social Survey confirm this. The GSS, based at the University of Chicago and sponsored by the National Science Foundation, is widely regarded as the single best source of data on societal trends. Although the numbers have increased over the decades, the patterns have held fairly steady. What follows are the divorce percentages among the following cohorts:[16]

58% Non-active Black Protestants

54% Non-active Evangelicals

51% No religious beliefs (e.g., atheists, agnostics)

48% Non-active other religions

48% All non-Christians

47% Active Black Protestants

42% All non-Christian religions

42% Non-active Mainline Protestants

41% All Christians

41% Non-active Catholics

39% Jewish

38% Active other religions

34% Active Evangelicals

32% Active Mainline Protestants

23% Active Catholics

For the Archdiocese of New York, marriage preparation is not an option. It is "required." The first part of the training involves practical advice for the engaged couple to help them acquire the skills needed to build a successful relationship. These sessions cover a range of useful topics, such as communication, conflict resolution, and decision making. The second part of the training is called "God's Plan for a Joy-Filled Marriage" and is designed to help couples appreciate a Catholic vision of married love.[17] The couple's participation in God's plan, at least for those who take their vows seriously, ennobles the relationship and strengthens it. Also, many Protestant churches today require marriage preparation courses.

Understanding Divorce

In September 1969, California governor Ronald Reagan signed the nation's most progressive no-fault divorce bill into law. The once-divorced governor came to regret signing it. He would tell his son Michael that it was "one of the worst mistakes he ever made in public office." Said Michael, "He wanted to do something to make the divorce process less acrimonious, less contentious, and less expensive."[18] He also made divorce a good deal more accessible, especially as other states began to copy California's law.

The numbers are troubling. In 1960 there were 1,523,000 marriages in America and only about 393,000 divorces—roughly four marriages for every divorce. Fifty years later, there were 2,077,000 marriages but more than a million divorces—1,043,000, to be precise—roughly two marriages for every divorce. More disturbing still, in 2009 there were 20 percent fewer marriages than in 1985, despite the fact that the nation's population had grown by 25 percent during that period.[19]

The numbers don't tell half the story. Michael Reagan, who, at age four, endured the divorce of his father from actress Jane Wyman, sums up the phenomenon from the child's perspective: "Divorce is where two adults take everything that matters to a child—the child's home, family, security, and sense of being loved and protected—and they smash it all up, leave it in ruins on the floor, then walk out and leave the child to clean up the mess."[20] Although good parents can find themselves with no other realistic solution than divorce, it is a fate best avoided when at all possible.

....

In *Loose Girl*, Kerry Cohen did an excellent job of explaining the impact of her parents' divorce. Her description bears out just about all of what Meeker and Wallerstein have reported in their works. Cohen's father left home just as she was coming of age, leaving behind "a house with no men." There were just Kerry, her older sister, and a "grief-stricken and frantic" mother, "busy with need."[21] The departure of the first parent left the two girls with the great anxiety that most children of divorce face, that of losing the second parent as well.

Even more damaging, her parents' divorce left Cohen feeling unwanted, unloved, and devoid of value. She moved from one boy to another in a desperate effort "to get evidence that I'm worth something." This she never really did. "I feel worthless, a discarded piece of trash," she lamented after one particularly futile relationship ended badly.[22] Her sister did no better. Both their marriages ended in divorce, as did the second marriage of her mother and the one long-term relationship of her father.

The divorce left both sisters angry. The mother eventually left the girls with their father, and their father was "barely there." Tellingly, each sister transferred her unspoken rage to some larger cause. Kerry became the editor of her college's alternative liberal newspaper. "I don't know as much as I should," she observed, "but it feels good to get behind something, to channel my anger into something real." Her "anticorporate" sister did the same, talking "loudly about all the ways she's getting screwed, about the environment, the government, everything but her real self."[23] Although Cohen did not generalize, one has to wonder whether a collective rage against the home, the father in particular, has soured feminists on traditional virtue and pushed the movement so uniformly leftward.

There are any number of resources to help divorced parents cope with the aftereffects of divorce, but as Dr. Judith Wallerstein urges, if at all possible feuding parents should stay together for the sake of the children.[24] Parents cannot communicate any meaningful messages to their children if they are not there to do so. This, the Cohen children fully understood. At one point, for instance, Cohen's mother attempted to assert her parental control over her girls, now living with their father. Cohen denied her that right: "Not when you're not around to parent us yourself."[25]

Divorce is nearly as rough on the women who have been left behind as it is on the children. With respect to economics alone, women suffer. An analysis of recent data suggests the woman's standard of living declines by 27 percent on average after divorce, while the man gains about 10 percent.[26] This gender gap does not seem to have changed much in recent decades. On the emotional front, women suffer even more. A woman's identity as a married person is typically stronger than her husband's, and her sense of abandonment and failure is correspondingly greater.

On the question of physical health, however, women do slightly better than men after divorce, but not as well as their married peers. According to *Neuroscience News*, a twenty-year-long study into longevity showed that only one-third of divorced men lived beyond the average male life span.[27] A review of more than 2 million death certificates in 2003 showed married men dying at an average of 77.6 years, with divorced men dying at the average of 67.1. The longevity study suggests that divorced women who never remarried lived almost as long as women who were consistently married, but the 2003 data give a nine-year advantage to married over divorced women (81 versus 72) and a nearly four-year advantage over women who never married (81 versus 77.4).[28]

Avoiding Divorce

Other than the Catholic Church and the Church of Jesus Christ of Latter-day Saints, America's principal faiths have not historically done a great job in preparing couples for marriage.

Arguably, no one has done more to help change that dynamic than Michael McManus, the founder of an organization called Marriage Savers. Marriage Savers begins by establishing a "community marriage policy" in a given locality. To date, Marriage Savers has worked with more than two hundred communities in forty-three states.

For the Marriage Savers plan to work, a critical mass of pastors, priests, and rabbis in a given area must sign a covenant to make healthy marriages a priority in their congregations and agree to implement a comprehensive marriage-saving program. If enough clerics do participate, young couples may find it difficult to identify a church that will marry them without participation in a premarital training program.

The churches in question must first recruit and train couples from among a congregation to serve as mentors. After rigorous training, these mentors work with other couples to prevent ill-advised marriages, strengthen existing ones, and even reconcile couples that have separated. Mentors will not work with couples who are living together before marriage. Neither will the pastor marry them unless they resume living apart. Although it seems counterinstinctive, couples who live together before marriage are more likely to divorce than couples that do not.

Mentors begin by testing the commitment and readiness of the couples hoping to marry. They do this by administering a fairly exhaustive inventory to both partners. Once completed, this inventory gives the partners an objective view of their respective strengths within the relationship and suggests areas for future growth. Historically, some 10 percent of the couples that have gone through this process decided not to marry. The available data suggest that those who break an engagement post roughly the same scores on the inventory as those who marry and subsequently divorce. The Marriage Savers program works under the premise that it is better not to marry than to marry badly.

For those couples who do successfully complete the program, Marriage Savers awards them "marriage insurance," a 95 percent guarantee that they will stay married. Of the 233 couples in Mike McManus's own church that went through the program starting in 1992, only seven to date have seen their marriages end in divorce, a 97 percent success rate. Some churches have reported no divorces at all over a four- to six-year period.[29]

Strengthening Existing Marriages

As part of the Marriage Savers program, participating congregations host marriage enrichment programs. One popular format goes by the name "10 Great Dates." As it works, couples gather at a given church for ten consecutive weekend nights, watch a video on topics such as conflict resolution or marital encouragement, and then each couple heads to a restaurant for a date during which the spouses discuss what they have just seen and its applicability to their own marriage. Reportedly, husbands like the program because the evening is crowned with a meal, and women like it because it helps address unresolved issues.

Marriage Savers also works with couples whose relationships are clearly in crisis. To make this program effective, pastors recruit "back-from-the-brink couples" as mentors. As should be obvious from the title, these are couples whose marriages almost fell apart but were saved by the heroic efforts of the partners to pull them back together. Given their own exposure to various marital stresses, they can show struggling couples just how they were able to rebuild the marriage. Marriage Savers has experienced a roughly 80 percent success rate with this part of the program.

The most challenging opportunity Marriage Savers has explored is the reconciliation of those already separated. In this twelve-week program, a trained mentor works with the separated spouse of his or her own sex in an effort to effect a stable reconciliation. Despite the obstacles, Marriage Savers reports a success rate in excess of 50 percent among those already separated.

As a final piece of the program, Marriage Savers helps organize "Stepfamily Support Groups" to help couples with children from previous marriages learn how to thrive in a blended family environment, a tall order under any circumstances. This program helps preserve an estimated 80 percent of the stepfamilies with which it works.

Starting at Home

For all the good that Marriage Savers or the various churches or Best Friends can do, no one can do more to model a healthy relationship than the mother and father of a young girl. Despite the wishes of our more radical feminist friends, young girls almost universally want to marry someday. Despite the efforts of a feminist educational establishment, they feel this way even when they graduate from high school, against almost universally negative messages about marriage or the need to marry.

In the December 3, 2012, issue of *Crisis Magazine*, Meg McDonnell reported,

> A ray of hope here is that desire for marriage remains high among young Americans. According to a 2009 report conducted by the non-partisan research firm Child Trends, 83 percent of young adults ages 20 to 24 responded that it was important or very important to them to be married at some point in their life. More than three-fourths of those young adults answered that love, fidelity and making a lifelong commitment are all "very important" components of a successful relationship. And in a 2010 survey, conducted by the National Healthy Marriage Resource Center, 82 percent of respondents, ages 18 to 32, answered that they intended to marry and remain married for life.[30]

Most of the encouragement young people get, they get from the married couples they see around them. Young girls are romantics. They want to believe their marriages will succeed, and they are more likely to draw inspiration from positive models than from negative ones. It is our responsibility to provide those models, to work at our own relationships, to know that young eyes will always be following us. If our daughters see us falter, they will go to their attics—or their own private places—and nervously add new strands to their balls of string, real or emotional. We ought not let this happen. As we say at Best Friends, if we give our children our best, they will give us their best.

Healthy Teenage Relationships

In a previous work, I stated,

> After more than 30 years of working with students I am convinced that young people really want to do the right thing. When character is not taught, children lack the foundation to exercise personal responsibility, and are ill-equipped to make decisions that may affect them and others for a lifetime. Our youth deserve an opportunity to develop these skills and have a childhood before they have a child. Unfortunately, sexual activity and drug and alcohol use rob children of this responsibility.[31]

Many teens have healthy dating relationships and do not engage in risky behavior. And given the right information and guidance by caring adults, youth are capable of making good decisions. Research confirms that teenagers respond to the challenge of high expectations by making positive choices and setting goals for their future.[32] In several studies by the National Campaign to Prevent Teen and Unplanned Pregnancy, teens have said that the best choice is not to engage in sexual activity in the high school years. Those who have tell us they regret having sex too young and wish they had waited.

Most would agree that teens are not ready for pregnancy and parenthood. The point of disagreement lies in whether youth programs should address *preventing pregnancy* by dispensing contraception, or *preventing the sexual activity* that leads to pregnancy. I believe the most responsible approach is to avoid the risk of sexual activity. So, what factors influence young people to engage in sex? Two critical areas which must be addressed are (1) the influence of media on the popular culture and (2) the lack of clear and consistent messages from adult authority figures, such as parents, teachers, clergy, and others.

The media's portrayal has a great impact on teens, who are bombarded with messages from movies, television, and music that glorify sex, violence, and drug and alcohol use. It has been said that next to parents, television is perhaps a child's most influential teacher. A recent study reported that the average child spends nearly forty-five hours per week with media, compared with seventeen hours with parents.[33] Primetime programming is heavily weighted with sexual references and innuendos. One recent study found that "verbal references to non-married partners outnumbered scenes depicting or implying sex between married partners by a ratio of nearly 4 to 1."[34] Nevertheless, nine out of ten students in a 2007 Best Friends survey want to be married someday. This indicates that our children still see marriage as a valuable goal. Why, then, is so little attention given to helping them reach that goal? The major media have simply not responded to the viewers' preference for family shows that depict positive relationships and healthy marriages.

Organizations that promote "comprehensive" sex education would argue that "personal responsibility" means to use birth control and/or condoms. In *Emerging Answers 2007*, Douglas Kirby reports that 30 percent of teens ages fifteen to nineteen who rely on oral contraception do not take a pill every day, which is necessary for protection.[35] Is it realistic to expect sexually active adolescents to be personally responsible? Wouldn't it be more responsible and healthier for parents and teachers to encourage and to expect youth to respond to the challenge of high expectations by not having sex until they are adults and in a committed relationship? We all know what that should mean—marriage.

What Schools Can Do

In May 2005, on the way home from a relaxing lakeside weekend with her girlfriends, Beth Twitty got a phone call that would forever change her life: her daughter, Natalee, had not shown up at her Aruba hotel for the bus that would take her to the airport. From that moment on, Beth would make a superwoman's effort to find out what happened to Natalee Holloway, but by that time all the fatal mistakes had already been made.

Natalee, then an eighteen-year-old senior at affluent Mountain Brook High School in Alabama, was a straight-A student and a member of the school dance team. According to Beth, she never drank, did not have a boyfriend, and had not had sex. Sadly, like so many parents, myself included, Beth could not see in her own child signs that she might quickly have seen in someone else's.

According to her friends, Natalee began drinking the moment she got to Aruba and rarely stopped. This was apparently not her first use of alcohol, but again, an unspoken code of silence helped keep Natalee's mother in the dark. What much of the public did not understand is that Natalee was on a school trip. Although in an unofficial capacity, 130 of her classmates and seven chaperones flew to Aruba with her. Apparently, the Aruba excursion was something of a senior class tradition at Mountain Brook. The chaperone to student ratio was much more responsible the previous year, according to a mother whose daughter participated. Jodi Bearman, the chaperone who organized the trip the next year, said "the chaperones were not supposed to keep up with their every move."[1] In Natalee's case, they fully succeeded. Natalee, after a night of carousing, was last seen riding away with three local males into the night. She was never seen again. Her body has still not been found.

Gerold Dompig, the Aruban deputy police chief in charge of the investigation, observed,

> [There was] wild partying, a lot of drinking, lots of room switching every night. We know the Holiday Inn told them they weren't welcome next year. Natalee, we know, she drank all day every day. We have statements she started every morning with cocktails—so much drinking that Natalee didn't show up for breakfast two mornings.[2]

Although much of the media furor was directed at Aruba, almost none was directed at the parents who sanctioned this madness. In the TV movie version, Natalee's divorced father, Dave Holloway, restates his objections to having let her go, but he is the only who questions the wisdom of sending these students—many of them under eighteen—on such an excursion. The fact that he was no longer living under the same roof as Natalee obviously weakened his authority.

Greta Van Susteren, one of my favorite TV interviewers, talked to chaperone Bob Plummer. His answers suggest how little responsibility any of the adults involved were prepared to assume:[3]

VAN SUSTEREN: All right. So when was the last time you remember seeing Natalee?

PLUMMER: I would have to say that it was probably that night in the casino.

VAN SUSTEREN: And was she drinking at the time?

PLUMMER: I couldn't specifically say if she was or not. The whole time we were down there, I never recall really seeing her drink a whole lot, period.

VAN SUSTEREN: All right. But as a practical matter, was there any sort of agreement or impediment to her drinking anyway? She was [an] 18-year-old adult. I mean, were there any specific instructions or anything like that?

PLUMMER: No, that was entirely up to the discretion of the students.

Beth Holloway (once more after her divorce from Twitty) now lectures student groups on the dangers of "overseas travel." In fact, she is currently constructing a website called Mayday360.com to help young people who travel abroad. Overlooked is the fact that Natalee could have suffered the same fate had her high school group traveled to Las Vegas or New Orleans or just down the road to Biloxi with the same goal in mind. Indeed, in the Holloway case, all of the major forces that put our daughters at risk came into play: a culture that glorifies recklessly bad behavior for teenagers; a high school culture that sanctions it; relentless peer pressure to indulge in it; and parents who either endorse it, ignore it, or lack the will to resist it. Natalee Holloway did not have to die, and Aruba was the least of the culprits.

Rethink Middle School

Much of the trouble our daughters will face begins in middle schools not unlike Portola Middle School in California's San Fernando Valley, the shooting location for the movie *Thirteen*. Portola Middle includes grades six through eight and educates, according to its website, "a culturally diverse student population in a positive and safe learning environment."[4]

As all suburban schools do, at least according to their literature, Portola provides "an academically rigorous, challenging, and enriched learning environment." The school website provides plenty of information for parents, but none of it offers a clue as to the turmoil that awaits incoming sixth-grade girls. More instructive perhaps is a thoroughly amateur YouTube video titled "Portola Middle School." The short video shows a boy teasing a girl and pulling her hair while uttering profanities and flashing gang symbols. Middle school is not what it used to be.[5]

Thirteen captures well the chaos that envelops many a younger girl who enters this environment without much in the way of parental or administrative guidance. Although Tracy, the protagonist, begins school as a studious innocent, she yields quickly to the pressure the school's "hot" girls apply to dress and act older than thirteen. Tracy faces little counterpressure from anyone. The fictional Tracy, unfortunately, has scores of real-life counterparts.

These counterparts are getting younger and younger all the time. For reasons not entirely clear—obesity and environmental chemicals that mimic hormones are the leading suspects—girls are reaching puberty much younger than they ever have before. The average age of pubertal onset in girls is now about ten and a half.[6] For black and Hispanic girls, puberty comes about a year earlier than it does for Caucasian, non-Hispanic girls. This means that girls today typically start middle school with newly sexualized bodies but scarcely a clue as to what to do with them. It is a rare middle school that is prepared to deal with this challenge.

Anyone who reads case studies on teen problems has to be struck by how often the transition from primary school to middle school disorients our daughters. The momentum to change has to come from somewhere. It will almost never come from the top of the educational establishment, and if it does, it is the kind of change most of us will come to regret. Parents and teachers must take the initiative to create positive change, even if those first steps seem daunting.

The following observations by adolescents and their parents or siblings appear in Mary Pipher's *Reviving Ophelia*, each from a different case study. Pipher used the phrase "junior high," which she employed generically to refer to the transitional school between primary and high school. Today, middle schools (grades six through eight) are much more common than junior highs (grades seven through eight or seven through nine). The problems are comparable at both.

> "Everything good in me died in junior high."
> "We've been worried since she began junior high, but last Saturday night we discovered that she was burning herself with cigarettes."
> "Junior high was the pits. I felt like I was on a different planet from the other kids. I was the untouchable of my school."
> "Before junior high, Gail was the star of the family."
> "In junior high . . . I wanted to be normal. All the normal kids were getting in trouble."
> "One of my sisters starts junior high the year I go to college. I wish I could help her through it."
> "Charlotte was okay till junior high, but then things started going wrong fast."
> "In junior high I wanted to kill myself because I was too tall."

Pipher describes junior high as "a crucible," a time and place where "confident, well-adjusted girls [are] transformed into sad and angry failures."[7] This transformative process affects every public middle school in America, affluent or impoverished. In every such school, girls face incredible pressures to be beautiful and popular, and these pressures often translate into sex, drugs, and bad grades. Not all girls succumb to the pressure, obviously, but all of them feel it.

It does not have to be this way. Many parochial schools and more and more public ones are structured on a kindergarten-through-eighth-grade model. As girls in these schools hit puberty, they are not thrown to the wolves in an alien, suddenly sexualized environment. Rather, as they reach the middle school grades, they become the school leaders. They assume responsibility. They take on the role of mentor to their kindergarten or first grade "buddies." In the process, they grow more connected to the school. When they do make the transition to a new school—that is, their high school—these girls are now fourteen or fifteen, not ten or eleven. They are more comfortable in their new bodies and more emotionally equipped to deal with transition. The boys they encounter will likewise be better behaved or at least more mature.

Many public schools are adopting this model. In Boston, for instance, there were once only three K–8 schools in the entire district. Today, there are more than thirty. One stated goal of the district, a good one, is to "provide educational continuity."[8] A side benefit, I am sure, is a safer environment for Boston schoolgirls. I have also seen firsthand, in the DC Public Schools, that the schools with a K–8 model allowed our Best Friends and Best Men participants the opportunity to become teenagers in a more protected environment with less peer pressure from older students.

Prepare Children and Parents for Middle School

If student behavior at Portola Middle School is no worse or better than average, administrators are doing an inadequate job in preparing parents for what their daughters will face. It may seem counterintuitive for them to warn incoming parents of the emotional disturbances their children will endure, but it is borderline negligent not to.

Here is the one warning that can now be found on the Portola website, and you have to look hard to find it: "Moving to middle school is difficult for all students. They need parental monitoring now more than ever."[9] The "monitoring" here refers to homework. Homework is not half the problem. Parents need to be told much more than that. They need to know about the kind of incidents that teachers and administrators see year after year. By most accounts, those incidents are increasing both in severity and in frequency. The schools need to address these issues with children and their parents in a systematic way before issues turn into crises.

Consider Uniforms

Almost all parochial schools have their girls wear uniforms. The very word *uniform* suggests one major advantage: girls can no longer compete with one another where school clothes are concerned. They can no longer vie to be one of the "hot" girls on campus. A plaid skirt, no matter how high girls might hike it when off school grounds, takes the wind out of that competition.

In the absence of uniforms, schools must draw up elaborate dress codes. The Portola Middle School, for instance, has a highly specific, eleven-point code that has literally more words in it than Lincoln's Gettysburg Address.[10] Among the provisions are a few that might give incoming parents cause for concern, like the following:

> 5. No see-through, mesh, or sleeveless shirts, tube tops, tank tops, shirts with spaghetti straps, leotards, pajamas or clothing showing bare midriff or undergarments may be worn....
> 11. No gang related apparel, such as white T-shirts, baggy pants or Dickies, gloves, jewelry, long belts, gang symbols or writing is permitted. No article of clothing or paraphernalia that symbolizes, characterizes or depicts profanity, sex, violence, tobacco products, drugs, or alcohol is permitted.

Remember, these prohibitions are for eleven- and twelve-year-olds. Although written by lawyers in an effort to head off specious "free speech" lawsuits, they speak to the environment that engulfs these children two hundred or so days a year. Portola is not your mother's middle school. Today, no middle school is.

More and more public schools have adopted school uniforms. President Bill Clinton endorsed the movement in his 1996 State of the Union speech. "If it means teenagers will stop killing each other over designer jackets," said the president, "then our public schools should be able to require their students to wear school uniforms."[11] Those who oppose school uniforms offer a variety of arguments against them, like limiting a student's right to freedom of expression, burdening the poor, and making students vulnerable to bullies from other schools. None of these arguments are particularly convincing.

Given that uniforms reduce the effect of affluence on appearance, one would think that feminists of a leftist bent might endorse them. But that does not seem to have happened. Uniforms represent a certain traditional view of sex roles—at least in schools where girls wear skirts—and that can bother progressive feminists. One picks up these arguments on feminist blogs when the school uniform issue emerges. "Mocking females for being female is sexist," argues one blogger. "But schools prescribing gender-specific uniforms reinforces sexism, and sexism doesn't combat sexism very well." Says another, "Girls have been wearing pants in school for the last 35 years, and anybody who would put them in a uniform has gotta be from the Stone Age."[12] That uniforms may help prevent young girls from being objectified as sex objects when they have barely hit puberty does not seem to overly trouble anyone in these conversations.

Wall Street Journal columnist Bret Stephens got a different take on uniforms from a young female West Pointer who was interning for him. Wearing a uniform, she told him, "helped her figure out what it was that really distinguished her as an individual." Stephens worries about a generation whose "mass conformism is masked by the appearance of mass non-conformism." In a May 2012 column, he implored them, "But if you can just manage to tone down your egos, shape up your minds, and think unfashionable thoughts, you just might be able to do something worthy with your lives. And even get a job."[13]

Consider Same-Sex Classrooms

After years of research all over the world, Dr. Leonard Sax has become an unabashed champion of same-sex schools. In his book *Girls on the Edge,* he cited a UCLA study that surveyed some twenty thousand girls across the United States. The results were unequivocal: girls who graduate from single-sex private schools, when compared with demographically comparable girls in coed schools, do better academically. In fact, all serious studies confirm this.

Sax answered the objection that coed schools better prepare girls for the real world with the question, what's real about a coed school? In no real-life circumstance do people work in an environment where everyone is single, available, immature, and the same age. "The co-ed school is a peculiar world," argued Sax, "where what really counts—if you're a girl—is who's cute, who's wearing the cool clothes, and who likes whom."[14]

Not only do girls do better academically in single-sex environments but they also do better emotionally. What researchers have discovered is that in coed schools the most important single determinant of a girl's self-esteem is appearance. In single-sex environments, says Sax, there is "a focus on who you *are* rather than how you *look*."[15]

At the very least, Sax believes that parents should have the choice as to whether their daughters can attend a same-sex school. More public school districts are moving in this direction. Today, at least five hundred public schools in the United States offer same-sex classes. In those districts without such classes, Sax urges parents to "organize."

Create a Nurturing Environment

Too many schools, from elementary through high schools, have responded to the ongoing sexual harassment of our daughters by overreacting on specific cases but underreacting in the creation of safe, sane environments. In North Carolina, for instance, a principal accused a nine-year-old of sexual harassment for calling a teacher "cute" and suspended him for three days. The district, overreacting itself, fired the principal.[16]

In Boston, a bully choked a seven-year-old and stole his gloves on the school bus. When the incident was reported to the interim principal, she ignored it. The next day, the seven-year-old kicked the bully in the testicles. The school reported the seven-year-old to the state Department of Children and Families for committing a sexual assault. Again, this case could have made sense only to school district lawyers.[17]

The best schools have the fewest rules. Their principals refrain from telling the kids what they should not do, but focus instead on showing them what they should do. They create environments in which students and teachers both feel obliged to live up to expectations. Teachers sit among the students at lunchtime, and principals walk the halls. The children know they care. Zero-tolerance policies have their value, but they work best in those schools where they are needed least.

Principals also need to enlist the parents in their efforts to sustain a wholesome school ethos. In talking to veteran school principals, they will tell you that the parents have changed more in the last generation than their children have. Too many of them now see the administrators as adversaries, not as allies. They will believe their child and condone his behavior regardless of the evidence against him. They would rather litigate than listen to reason. That is all the more reason for principals to educate parents in the very beginning on the real problems schools face and enlist them in the search for solutions.

Preserve Their Innocence

Padre Pio Academy is a small Catholic grade school in Shawnee, Kansas. It has as its motto: "Excellence, Innocence, Reverence."

The "excellence" and "reverence" one might expect from a parochial school, but the "innocence" is eye-catching. Many involved parties believe, as JoAnn Deak does, that school should be a "sanctuary from much of the junk we all have to face in the rest of the world," but Padre Pio Academy has a much deeper understanding of "sanctuary" than do Deak and most secular psychologists and an entirely different take on the word "junk."

Deak, for instance, talks about one coed class of seventh graders that she led in a discussion about the different ways girls and boys kiss. She calls the session "magical" because she was able to get the students to talk about so sensitive a subject. "That opened the floodgates," she enthused. She was then able to educate them on the "gender difference in the sensitivity of the face," a touch of science that reportedly helped ease the tensions between the sexes.[18]

From Padre Pio Academy's perspective, however, a conversation on kissing in the seventh grade would be unthinkable. It would be seen as part of the "junk" that children need protecting from. Innocence, here, ought not be confused with ignorance. The children know what is out there. They will have plenty of time to confront it. In the interim, in these truly magical years, they can receive the kind of "spiritual, intellectual, moral, and physical formation"[19] that will enable them to transcend the junk when they do face it.

Rethink Sex Ed

Consider the plight of a public middle school teacher assigned to teach sex education to sixth graders. The students come from a variety of different backgrounds: some as traditional as those who send their children to Padre Pio—Christian, Muslim, or Orthodox Jewish; some thoroughly progressive and permissive. The children themselves will be at dramatically different stages in development: some of the girls will be prepubescent and indifferent to boys; others will be physically fully mature and sexually active. This very challenge speaks to the inherent flaw in homogenized public education, especially when administrators seek to involve themselves in subject areas that many parents feel should be taught at home.

Too often, however, those parents are shut out of the debate. In 2011 the New York City public school system mandated that sex education—including lessons on how to use condoms—was to be taught in all the city's middle and high schools. No voice at all was given to those parents who "don't want sex education in schools."[20] There is something sad to me about requiring all eleven-year-olds to learn how to use condoms.

Compounding the problem is that public education management has become increasingly top-down over the years. Local districts have little control over curriculum. They can and have been sued for attempting even minor variations on the prevailing orthodoxy. A few years back, for instance, the local school board in Dover, Pennsylvania, merely required that a statement presenting intelligent design as "an explanation of the origin of life that differs from Darwin's view" be read aloud in ninth-grade science classes when evolution was taught. The ACLU came after the board, and the board was forced, on the decision of one judge, to pay the plaintiffs more than $1 million in legal fees.[21]

On the sex education front, the ACLU has been even more active. It recently sued the Silver Ring Thing (SRT), a successful abstinence pledge program that draws on Christian theology, and won. The SRT was denied all federal funding. The ACLU fretted that the SRT had no business showing how abstinence fit into Christian teaching. "The Silver Ring Thing has been quite public about the fact that it considers its abstinence education as a vehicle for bringing students to Christ," said Julie Sternberg of the ACLU, "in which case it should never have received federal funding."[22]

In fact, however, there has been a huge lobbying effort on the part of the contraception education proponents to deny abstinence funding even to those programs, like Best Friends, that are thoroughly secular. As I mentioned earlier, after the election of Barack Obama, we were no longer able to discuss abstinence or even to talk about the risks inherent in teen sex. Unfortunately for our daughters, the public educational establishment and the contraception-friendly feminist lobby are political allies. Add the ACLU and the media to the mix, and one can all but predict the kind of sex education our youth are getting in our public schools—and understand as well the growth of the home school movement.

A 2004 NPR report shows just how uneven the battlefield is on the subject of sex education. The report begins presumptuously, "The debate over whether to have sex education in American schools is over." A new poll, we are told, finds that only 7 percent of Americans say sex education should not be taught in schools. The report continues that there is little debate about what kind of sex education should be taught in that "parents are generally content with whatever sex education is offered by their children's school." In the fine print of this article, however, we can see that the reason parents seem so quiescent is that they are almost surely being misled about their children's education. In the same poll, 61 percent of the parents believed that schools should teach either abstinence-only sex education or "abstinence-plus."[23]

New York City's Department of Education, for instance, promotes its new program as abstinence first. When *New York Post* reporters got a hold of some of the new workbooks, however, they discovered the city's rather curious take on the word *abstinence*. Some choice revelations:

- High-school students go to stores and jot down condom brands, prices and features such as lubrication.
- Teens research a route from school to a clinic that provides birth control and STD tests, and write down its confidentiality policy.
- Students ages 11 and 12 sort "risk cards" to rate the safety of various activities, including "intercourse using a condom and an oil-based lubricant," mutual masturbation, French kissing, oral sex and anal sex.

- Teens are referred to resources such as Columbia University's Web site "Go Ask Alice."[24]

The "Alice" in question deserves special attention. In fact, it is really a team of Columbia University health care professionals whose collective wisdom, unfortunately, mirrors that of the age. "Radical politics pervades my profession," laments Dr. Miriam Grossman, "and common sense has vanished."[25]

When asked about a ménage à trois, for instance, Alice responds, "Nothing wrong with giving it a try, as long as you're practicing safer sex." The uneducated have to be forgiven for asking themselves, "Safer than what?" Alice responds to one reader who "will try anything once" with advice on proper "swing club etiquette," as if etiquette were more important than morality or even sexual hygiene.[26] It gets much worse than this.

Challenge Authority

In her book *Unprotected*, Dr. Grossman leveled a challenge to Columbia University for hosting such a site. Grossman wanted to know how "Alice," given the national pandemics of herpes and HPV, could advise a high school senior with three previous boyfriends to "experiment" and "explore" her sexuality. Alice's promise of "future well-being and peace of mind" for the girl was based on nothing vaguely resembling science. Asked Grossman, "Are parents aware . . . of the guidance their daughters will find on this award-winning health education Web site of one of the most esteemed institutions in the world?"[27]

The advice Alice dispenses is not unique to Columbia University. In her exploration of college websites, Grossman discovered that at Virginia Commonwealth University, cross-dressing is considered a "recreational activity." At the University of Wisconsin, coeds are advised how to pick up "that cute girl you noticed in your English class." And at the University of Missouri, "external water sports"—that is, urinating on a partner—is described as a form of "safer sex."[28]

To a large degree, parents remain unaware of how much of the progressive agenda seeps down into high school and middle school, and this undoubtedly accounts for the minimal resistance school principals report. They should face more. Admittedly, parents take the risk of embarrassing their children, but sometimes it is a risk that should be taken. Parents would do well to inquire first into what their children are learning. They may be surprised.

Consider Homeschooling

One reason principals get so little flak on sex education is that many of the parents most passionate about preserving their children's innocence have withdrawn from the public school system. Although the numbers are imprecise, roughly 2 million American children are now being homeschooled, a 100 percent increase in the last twelve years. While public school population grows at about 1 percent a year, home school population has been growing at about 8 percent.[29]

A recent *Education Week* article notes that while the most vocal and organized homeschoolers are typically conservative Christians, a more secular class of homeschoolers is emerging among those parents concerned "about violence, peer pressure, and poor academic quality in their schools."[30] The fact that parents are pulling their children from the supposedly "good" public schools in record numbers, despite the fact that they are paying for those schools, should serve as something of a wake-up call to the educational establishment. Instead, many within that establishment exploit the absence of these parents to push an increasingly extreme agenda. Although homeschooling is obviously not for everyone, in some districts it may be the best way for parents to preserve the moral integrity of their daughters and their sons.

Partner with Groups That Can Help

Having worked in Best Friends in more than a hundred urban schools, I know how very difficult it is for even the best of principals to create and sustain a nurturing environment for our daughters and our sons. That is why it can be highly useful for school districts to partner with groups like Best Friends.

Given our structure and our voluntary nature, we are in a better position than administrators to work on character issues. The strong and enthusiastic support of principals is critical for partners like us to succeed. We depend as well on the support of teachers and school personnel to serve as coordinators and mentors. Our motto is "helping girls develop self-control through self-respect." The more self-control our participants can exercise, the less external control they will need from authorities.

"Diamond Girls is important to me because it helps me stay on track" wrote Tyiesha Russell of Milwaukee in her award-winning essay. "My Diamond Girl friends help me make the right choices when I have decisions to make. They lead me to the right path so that I don't do anything wrong." Students who lead themselves on the right path do not have to be led.

RoseMarie Peterkin, the outstanding Best Friends program director in Newark, New Jersey, can attest to this. She tells the story of a sixth-grade girl whose mother and father were both deeply entrenched in the drug culture and, as a result, died from AIDS within months of each other. Through Best Friends, Peterkin and her colleagues were able to encourage the girl in school, foster excellence in academics, and help her resist drugs and alcohol right through college.

One of Peterkin's "proudest moments" was going to the girl's graduation at Wilberforce University. As a senior class officer, she attributed her success to Best Friends in front of a huge audience and noted that her seven Best Friends mentors were really "angels" for always being there for her. Peterkin calls Best Friends "the magic thread" that allowed staff, volunteers, parents, and participants "to change the norm of despondency and defeat to one of personal responsibility and positive action."[31]

Diane Glover, an excellent, ten-year program director for Best Friends in Charlotte—who just happens to be my beloved sister—reports a similar outcome. "Students have found their talent and self-confidence through the program," she observes. "That is what makes Best Friends unique from other youth development programs. It has the component that really gives students a chance to shine and develop their skills while, at the same time, they learn the importance of lessons taught."[32] As civil rights pioneer and educator, Mary McLeod Bethune, reminded us, "Invest in the human soul. Who knows, it might be a diamond in the rough."[33] Our Diamond Girls are a testament to that observation.

Reinforce "Connectedness"

The word that keeps recurring in the Add Health study is *connectedness*. The research has shown conclusively that adolescents who feel connected to their school delay having sex and prove less likely to drink, smoke, take drugs, and engage in violent behavior. Of course, it is much easier to urge schools to maintain a strong bond with their students than to actually accomplish that, but the effort is worth it.

Therapists who work with adolescents reinforce this notion. Almost universally, they encourage their charges to immerse themselves in school activities as a way of countering the alienation they feel. The Best Friends program is merely one way out of many for students to stay bonded to school. Sports are often hugely helpful. So are any number of school activities—band, glee club, newspaper, cheerleading, science club. The list goes on. From my experience, I would recommend that administrators take a more active role in encouraging this kind of involvement.

Students are more likely to feel connected to schools where they sense that others know and care for them. American Indian Public Charter School (AIPCS) in Oakland, California is one such school. When Ben Chavis, former executive director of the NAACP and a Lumbee Indian, took over at AIPCS about fifteen years ago, it was the worst-performing middle school in the Bay Area. Today, it is among the best.[34] Among other reforms, he set out consciously to strengthen the bonds between the students and the school.

Chavis prefers the word *family* to *connectedness*. Given the family breakdown he saw all around him, he felt that the school had to compensate if it were to succeed. "I create an extended family for my class," says Chavis.[35] Knowing that many of his students have dysfunctional parents, he reaches beyond them to involve the grandparents, even the aunts and uncles. If a kid has problems at school, Chavis will call whomever he must to get the necessary response.

To reinforce the sense of family, the students remain together as one class for all three years of middle school. They even stay with the same teacher and do not rotate among classes. "At this school, we are like a family," wrote one girl proudly in a school publication. "We work through things because we care for each other."[36] With students so well bonded to one another and to the school, instances of harassment and abuse are extremely rare.

There is no better proof of connectedness at AIPCS than attendance. The daily absentee rate at some urban schools hovers around 20 percent. Schools with daily absentee rates of less than 10 percent brag about them. At the American Indian Public Charter School, the daily absentee rate runs at about 1 percent.[37]

California allows its charter schools more freedom than do many states. Yet every public school in America has some flexibility to make their students feel at home. Those students who feel connected, who take pride in their school, and who engage in meaningful extracurricular activities are much less likely to harass their peers or to harm themselves through risky behavior.

What Universities Can Do

In a classic bit of Orwellian doublethink, university administrators tend to embrace both of the two competing feminist ideas on sex—the sex-positive and the anti-pornography—without seeing the internal contradiction. On the one hand, they support coed dorms, open visitations, and a casual hookup ethos. "Sex! Sex! It was in the air along with the nitrogen and the oxygen," wrote Tom Wolfe in *I Am Charlotte Simmons*, of Dupont, his fictional university. "The whole campus was humid with it."[1]

Dr. Miriam Grossman has confirmed Wolfe's perspective, but without the ironic distance. Said she bluntly of campus life, "The exaggerated place of sexuality is grotesque and destructive."[2] As she's observed, some 40 percent of college women have experienced a sexual encounter without commitment, and 10 percent have done so on at least six occasions.[3] And yet despite the emotional and health risks of such encounters, university health officials provide no useful counseling whatsoever.

While university administrators routinely denounce the objectification and exploitation of women and seem distressed that male students no longer view female students with respect, they are reluctant to address indiscriminate sexual activity among their students.

Unable or unwilling to recognize their own incoherence, many administrators refuse to recognize the root causes of the moral breakdown. Mary Eberstadt, among other critics, has little respect for them. "At Toxic U," says Eberstadt, "there are no authorities; instead, there are predators and prey."[4] Administrators find it safer to paper over the problem with meaningless platitudes, empty petitions (like the Amethyst Initiative), and unenforceable rules. Asks Grossman, "Why no pamphlets in our waiting room directed at freshman women with data about their 'increased vulnerability' in romance?"[5]

On its website, the University of Virginia tells us that "sexual harassment is so commonplace that often we fail to even recognize harassing behavior as wrong."[6] There is a logic problem with this sentence. It would make more sense if its order were reversed; to wit, the fact that we fail to recognize harassing behavior as wrong has caused such behavior to be more commonplace. Regrettably, women account for nearly 50 percent of Tucker Max's book sales.[7]

"Sexual harassment in any form is unacceptable behavior and should not be tolerated by anyone," says the university. "It undermines our ability to study, to work, and to feel like effective, empowered people in the world."[8]

The university also offers formal information on a "sexual assault" website that includes definitions of *sexual harassment* and *stalking* as well as *sexual assault* and *domestic violence*. Under "legal rights," the site refers students to the Virginia Criminal Code.[9] I am sure Liz Seccuro would find great solace in knowing this information is now available to girls who have been assaulted.

Insist On Common Sense

Virginia Tech University senior Seung-Hui Cho had any number of problems that should have been red-flagged long before he shot fifty-seven of his teachers and fellow students in April 2007, killing thirty-two of them. In high school he had suffered from chronic mental health issues but chose to discontinue therapy. Due to privacy laws, Cho arrived on the Virginia Tech campus without school officials knowing of his problems or his refusal to treat them.

Being away from home did not help. What authorities euphemistically refer to as the "lifestyle irregularities" of the college experience can trigger manic and depressive episodes in students genetically predisposed.

Cho's problems manifested themselves in obvious ways at Virginia Tech. He became a stalker. At least two female students complained about him to campus police, one in November 2005, the next a month later. When the students both refused to press charges, the police talked to Cho, but that was it. He was referred to the university disciplinary system, where nothing of consequence happened.

Cho was clearly falling apart, and his teachers and fellow students were noticing. One creative-writing teacher referred him to the school's counseling service because his essays were so obviously troubled, but he would not go. She was sufficiently concerned to report him to the counseling office, but they told her they could do nothing unless Cho agreed to participate. This is often the crux of the problem on college campuses. Students are considered adults at eighteen and cannot be forced into treatment against their will. However, teachers and administrators could have called Cho's parents to alert them to his breakdown. In 2005 Cho was actually referred by a judge for evaluation and treatment. Because student records are shielded by the student privacy law there was never any follow-up. It appears the university was never notified.[10]

Dr. Fuller Torrey, executive director of the Treatment Advocacy Center, is an outspoken advocate for civil commitment. He believes this would enable the seriously mentally ill to receive and continue to take the all important medication that ensures their safety and that of others. A psychiatrist whom I greatly admire, Dr. Robert DuPont, a leading authority on drug treatment, told me, "Very few mentally ill people are ever violent. It is when mental illness is combined with illegal drugs there is a danger of violence."

In the Virginia Tech case, it appears the most consequential mistake authorities made was their failure to alert students after Cho killed his first two victims in a coed student dorm two hours before he would return to campus with massacre on his mind. The police had somehow convinced themselves that Emily Hilscher and resident assistant Ryan Clark had been killed by a jealous boyfriend. One wonders whether dating violence is sufficiently common on campus that police presume it to be the cause of all major crime.

Ironically, like the iconic Travis Bickle in Martin Scorsese's *Taxi Driver*, Cho saw himself as an avenger, the man who would purge the campus of its decadence. "You had everything you wanted," he would write to his fellow students in his suicide note. "Your Mercedes wasn't enough, you brats. Your golden necklaces weren't enough, you snobs. Your trust fund wasn't enough. Your vodka and cognac weren't enough. All your debaucheries weren't enough. Those weren't enough to fulfill your hedonistic needs. You had everything."[11]

A mature, intelligent young woman I know, who was at Virginia Tech at the time, told me Cho's rant of depicting the students as wealthy snobs was a total figment of his imagination.

In fact, the tolerance of his disturbing behavior by the students, the fear of offending, the anxiety about violating unspecified privacy laws, the lack of attention paid to the professor who was concerned about Cho's writing, the reluctance to say the obvious about a deranged young man—all led to a thoroughly senseless tragedy.

Protect Proactively

Universities all have some student protection plans in place. To its credit, the University of Virginia Police Department now offers a range of services to its students that have the potential to decrease the risk of assault on campus. These include rape aggression defense classes, basic self-defense instruction, frequent security surveys, a third-party sexual assault reporting program, some four hundred blue-light phones around the campus, and a variety of educational seminars, including those on alcohol awareness, illegal drugs, hazing, sexual assault prevention, driving under the influence, and self-defense.

Princeton University, like many universities, has a rigorous sexual misconduct code as well as a SHARE (Sexual Harassment/ Assault Advising, Resources, and Education) office through which grievances are addressed. "All forms of sexual misconduct are regarded as serious University offenses," reads the opening paragraph of the highly detailed code, "and violations are likely to result in discipline, including the possibility of suspension, expulsion, or termination of employment."[12] The code defines misconduct, addresses the issues of incapacitation and consent, describes the grievance process, and outlines the steps to resolution. Princeton also provides its young women information about counseling, medical services, accommodations with respect to classes, and the issuing of a "Dean's no contact order" (DNCO). This is an especially helpful policy in my mind, as the student takes no risk in legal action. The student who is harassing the other student must stay away or expulsion from the university is recommended.

Many universities have in place what is called at Davidson College a "Good Samaritan Policy." What this means is that a student who calls 911 when a fellow student is having an alcohol-related medical emergency cannot get in trouble with the police regardless of his or her own state of sobriety.[13] To be sure, this represents something of a watered-down version of the original concept of a Good Samaritan, but at least it is a start in the right direction.

What is hard to discern from a distance is just how proactive these programs are and if the campus culture allows for their utilization. This is where leadership makes a difference, not just of the police department, or of the SHARE office, but of the university. Safety has to be a campus-wide concern.

Given the many sophisticated technical people on a college campus, I was wondering if someone somewhere could devise a simple interactive system that allowed students to report problems instantaneously through texting or social media messaging. No sooner did I think this thought out loud than I read that the University of Maryland was planning to roll out a mobile phone application called "the Escort-M program." With a few taps on her phone, a student leaving a late class or venturing out on an errand will be able to alert campus security to watch her on live video.

The Escort-M application follows the "M-Urgency app" university police recently began to offer as a more sophisticated way to call 911. With a few clicks, a student can connect to public safety dispatchers and provide them with live audio, video, and the GPS-driven location of the phone in question. The recorded video can be used to give police a sense of the situation's seriousness, help ID a perpetrator, and save the caller from having to describe the event.[14] I only wonder how much tragedy this system could have avoided if Eve Carson had had access to it, or Morgan Harrington or the students at Virginia Tech. The smart phone technology can surely be utilized for the safety of our daughters and our sons.

Protect the Whole Woman

"If someone's my patient, I'm responsible for her—*all of her*," wrote Dr. Miriam Grossman. "Who says I should worry about alcoholic binges but not hookups? What, her liver's more important than her cervix or fallopian tubes?"[15] In her impassioned challenge to the world of academic health, Grossman tackled the fundamental questions universities have ceased to ask.

In *Unprotected*, Grossman made the case that biologically, not just culturally, women "are designed to bond." In many of the young women she has interviewed, the end of a relationship has left the female depressed and dysfunctional but has scarcely troubled the male at all. Research, she reminds us, "implies that sexual activity, especially in women, might be more complex than, say, working out. It suggests women may be vulnerable, unprotected."[16] And yet many universities systematically put ideology over health in the treatment of young women. If this is going to change, more professionals like Grossman are going to have to speak out, and more administrators are going to have to listen.

Acknowledge Gender Differences

Administrators and health professionals are systematically misinforming their female students. They stress the need to abstain from tobacco but wink at reckless sex despite its more immediate dangers. They encourage girls to plan for the future but neglect to factor motherhood into those plans. They fret about their students' emotional health but deny the role of gender differences in their students' emotional makeup. They recommend abortion as a solution to a problem but fail to warn their girls about the enduring psychological distress that abortion often causes. Says the pro-choice Grossman, "The denial of the trauma of abortion is entrenched dogma."[17]

As Grossman sees it, university officials will fail their female students until they begin to "acknowledge gender differences."[18] As long as males and females are treated the same, females will suffer, both emotionally and physically. To acknowledge gender differences, however, is a risky proposition on the contemporary campus. Harvard president Lawrence Summers learned just how risky at a diversity in science conference in 2005. For merely suggesting that a gender difference in scientific aptitude might be a causative factor in female underrepresentation in the profession, he was accused of sexism. Despite his repeated apologies, he was eventually forced to resign.[19] A public rebuke at this level puts a chill on honest discussion of gender differences in just about any campus environment.

As Grossman has detailed, there is a widespread reluctance to dissent from prevailing gender orthodoxies on just about all American campuses. "We were afraid," she wrote of her fellow dissidents, "of challenging the entrenched dogma of our profession."[20] That she proved willing to speak out is a good sign. More will follow. Said Grossman defiantly at the end of *Unprotected*, "And one last thing: don't tell me how to speak and what to think."[21]

Strengthen the School's Academics

One indirect way to change campus culture, whether college or high school, is to insist on academic rigor. The well-received 2011 book *Academically Adrift*, by Richard Arum and Josipa Roksa, shows just how unrigorous college education has become. "How much are students actually learning in contemporary higher education?" ask the authors. "The answer for many undergraduates, we have concluded, is not much."[22]

The survey data, taken from a broad cross section of students, reveal that 32 percent of students in a given semester do not take any courses with more than forty pages of reading assigned a week. More troubling still, half of all students do not take a single course in which they must write more than twenty pages over the course of a semester. On average, students study only about 12 to 14 hours a week, and much of that time is in groups, a practice that produces little in the way of results. In other words, of the roughly 100 to 120 waking hours a student spends on campus in a given week, only about 30 are given over to academics. This leaves the academically unmotivated with an excess of free time, and few students do anything productive with it.[23]

Speaking of which, the study also found that students who were more deeply involved in fraternities and sororities show smaller gains than other students. At least since the 1978 film *Animal House*, the media have tended to celebrate the dysfunctional side of Greek life. I suspect, however, that even the young men from Delta Tau Chi would be a bit surprised to see how crude campuses have become. They would find little to rebel against.

The Arum and Roksa study suggested that colleges de-emphasize "social engagement"—that is, all things nonacademic—and focus on academics. In their competition for students, universities often promote all sorts of attractive campus features—sports, rec centers, swimming pools, local night life—that have little to do with the mission of the university. Administrators fear, and not without good cause, that a refocus on academics could cost them in student admissions. This is a possibility they will one day have to face in any case.

Coach for Character

On Dom Starsia's lacrosse camp website, the reader learns in the very first sentence that Starsia "is one of the most successful college lacrosse coaches in the country."[24] In terms of wins and losses, that would be hard to argue with. Starsia led the University of Virginia Cavaliers to the 2011 national title, and three others before that.

In talking to former players, I get the strong sense that Coach Starsia is well loved and respected. One star player told me that in summer training, even before Yeardley Love's death, Starsia insisted that he would tolerate neither violence against women nor drunk driving. He may not have understood, however, that adolescents need redundancy. They need repeated reminders that certain activities are clearly off-limits. Starsia's players did him no favor by keeping Huguely's behavior to themselves. They did Huguely no favor either. I wonder if students today have given the "code of silence" higher priority than the campus honor codes.

In his four years playing under Starsia, George Huguely apparently became an alcoholic in serious need of treatment. In February 2009, for instance, Huguely viciously pummeled the face of a sleeping teammate because he knew he had been intimate with Yeardley Love. The unblemished Huguely and the brutalized teammate acknowledged the "fight" to Coach Starsia, claimed they had settled the matter between them, and that was that. The teammates seemed to know what happened, but Starsia was unaware. The coach also said he was unaware of Huguely's earlier run-in with a police officer in Lexington, Virginia, in the course of which Huguely had to be tasered into submission.

"I never knew about the incident at W & L," Starsia would say later in reference to Huguely's ugly encounter with the policeofficer in Lexington, Virginia. "If I had known, maybe I'd have done something."[25] Not unlike coach Joe Paterno of Penn State, who seemed unable to grasp the unthinkable abuse being perpetrated by a former coach, Starsia failed to imagine just how deranged Huguely could become when drunk. These things were not supposed to happen on college campuses.

Love's coach, Julie Myers, appeared as unknowing as Starsia was to the impending disaster. "He was shaking and just like we were," Myers said of Starsia immediately after the killing. "I mean, everyone had this tremendous sense of loss and, how does this happen?"[26] Apparently she was never told that Yeardley was nearly choked to death by Huguely earlier that year. None of Yeardley's teammates believed this incident was serious enough to inform their coach, or that their relationship with this coach should include the sharing of personal concerns about teammates. Again the code of silence reigned supreme. In answer to Coach Myers's question, "How does this happen?": Possibly, it happens because the code of silence does not allow the coaches to know the signs of impending tragedy. If coaches had absolutely no idea about George's alcoholism and Yeardley's victimization, why did their players not come forward and tell them? Many an abused girl has disclosed a dangerous situation when an alert teacher or authority figure has questioned her. We have experienced this first hand in the Best Friends program.

Athletes often look to coaches to fill the void left by unavailable or inadequate fathers and mothers. Coaches and other youth leaders spend more time with college students and often have more control over them than their parents do. Like many universities, UVA has a Student Athlete Mentor (SAM) program. I have talked to student athletes at UVA who have taken advantage of the program to help them steer clear of the various seductions campus life offers. For students today, these programs cannot be voluntary. They should be required. And coaches at both universities and high schools have to pay more attention to the needs and behavior of the individuals on their teams.

Some do as a matter of course. Others obviously do not. My sons' coaches, particularly Kevin Giblin and Dan Perot, are among those who do. As both my sons are athletes—the older one a four-year lacrosse starter in high school and college, the younger one a college football and high school football and lacrosse player—I have watched hundreds of games. I have seen boys grow into fine young men who work hard, play hard, and pray hard, just as their coaches taught them.

Some coaches, like Bill Tierney when he was at Princeton, made sure that parents and players behaved responsibly by prohibiting drinking at pre- and post-game tailgate parties. "I want not only to teach these boys to be great football players, but also to be good men," said the new football coach at UNC, Chapel Hill, Larry Fedora. We need more coaches to say the same and mean it.

In *The Book of Man: Readings on the Path to Manhood*, my husband, Bill, profiles a few coaches who understand their larger responsibility. Michael Faulkner starred at Virginia Tech University, played a year in the NFL, and then found his true calling in the ministry. For the last thirty years, he has fearlessly taken his gospel message to the streets of Harlem. In recent years, he has been working with young people, particularly young men, through his nonprofit organization, the Institute for Leadership. He has worked hard to help his charges learn planning and decision making by applying biblical principles.

Faulkner has witnessed an increasing failure by men to accept responsibility for raising the next generation. "The problem right now is that men are afraid to be men," says Faulkner. "We are afraid to confront that kid on the train that's cursing; we're afraid to say to him that's not the way we're supposed to behave." As Bill has observed, Faulkner "wants to see men assert themselves as guardians of social and civic decency in the age of moral relativism." Faulkner has done just that in one of the nation's toughest environments.[27]

In the high-pressure environment of Texas high school football, Ken Purcell has made many of the same leadership decisions that Faulkner has. Purcell coached high school ball for twenty-four years before becoming athletic director for the Denton school system. "If we're not teaching values," says Purcell, "then we're wasting too much money on a game." Purcell is specific about what values he and the coaches he has hired should teach: "discipline, poise, class, accountability, and decision-making skills." Purcell's goal is not to create star football players but to create men of honor. "Part of being a man means that you have integrity," says Purcell. "It means that you honor your commitments, you follow through on what you say you're going to do."[28] I do not wish to imply that athleticism or being a member of a sports team can lead to violence against women. My husband, Bill, wrote an essay "On the Defense of Sports" many years ago that is true today. He wrote,

> Sheer uncontrolled violence in sports, often called unnecessary roughness, unsportsmanlike conduct, is not a part of the game. On the contrary it stops the game, nullifies the play . . . Sports is still an activity in which excellence can be seen and reached for and approximated each day; sports has been relatively unaffected by the general erosion of standards in the culture at large. . . . Sports is a way to scorn indifference and occasionally, indeed, can even discern in

competition those elements of grace, skill, beauty, and courage that mirror the greater affirmations of human spirit and passion.

Change the Culture

I am not going to pretend this is easy, and I do not have any quick solutions, but university administrators must start looking within. In her observant essay on the Yeardley Love tragedy, Alexandra Petri spoke of "the strange mess of college life."[29] Tom Wolfe, who wrote an alarmingly detailed and prophetic novel on the larger chaos of college life, repeatedly used the word "mess" to describe its particulars—"noxious mess," "virulent mess," "crumpled little mess."[30] Grossman got specific about the mess, describing a "campus culture of permissiveness, experimentation, androgyny, and spiritual bankruptcy."[31]

This mess is visible to anyone who cares to look, but too few administrators, alumni, and parents choose to see. They content themselves with knowing too little. Nowhere did this willful blindness have more devastating consequences than at Penn State University. By not being proactive against child molester Jerry Sandusky, Penn State coaches and administrators not only endangered scores of children but they also wrecked the reputation of the university.

At Penn State, the problem started at the top. University president Graham Spanier, while a young sociology professor, mirrored the moral relativism of much of academia when he wrote, "We choose to view deviant behavior simply as behavior that some value and others consider wrong. An individual's behavior becomes deviant only when others define it as deviant."[32] As Spanier learned, the rest of America is not as "tolerant" as the faculty lounge. Unfortunately, too few administrators elsewhere will see the connection between Penn State's inaction on the child abuse case and their own inaction on the ongoing dangers their students face.

An impending tuition bubble may cause parents to pay attention, but administrators are too engaged in sustainability to worry about what it is they are sustaining. As to alumni, as long as the sports teams keep winning, that is enough for too many of them. The NCAA's sanctions will prevent Penn State's football team from winning much of anything for years to come. Hopefully, that will stir some alumni out of their slumber.

But not all young athletes make bad decisions. Mary Katherine Macklen, when captain of her Dutch Fork High School soccer team in South Carolina, made a good decision, one that many of the students who went to Aruba with Natalee Holloway might wish they had made. Instead of going to Aruba to party on her senior trip, she went to Haiti to teach. "We worked with an orphanage," Macklen said. "I love working with kids. Shows me what I want to do for the rest of my life. Be with those kids." Macklen brought sports equipment with her on the trip and shared it with children who may have never seen anything new in their whole lives. "You don't realize how other people live in the world," said Macklen. "It's so different in America. It just changed my whole world view."[33]

To be sure, Haiti is at least as dangerous as Aruba, maybe more so, but the risks our daughters run, no matter where they are, derive more from what's going on inside their heads than what is going on in the world around them. If a school really wants to change its culture, it should teach the students skills other than partying and virtues other than popularity and send them some place where they can put those skills and virtues to work, even if that place is a homeless shelter or a children's hospital in their own hometown. Our young people should be taught to realize that concern for others makes them better people. "'Twas her thinking of others made you think of her,"[34] said Elizabeth Barrett Browning in a bit of advice that never grows old.

Put Teeth in Their Policies

In reviewing the policies of any number of universities, I see a trend toward more recognition of campus-wide problems and more policies to address them. What is less obvious is whether the universities are enforcing these policies. Still, some of the changes afoot are encouraging.

Many universities now have a SHARE—"Sexual Harassment/Assault Advising, Resources, and Education"—program, but Princeton University has one that is committed and comprehensive. The program has a designated space, regular hours, a viable hotline, and 24/7 emergency services. On the plus side, too, the university has banned its notorious "Nude Olympics."[35]

The University of North Carolina seems to have taken an equally proactive stance in educating its students about relationship violence and training its students to do something about it. The Sexual Assault and Relationship Violence Training and Education (SARVTAE) committee is an interdisciplinary, interdepartmental, and collaborative task force. It includes members of the UNC and Chapel Hill communities, who take their responsibility seriously.[36]

Among UNC's more distinctive programs is one called HAVEN, a campus-wide initiative to provide support for students who have been victims of sexual abuse and dating violence. The goal is to create multiple "safe spaces" around the campus for students to go for information, discussion, and referral.[37]

Although the Yeardley Love, Morgan Harrington, and Liz Seccuro cases caused the University of Virginia to be more visible on the issue of campus violence, its environment differs little from comparable universities. To its credit, the university has responded with some useful correctives, among them a safe ride program, in which students can be driven home late at night from certain pickup points,[38] and self-defense classes for women taught by campus and Charlottesville police.[39]

Of all the changes I have seen, however, very few address the campus culture in a substantial way. One university that has taken a dramatic and concrete step to turn the culture around is the Catholic University of America. University president John Garvey took to the pages of the *Wall Street Journal* to explain why CUA was embarking on the change at hand.

"I would have thought that young women would have a civilizing influence on young men," said Garvey shrewdly. "Yet the causal arrow seems to run the other way. Young women are trying to keep up—and young men are encouraging them."[40] One platform for their mutual undoing has been the coed dorm, now the norm on university campuses. Garvey cited a recent study by Christopher Kaczor at Loyola Marymount to make his case. According to that study, students in coed dorms are more than twice as likely both to indulge in weekly binge drinking and to have had three or more sexual partners in the past year.[41]

Garvey is the rare university president to cite "binge drinking and the culture of hooking up" as "the two most serious ethical challenges college students face." He is rare, too, in making the connection between intellect and virtue. "They influence one another," says Garvey. Accordingly, CUA has switched to single-sex residence halls. "The change will cost more money," Garvey concedes. "But our students will be better off."[42]

What Peer Groups Can Do

The need for young people to find reassurance from their friends is unrestricted by time or place, as is our need to monitor the same. In *West Side Story*, for instance, the "Jets" memorably promised themselves to watch out for each other, "You're never alone/ You're never disconnected/ You're home with your own/ When company's expected/ You're well protected!"[1] As the Add Health study insists, the need for "connectedness" is an essential part of adolescence; it always has been.[2]

West Side Story, of course, was based on a play written thousands of miles away and nearly four centuries earlier, Shakespeare's *Romeo and Juliet*. In both dramas, the youthful peer groups—the Jets and the Montagues, respectively—unite to protect their cherished friend— Tony/Romeo—but in each case, the protection fails, and tragedy ensues. The irony is that the Tony/Romeo character tries to introduce a bond among friends based on love, not fear. When Juliet's cousin, Tybalt, threatens Romeo, Romeo insists, "I do protest, I never injured thee, but love thee better than thou canst devise, till thou shalt know the reason of my love: And so, good Capulet—which name I tender as dearly as my own—be satisfied."[3] A bit less eloquently, Tony insists to Bernardo, "There's nothin' to fight about."[4]

These pleas obviously failed, and they did so because they were delivered entirely out of context. Each of the peer groups in question—Jets, Sharks, Montagues, and Capulets—was formed in a violent society that had yet to recognize the prospect of virtuous behavior and peaceful resolution. Today, our prospects for introducing change are brighter, but our challenges are at least as daunting. That much said, peers have an obligation to protect their friends, and parents and educators should do everything they can to make sure that happens.

Intervene When Necessary

If anyone were to have a protective peer group, it should have been Yeardley Love. The University of Virginia lacrosse teams, male and female, hung out together and watched out for each other. Well liked and respected by just about everyone in her orbit, Yeardley had brothers and sisters everywhere.

"Yeardley lived with two roommates and seems to have traveled in a pack, constantly surrounded by friends and other members of the women's lacrosse team," wrote Melinda Henneberger in the *Washington Post*, seemingly astonished that someone like Yeardley could be killed.[5] That pack included the best and brightest, almost all of them from middle-class families—smart, athletic youth, well educated, disciplined in their sport, future-oriented—and yet for all their professed affection for Yeardley they let her down.

She was killed by one of her own. "He's not complicated. He's not complex. He's a lacrosse player,"[6] said George Huguely's attorney at the start of the trial, as if to imply that his behavior the night he killed Yeardley was somehow normative for a lacrosse player. As a lacrosse mother, I can tell you it was not the norm. But a female student athlete who knew Yeardley and George told me, "A lot of guys get very aggressive toward girls when they have been drinking. George wasn't the only one." Later in the trial, a witness testified that he saw Yeardley being choked by Huguely months before the killing, but he made no effort to bring this behavior to light. At the same trial, Huguely's teammates conceded that their friend had been binge drinking about four days a week throughout his senior year, and that they had considered an intervention for after graduation, but sadly, it was too late.[7]

Get (Really) Grounded

Following the murder, grieving students launched a "Let's Get Grounded Coalition" to promote bystander intervention, but they were hard-pressed to determine in precisely which values they wanted their peers to be grounded. The coalition mission statement demands that students "take a stand," but students could not be faulted for saying, "Against what, exactly?"

The statement reads like a parody of a contemporary campus mission statement. It claims that the press-worthy "incidents" on campus resulted from "a culmination of different behaviors." These behaviors, in turn, resulted from "misunderstandings and disrespectful norms that cross the line into action." These misunderstandings, of course, "include misconceptions of race, ethnicity, gender, religion, economic status and sexual orientation."[8]

The irony is that the incident included none of those trendy misconceptions. If there were a misconception, it was that a male student could demand a traditional monogamous relationship in a hookup culture when he himself was not prepared to honor that relationship. If there were a second misconception, it was that Huguely's peers could remain nonjudgmental in the face of his increasingly brutish behavior, and do so without consequence. There was a timeless struggle taking place on a campus whose punishable offenses have been recently manufactured to pacify powerful progressive interest groups. Reality was never in play here.

As part of the "Get Grounded" response to Yeardley's death,

student leaders were to have joined with the UVA athletics department and the school's Gordie Center for Alcohol and Substance Education (named for eighteen-year-old Gordie Bailey, who died in 2004 following a hazing incident involving alcohol in the Chi Psi fraternity at the University of Colorado) to participate in a national "Step Up!" training program to promote peer intervention. Despite the exclamation point in the program's name, little or no actual training seems to have taken place. The calendar of events for the Let's Get Grounded Coalition lists no events for February 2012, the month of George Huguely's trial, and in fact no events for 2012 at all.[9] As of this writing, the website's Step Up! page appears to have been last modified on April 28, 2011.[10] Values that are improvised on the spot are not likely to endure.

Once our daughters have moved beyond our immediate control, peer groups should play an important role in protecting them, but they rarely do. Candlelight vigils and thronged courtrooms don't count. They come much too late and accomplish far too little. If instead we could encourage an entire generation of youth to care for their friends and be concerned for their safety, the rewards to our society would be extraordinary. To care for their friends, however, they must first ground themselves in something deeper than pretend virtue.

It was for this reason that the Best Friends Foundation launched the "Stop the Silence. Prevent the Violence" program. As we explain in the program, 40 percent of teenage girls know someone their own age who has been hit or beaten by her partner. We know there are specific steps we can take to empower teens to speak up and protect their peers.

Get Specific

Young people are willing and able to step up and protect their friends. They need, however, to be encouraged to do so and to be educated in what to look for. Here are some of the practical questions we invite our young people to ask themselves.[11]

- Does the individual have unexplained bruises, scratches, or injuries?
- Do you see signs that the individual is afraid of his/her boyfriend or girlfriend?
- Does the boyfriend or girlfriend lash out, or insult the individual?
- Has the individual's appearance or behavior suddenly changed?
- Has the individual stopped spending time with friends and family?
- Has the individual recently started using alcohol or drugs?
- Have you seen the boyfriend or girlfriend become abusive towards other people or things?
- Does the individual seem to have lost interest or to be giving up things that were once important?
- Has he/she lost interest in school or other activities?
- Does the boyfriend or girlfriend seem to try to control the individual's behavior, making all the decisions, checking up on his/her behavior, demanding to know who the individual has been with, and acting jealous and possessive?
- Does the individual apologize for the boyfriend or girlfriend's behavior to you and others?
- Has the individual casually mentioned the boyfriend or girlfriend's temper or violent behavior, but then laughed it off as a joke?
- Have you seen sudden changes in the individual's mood or personality? Is the individual becoming anxious or depressed, acting out, or being secretive? Is the individual avoiding eye contact, having "crying jags" or getting "hysterical"?

We encourage our young people to step forward when they learn that a friend is being abused. To facilitate them, we have developed a specific protocol for our coordinators to follow once they have been informed. This protocol, provided in the resource section of this book, assures that the students feel comfortable coming forward and the proper authorities are promptly made aware of the situation. All organizations, universities included, should so the same. If they don't, nothing will change.

Encourage Sound Decision Making

Sound decision making is not something that comes naturally to young people. Jean Piaget's developmental research has shown that teenagers have a limited ability to make decisions, especially in regard to sexual relationships.

Developmental psychologist Wanda Franz defines the problem-solving dynamics of Piaget's development stages as the movement from the so-called concrete operations stage to the formal operations stage. In the concrete stage, one typically experienced in grades three through seven, children have all they can handle with the immediate concrete experiences they encounter. They tend to process information haphazardly and not anticipate future outcomes.[12]

At Best Friends, our goal is to help our girls reach the formal operations stage, one in which they anticipate possible outcomes, weigh their value, consider complex interactions, and begin to reason realistically about the future. To accomplish this, we teach effective problem-solving skills and goal setting. We use group discussion as a way to help girls reinforce each other in what they have learned and how that learning might be applied.

Michael Oher has added a nice little bit of wisdom on this subject. "If you make the wrong decision," he wrote, "it's never too late to make the right one."[13]

Reinforce Your Daughters

If we are to protect our daughters, we must make them strong enough to shape their own peer groups. This starts at home. Children imitate what they see. Abusive parents often beget abusive, bullying children.

Conversely, parents who treat their partners with obvious respect, who affirmatively care for their children, and who extend an unforced empathy to their friends and family members have a much greater chance of raising children who do the same.

That is a good start, but it is not sufficient. Our daughters must have the strength to take these values with them out into the culture. At a transitional moment in a girl's life, and none is more transitional or potentially traumatic than beginning middle school or a new high school, parents need to instruct their daughters in what they are about to face before they face it.

Parents ought first to acquaint themselves with just how rough that culture can be. It will almost inevitably be more vulgar, violent, and sexualized than the one they experienced back in the vulgar, violent, and sexualized days of their own youth. If parents do not understand this, they will have a hard time empathizing with the transition their daughter faces. They need to reassure their daughter she has the character to prosper even in a hostile environment, and also has parental love and protection should she ever need it.

To make this assignment that much trickier for parents, they will have to teach their daughter about the trials she may face without scaring her or destroying her confidence in the goodness of humanity—even at its most adolescent awful. A big assignment, I know, but if we as parents could get our daughters to model self-respect and self-control among their peers, we would revolutionize our times.

Support Faith Groups

It should come as no surprise to anyone familiar with the way our deeply secular universities work that there has been a genuine lack of serious studies on the relationship between religion and risky sexual behavior. Not to be cynical, but I suspect that many researchers are afraid either of what they would find or what their peers and superiors would say about their findings. Dr. Miriam Grossman traces part of the problem to the disproportionate number of atheists and agnostics among the psychology profession, almost five times as many as among the general population.[14] Some of these people treat a deep and genuine faith as a pathology.

As Dr. Clea McNeely and her coauthor, Jayne Blanchard, observed, "The research that does exist suggests that faith-based organizations can provide young people with role models, moral direction, spiritual experiences, positive social and organizational ties, and community and leadership skills."[15] Confirming this fact is not necessarily the best way to assure tenure.

Undaunted, Sharon Scales Rostosky et al chose to mine the Add Health survey for information on the role faith plays in protecting our daughters. What Rostosky and her peers found, of course, is that in virtually all studies, both boys and girls who attended church and associated with others who did the same were, in the jargon of the academy, "more likely to delay coital debut." Rostosky made the point that in contrast to the "generally prohibitive sexual ideologies" of most faith groups, "American popular culture and mass media often are understood to actively promote a sexual ideology characterized by pleasure." In some contexts—the Amish, for instance, or Orthodox Jews—the faith has the edge over the culture. In other, less-disciplined faiths, the culture maintains the edge.[16]

Despite the pressure to yield to cultural forces, some three-quarters of college students continue to pray, at least according to a study involving thousands of students nationwide. The same study states that those who are deeply involved in religion report better mental health. In fact, they do dramatically better than their non-churchgoing peers who are twice as likely to be depressed, three times more likely to rate themselves emotionally below par, and seven times more likely to feel "overwhelmed."[17]

As Grossman explains, a place of worship offers the student a sense of community and an opportunity to share experiences with likeminded people. Commitment to just about any mainstream faith encourages healthy behaviors and, if not abstinence, at least the avoidance of risky behavior. By lowering disease risk, religious commitment also inevitably increases well-being. In a chapter titled "Memo to the APA" (American Psychological and Psychiatric Associations), Grossman says, "Believing in God is good for you."[18]

Resist the Oppressors

In no known case do American youth who take their faith seriously, whatever that faith, indulge on average in more risky behaviors than their secular peers. Given this fact, one would think that educators would encourage young people to join faith groups and associate with other children who do.

To think this true is to ignore the profound antireligious wave emanating from our educational and media establishments. Grossman calls it an "irrational antagonism,"[19] one that is all the more problematic for its being so widespread. A few years back, for instance, the city of Berkeley, California, undid a longstanding agreement it had with a local Sea Scout chapter to provide free berthing at the city's marina. Many of the children in this racially diverse troop come from impoverished families and were in need of just the kind of positive peer group reinforcement the Scouts provide, but that mattered less to the city of Berkeley than to the restrictive clause in the Scout Oath.

In the Oath, boys must promise to do their "duty to God" and to keep themselves "morally straight." In California, those are fighting words. When the Sea Scouts appealed, the League of California Cities, the California Association of Counties, the Anti-Defamation League, the Lawyers' Committee for Civil Rights, and three foundations of the ACLU came to the defense of Berkeley as did the California Supreme Court, which ruled unanimously in the city's favor.[20]

Children of faith, Christians in particular, do not get much support from the media either. On the popular TV show *Glee*, for instance, Christians are invariably shown to be cold and hypocritical. The one self-identified Christian on the show, the perky, blond president of the celibacy club, is impregnated by one classmate but pretends the father is another. When she begs her parents' forgiveness, they throw her out of the house.

Nevertheless, in her review of the show for *Time* magazine—"The Gospel of *Glee*: Is It Anti-Christian?"—Nancy Gibbs scolded those Christians who think it might be. "The point [of the show]," wrote Gibbs, "lies in the surprises that jostle us out of our smug little certainties and invite us to weigh what we value, whatever our faith tradition." Gibbs casually overlooked the fact that most everything a young believer sees on TV or hears in school jostles her out of her "smug little certainties."[21] Jostled free of her moral security, and shoved out into what Mary Pipher describes as "a media-drenched world flooded with junk values,"[22] where exactly would Ms. Gibbs recommend that our daughters turn for reassurance?

One place they might *not* want to turn is to the short-lived ABC comedy titled, finally, *GCB*, which is shorthand for its original title, *Good Christian B____es*. This show tells the tale of one Leslie Bibb, formerly the "queen b____" of her Dallas high school, who has moved back to Dallas with her two teenage children after her good Christian husband has been killed in a car accident with his mistress after stealing billions of dollars from investors. Typical Christian behavior, or so the media would tell us. Still, as Gayle Trotter pointed out in the *Washington Post*, if *GCB* forces Christians to question their own deviations from the Christian ideal, "then the show will serve a good purpose, perhaps despite the intentions of the show's creators."[23] Too bad Hollywood does not examine its own hypocrisies with the same glee.

Those of our daughters who have shut out the media and ignored the insults of their schoolmates have found the kind of peer group reassurance all teens crave in a wide variety of faith-based programs for adolescence. Curiously, many of the same progressives who denounce the effect of the culture on our young people openly mock Christianity.

Look for Peer Groups That Work

Michael Oher has written eloquently on the subject of friendships that make sense. His first step on the ladder out of chaos was making friends with boys in his community who had good values and strong fathers. The two often go together. As he climbed to success, he began to attract a whole range of people wanting to be his friends, but he had to discipline himself to stick to a virtuous path. "It's impossible to stress how important it is that you choose the right friends," he would tell the young men and women who identified with his ascent. "You have to keep your eyes open for the right kind of friends if you want to go against the trends around you."[24]

As parents, we always want to steer our children into groups that resist negative trends and that rely on learned values. Yet despite a parent's best efforts, this doesn't always happen. In this regard, our age is not unique. Left to their own devices, unsupervised adolescents can rapidly become uncivilized in the hallways of their local middle schools. To prevent more routine kinds of social meltdown, McNeely and Blanchard recommend that those in a position to do so create opportunities for girls to "develop a set of core assets." They identify these as the classic "5 Cs"—*competence, confidence, connection, character,* and *caring.*[25]

In fact, we launched the Best Friends Foundation as just such an opportunity. Given the stresses on home and family, and the limitations of the educational establishment, we set about to help create positive peer groups in environments where they might not naturally form. We know that ours is not the only solution, but we know that it works. We believe it holds potential for any organization looking for a model, especially those that must work in a secular environment.

We begin with girls in the sixth grade, just as they embark on adolescence and need protection beyond what their parents can reasonably provide. Dr. Pipher has shrewdly observed that if it takes a "village" to raise a child, "most girls no longer have a village."[26] In Best Friends, we strive to provide the support system young people are looking for through an intensive peer support structure and long-term adult involvement.

Our program is school based and character oriented and continues through high school graduation. It involves any number of components, all designed to keep our girls engaged, active, and aware of themselves and the world around them. Adults play a critical role. Each girl selects a mentor from those faculty who have agreed to participate in the program. The mentor then meets with the girl for thirty to forty-five minutes each week.

At least once a month, during school time, the girls come together for a structured discussion group. Here, they receive guidance on the topics of friendship, love and dating, self-respect, decision making, alcohol abuse, drug abuse, physical fitness, nutrition, and HIV and STDs, among other subjects. They also provide useful feedback on what is happening in their own lives.

At least twice a year, a distinguished woman from the community meets with the girls to share her own experiences, particularly the decisions she made when she was young, and to hear from the girls themselves. One of our first role models was Alma Powell, wife of former Secretary of State General Colin Powell. Her story of growing up in segregated Birmingham, Alabama, intrigued the students. She told of the fire-bombing of her church, which killed four little girls. She had stood many times before in front of the same mirror where the little girls were fixing their hair when the bomb exploded. The Best Friends students were fascinated at the fact that she could not attend the state university but was provided funds to go to Emerson College in Boston where she met Colin Powell, a young, handsome soldier. She made it clear to the girls, who were mostly African American, that after the storm one must look for the rainbow. She would never have met Colin if she had not had to pursue her education outside of her state. Alma became an active and enthusiastic member of our board of directors at Best Friends. I am forever grateful to her and to Colin for their support.

When Best Friends girls reach ninth grade, they are eligible for the Diamond Girl Leadership program. I designed this program to keep girls moving in a wholesome, structured orbit in high school, when adolescents usually begin to pull away from societal restraints. All Diamond Girls are encouraged to participate in the Diamond Girl Jazz Choir or Performance Dance Troupe. These activities foster discipline, help the girls with their social skills, improve their ability to present themselves, but most important, offer fun—upbeat singing and dancing. As one Diamond Girl told me, "This brings my joy up."

Our girls undertake at least one community service project each year. This could take the form of a clothing drive to benefit the homeless, volunteer work at a community day care center, reading sessions with small children, or many other worthy programs. Although we shrink back from the kind of excessive praise that renders real praise meaningless, we end the school year with recognition of a job well done for all those girls who have stuck it out. Our program, like many of the more durable programs for young people, encourages and rewards persistence and consistently provides positive reinforcement for positive behaviors. Since so many adolescents today lack the wherewithal to complete even short-term projects, we have found real value in acknowledging the perseverance of the Best Friends and Best Men. For some of them, the honors they receive at our Family and School Recognition Program are the first real honors they have received anywhere. In that these honors include college scholarships and other awards of value, students learn the connection between effort extended and rewards received.

Our goal, finally, is for all Diamond Girls and Best Men Leaders to graduate from high school with specific college, vocational, or career plans and with their characters intact. What makes our program distinctive, I believe, is that we encourage the young women and men to be better friends to their friends, the kind who exhibit virtue, initiate charity, practice restraint, and stand up for their friends when necessary. One of the slogans in our leadership programs is "If you do not stand for something, you will stand for anything."

Stand Up to Bullying

Although our daughters are not as inclined to physical violence as our sons, their capacity to inflict emotional violence likely exceeds that of their brothers. To be sure, everyone who has a child, knows a child, or was a child has experienced bullying, but it has taken on new and more sinister overtones, especially among girls.

In *Reviving Ophelia*, Mary Pipher argues that young girls, as new converts to the corrupt culture that awaits all of today's adolescents, can become the culture's "biggest enforcers and proselytizers."[27] As insecure as they are about adapting to the new norms, young girls are as insistent that others do the same. The norms these girls set can be pretty narrow. One can be punished for being too slutty or too proper, too smart or too slow, too pretty or not pretty enough. Today's parents, as Pipher has observed, are almost always unaware of how cruel youth culture has become. We all need to heighten our vigilance.

Punishment for nonconformance with the standards set by adolescents can get extreme. In December 2011, for instance, a sophomore at Port Richmond High School in Staten Island got into a "he said, she said" kind of altercation with some other girls at the school. The bullying got so intense that the sophomore, given her heart condition, stayed home for five days. Apparently missing their victim, the girl's tormentors assembled many of their friends and assaulted the girl's home in a middle-class neighborhood. "We're gonna punch you in the chest," the girls yelled. "We're gonna fix your heart condition." A fire truck had to disperse the group with water cannons. The police arrested nine of them. Two officers were injured in the melee. It should never have come to this point. When police and firefighters have to intervene, a whole lot of educators and parents have failed.[28]

As Pipher contends, girls get the message that "not pleasing others is social suicide."[29] Sometimes, the suicide is more than just social. Just weeks after the Port Richmond incident, also on Staten Island, a fifteen-year-old New Dorp High School student, Amanda Cummings, jumped in front of a bus and killed herself. She had been dating a nineteen-year-old, whose other girlfriend had apparently been bullying her. Amanda's family was convinced that bullies had killed Amanda. Whether bullying led to Amanda's death is a matter of speculation, but what can be said with confidence is that her peers did nothing to protect her. As her post-mortem Facebook page suggests, just the opposite was true. Wrote one soulless peer, "Bus was cummin' Bitch was watchin' Oh hurry Amanda Your bus cummin'."[30]

In fact, Amanda was spiraling downward in full view of friends and family. She was a broken girl, falling hard for boys, smoking, drinking to excess, and posting comments like, "ill just go f__k myself, just like u said baby, then ill go kill myself, with these pills, this knife, this life has already done half the job."[31]

Based on the Add Health research, Dr. McNeely and her coauthor, Jayne Blanchard, have concluded that bullying must not be dismissed as a normal adolescent mischief. "It is abusive behavior that is likely to create emotional and social problems during the teen years and later in life for both the victim and the aggressor," they wrote.[32]

When authorities respond to these attacks, they tend to focus on the problem most immediately at hand: gangs, the school, the technology, and the like. Real change, however, demands a more global approach. Our goal should be not just to stop bullying but to turn our children's peer groups into sources of moral strength and security. We want these groups to surround our daughters with care and reinforce the better angels of their nature. As the previous examples have shown, this will not be easy, especially in those environments where a majority of the youth come from dysfunctional homes, but it can be done.

Dr. Leonard Sax has seen good working examples of the same. In *Girls on the Edge*, Sax observes that girls compete very indirectly. Instead of fighting, say, a new girl who threatens the status of a group's alpha female, the alpha girl might start a smear campaign or a social boycott—this was the basic plot line of *GCB*, by the way. For the victim, these can all be devastating, but there is much a school can do to intervene. Sax cited one school strategy that works.

The effective teacher does not lay down rules for the class, but rather invites the students to create the rules for themselves.[33] As actress Patricia Neal once said, "A master can tell you what he expects of you. A teacher, though, awakens your own expectations."[34]

With effective steering, students will write guidelines such as, "If a bullying situation arises, we will intervene and/or get help from a teacher or school administrator or counselor." The teacher then prints out the contract on a poster and has the students sign it. Once bound to a contract they have devised themselves, the girls are much likelier to honor it.

In our Best Friends and Best Men programs, our Best Men research data showed that bullying decreased by 50 percent from fall to spring—13.2 percent to 6.3 percent. The linked data also showed a drop in students who reported being seriously bullied twelve or more times from forty students in the fall to twenty-four students in the spring. This is particularly noteworthy given the passage of the school year. Friendship is at the foundation of our program. The fact that we reiterate the importance of friends standing up to collective bad behavior has led to the distinct improvement the survey data demonstrate.

Beware of Social Media

As I have mentioned elsewhere, bullying has taken on a new and rougher tone in the social media era. There is something about faceless, voiceless contact that seems to unleash a person's darker forces.

Young people especially seem empowered to say the vilest things that come to mind, regardless of the consequences.

Andrea McCarren, a veteran TV reporter in the Washington area, got to experience this vileness firsthand. In early 2012, she hosted a series on teen drinking for WUSA Channel 9. The response from teen drinkers whose alcohol sources were being threatened was swift and voluminous. "You can't try and take away something that teens love without retaliation," said one of the more civil respondents. "Haven't you ever heard of teenage rebellion?" So hostile was the response on her children's Facebook pages that McCarren felt compelled to hand the latest installment in the series off to a colleague. "My kids were targeted," McCarren said. "That's where I drew the line."[35]

So-called cyberbullying can quickly escalate into what is sometimes referred to as a "flame war," a highly public, participative, online conflict. More often than not, girls are the victims in these wars. In its most brutal form, a gang of assassins will try to humiliate a single victim and drive her out of the particular medium. As much as parents would like to intervene, legitimate privacy issues make their involvement highly problematic. In this case, peers are in a much better position to intervene. As cyber "friends," they often have ringside seats. That is why it is all the more important that we help our children create trustworthy peer groups.

Encourage Fitness

As if our daughters did not have enough to worry about, there is now a very real obesity epidemic abroad in the land. Approximately 17 percent of children under nineteen are considered obese, three times the number just thirty years ago.[36] To compound the problem, obese girls are quicker to reach puberty.[37] Ironically, for the first time in world history, the poor are more likely to be obese than the affluent.

Peers can help. A recent Brown University study found that

team-based weight loss competitions can inspire individuals to lose weight in a relatively stress-free way.[38] Accordingly, at Best Friends we have made physical fitness and nutrition a major component in our self-improvement program. Our fitness program is designed as an interactive and immediate gratification component of the curriculum. Students meet weekly. The music is inspirational, even cool. Participants have fun and reinforce each other's behavior in the Bandura model. The Best Friends theme song, which stresses self-respect through self-control, is sung at the end of every session for further reinforcement. It all helps.

Stress Peer Responsibility

The day before I learned of Yeardley Love's murder, I had an eye-opening discussion at a Washington, DC, public school with the girls in our Best Friends program and the boys in our Best Men program. I was reminded how much programs like ours are needed. I asked these teenagers, "What are some of the signs of dating violence?" One of the senior boys said, "When he is hittin' on her because she doesn't want to be with him anymore."

The girls all started talking at once, and I heard things like, "The reason she doesn't want to be with him is *because* he's hitting her."

That generated the response, "Yeah, but what is *she* doing to make him hit her?" The students then began to mention names, and it became clear they were not talking hypothetically. They were speaking about real couples in their school who were suffering abuse in their relationships.

The students were particularly upset about a girl named Mary[39] who was being stalked by a violent former boyfriend. As the details of the situation began to spill out, I said, "She's your friend. What are you doing to help her?"

One of the girls snapped back, "She's got to help herself. We can't do anything."

"Well then, you're off the hook," I said with more than a hint of irony. "Whatever happens, happens, right?" Then I looked at the boys, and asked, "Do you have any responsibility to protect her?" One of the leaders in our Best Men program chose to answer, "She probably beat on him too."

"So she deserves to be tormented, right?" I continued, "How big is this guy?"

"Oh, he's big; he's over two hundred pounds," said one of the younger guys. The girl in question, I learned, was "a little skinny thing." Although I had come to the school to produce a video, reality intruded and replaced art. The video was no longer important. This was an opportunity to teach a life lesson. The students and I went on to have a spirited and in-depth discussion, the kind that inspires teachers to continue teaching, the kind I later deeply regretted was not caught on tape.

The session ended, and the group moved on to the auditorium. I walked into the hallway, and a male student whom I had considered particularly bright and able, and who was president of the Best Men Leadership program, was waiting for me. "Mrs. Bennett," he said, "Mary could get really hurt by this guy."

"Cameron," I answered, "you must protect her. That is what a Best Men Leader does." I told him to call the Domestic Violence Hotline number and to report this boy to the guidance counselor at the high school. I had the sense he was the type to follow through, and I also knew what *I* had to do on Monday to protect Mary. The friend's role, like the mentor's role, only begins with that phone call. Mary's well-being is the responsibility of everyone who knows her. (See the resource list in the back of the book for hotline help numbers.)

Remind Males of Their Role as Protectors

Although feminists recoil from the fairy-tale scenario in which the handsome prince rides to the rescue of the distressed damsel, our daughters are not always strong enough to save themselves. There is no clearer example of this than the Yeardley Love case. Friends, particularly her male ones, needed to intervene, but none did. The code of silence, powerful even among adults as evidenced at Penn State, apparently overrode their good judgment.

When the *Titanic* sank a century ago, 100 percent of the children and 93 percent of the women in first- and second-class lodgings were saved, but only 20 percent of the men. Many of those men who did survive would forever be shamed for surviving. When the MS *Estonia* sank in the Baltic Sea in 1994, the outcome was altogether different. Despite equal numbers of males and females on board, males were four times more likely to survive.[40]

The acculturation of the males makes all the difference. If it is "every man for himself," physical strength will give men the advantage. If, on the other hand, the strong help the more vulnerable first, the more vulnerable will survive. This was evident at the horrific mass shooting that occurred at a midnight showing of the newest Batman movie in Aurora, Colorado. Three young men—Jon Blunk, Matt McQuinn, and Alex Teves—all died shielding their girlfriends from the raging gunfire. Their sacrifice is proof that the heroic instinct to protect women still lives, and in this case, the media were sensitive enough to honor it.

Young men tend to treat young women according to the messages they receive from these women. I will never forget Kamillah and the story she shared with a large group of Best Friends girls in one of my curriculum sessions at a middle school.

Kamillah, a Best Friends alum, was now in high school and a Diamond Girl. She arrived with her guidance counselor a few minutes before we were to start. "Mrs. Bennett," she asked, "would it be all right with you if I had a few minutes to speak to the Best Friends?" I hesitated because I was conscious of the time necessary to present our curriculum effectively. But something told me to let Kamillah go first. Here is what she told the middle schoolers.

"Girls, I really want you to listen to what Mrs. Bennett and Ms. Rice have to say. I was a Best Friends girl before high school, and I honor my commitment not to sleep with my boyfriend. Not too long ago, I went to a party with my friend who was also in Best Friends. She doesn't sleep with her boyfriend either. The rest of the girls do.

"While we were at the party, shooting started. The boys ran out in a flash and left the girls behind—but not all the boys. My boyfriend and my friend's boyfriend stayed with us and helped us get out. My boyfriend was calling my name to get me to a safe place. Those other boys left those girls flat. Girls, I just want to say, if you do not respect your body, no one else will either."[41]

The girls were listening so intently you could almost hear their hearts beat. I was awestruck. I said a silent prayer of thanks that I'd let Kamillah speak. Her personal story had more impact than anything I could have said. It was exactly what I hoped for: girls giving back and sharing their knowledge with younger girls.

Strong mentors make a difference. They were who saved Michael Oher from the street Darwinism that seemed to be his destiny. Perhaps the most important one was "Big Tony" Henderson, who took an interest in Oher when he was still in grade school. Tony coached him, counseled him, got him into a better high school, and introduced Oher to his son, Steve, who would become a lifelong friend. Perhaps more important, Big Tony showed Oher the possibility of concepts such as trust and hope. These were concepts that Oher would one day share with the young men and women who drew inspiration from his life story. In fact, in his book, he wrote about one girl who, after watching *Blind Side*, now saw "that there was a hopeful future for kids like us if we just accepted the help and support of the people around us."[42]

We started the Best Men program in no small part to transform young boys from potential predators to likely protectors. It is not enough to tell our children what they ought not do—smoke, drink, do drugs, have sex—we must also provide them a model of what they should do and a peer group setting in which that behavior is reinforced. The testimony of our Best Men continues to encourage me. I could list many more, but here are just a few:[43]

"I learned a lot. Not just about marriage and relationships, but life itself. Now, you've got friends—use them. They will help you."

D'Angelo Anderson, senior, McKinley Technology High School

"Just 2 years ago inside I was sad, angry and had a lot of hatred. I used to hide it. I learned how to be a happier person, a better person. This is only my second year. I learned a lot. I'll never forget how I changed."

Nathan DuPree, sophomore, McKinley Technology High School

"[The Best Men program] means a lot to me. It's the foundation for my leadership skills, the principles I live my life by and the guidelines to a better future. Best Men gives young males a support system they can trust in and believe in as well as relate to."

Julian Mujihad, senior, McKinley Technology High School

Encourage Rational Decision Making

In both our Best Friends and Best Men programs, we stress the value of making wise decisions. To make wise decisions, adolescents must anticipate possible outcomes, weigh the value of each, and consider the long-term ramifications of a given behavior. If they do this for themselves, they are in a much better position to help their friends do the same. In anticipating particular scenarios, bullying, for instance, or sexual harassment, they will be able to respond more quickly and more effectively.

It is critical, too, that young people share relevant information with their peers and with adults in authority. I am sure there are boys who would have helped Yeardley Love had they known her plight, but too many of the players, male and female, kept quiet for the sake of the "team." The unfortunate trend of youths keeping parents and other authorities at bay needs to be reversed.

Girls are instructed in the Best Friends program to "tell" if some-one is being abused—and to keep telling until someone listens. This sense of taking action for a friend in trouble must be developed in early adolescence. Adolescents need to have a sense of trust that adults will help when asked, and, as adults, it is our responsibility to respond when asked for help or when we sense there is trouble.

The bottom line is that children today spend much more time com-municating with their peers than they do with their parents or other authorities. This does not lessen the accountability of adults for ado-lescents. Parents should try to exercise as much control as possible over their children's selection of friends.

Reinforce the Basics

We sometimes presume that once girls reach high school age, they know enough to deflect peer group pressure, especially of the sort that leads to destructive behavior. That is not always true. In the Best Friends program we have found value in reinforcing some common-sense basics so our girls will know how to respond to pressure the moment they feel it:[44]

- Ask 101 questions: When a friend suggests some new, risky behavior, the girl being put on the spot should push back and ask some hard risk-benefit questions.
- Say no, and mean it: Tempters can sense weakness. Don't let them see it.
- Back up a "no" with a positive: Rejecting a temptation is more effective when the tempter is told why.
- Be repetitive: The tempter will keep pushing. The tempted has to keep pushing back.
- Practice saying no: Saying no to small requests will help you prepare for the big requests.

- Get away from the pressure zone: Sometimes the best way to avoid a potentially nasty situation is to walk away from it.
- Avoid the pressure zone: An even better way to avoid a troubling situation is to not go near it in the first place.
- Use the buddy system: It pays to find a friend who shares your values and will watch your back.
- Confront the leader of the pack: Often a single bully sets the tone for a peer group. There is value in talking to her, but always when the two of you are alone.
- Consider the results of giving in: A little cost-benefit analysis can go a long way in the decision to avoid risky behavior.
- Look for positive role models: In the long run, the most successful kids at school are the ones who listen to the beat of their own drum and follow it.
- [Understand that] everyone's *not* doing it: Whether it is sex or drinking or drugs, not everyone is doing "it," and those who are not have fewer regrets than those who are.
- Seek support: Peer pressure falls heavily on every member of a group. Friends benefit from sharing their experiences.
- Be your own best friend: Every girl has a lot going for her. Sometimes she has to remind herself.
- Find ways to excel: No one excels at everything, but we all excel at something. The challenge is to identify it and pursue it.
- Don't pressure others: Most young women know what is in their best interests. Do not try to convince them otherwise.
- Speak out: Underdogs rarely forget the favor and are not shy about spreading the glory.
- Watch your moods: Mood swings can cause a young woman to lose self-confidence. Self-awareness is the best defense.

- Evaluate friendships: A good friend is not someone who consistently thinks of herself first.
- Find new friends: So many of our friends are simply those who fall within our sphere. Self-confident girls are those willing, when necessary, to look beyond.

What the Rest of Us Can Do

Whether we like his politics or not, President Barack Obama has given every impression of being a faithful husband and loving father of two young daughters. As such, he is in an excellent position to instruct American young people, especially African Americans, about the value of marriage, family, and future-oriented thinking.

Early in the 2008 presidential campaign, Obama was doing just that. In a Father's Day speech that year at a black church, Obama chastised absent black fathers, saying, "We need them to realize that what makes you a man is not the ability to have a child—it's the courage to raise one."[1] With more than 70 percent of black children being born to unmarried mothers, this message could not have come from a better person at a better time.[2] In other church settings, Obama had been advising parents to encourage their kids to read books rather than play video games and to focus on school rather than on elusive, would-be careers, such as rock stars or pro athletes.

Jesse Jackson, the self-appointed leader of black America, was not pleased. In July of that year, while waiting for an interview with a Fox News correspondent, Jackson was caught on a hot microphone, whispering to a fellow interviewee, "See, Barack been, um, talking down to black people on this faith based . . ." Jackson went on to make a crude remark about what he would like to do to Obama. Of course, Jackson quickly, if insincerely, apologized. "My support for Senator Obama's campaign is wide, deep and unequivocal," he said. "I cherish this redemptive and historical moment."[3] He went on to explain, however, that Obama's message to black voters must transcend mere "moral challenge" and focus on "some real serious issues" like unemployment, home foreclosures, and violence.[4] The fact that all of these problems flow from the same source—namely, the collapse of the family, particularly in black America—did not seem to enter Jackson's thinking.

As quickly as Jackson apologized, Obama welcomed him back into the fold. Campaign spokesman Bill Burton said that the senator from Illinois "of course accepts Rev. Jackson's apology."[5] The damage, however, had been done. Senator Obama had gotten the message. From that point on, he would downplay the "moral challenge" and refocus on class warfare, a more comfortable theme for political allies like Jackson. Class, like race, is perennial. It takes no introspection to talk about class differences. Class warriors do not ask their followers what they can personally do to save our daughters and to save their communities. Their followers are all "victims," and it is wrong, of course, to blame the victim.

This is a shame. There is much that individuals working with our sons and daughters can personally do. To accomplish anything, however, they cannot yield to defeat or despair or seek government solutions to everyday problems. They have to believe they can make a difference. Best Men coordinator and program director in Milwaukee, Kyle Witty, can attest to this. "Best Men and Best Friends was one of the real beacons of hope in this community," he tells us. "For the first time many of the teenage youth, both males and females, were able to sit down with positive male and female role models and talk about the struggles that they faced in their everyday life." Kyle later wrote me, "People can say what they want to but I know that the Best Friends program had more to do with the big reduction in teen pregnancy in Milwaukee than any one will ever know. Thanks for your belief in Milwaukee. I still have high school kids that ask me if they can get involved."[6] Best Friends, of course, is just one program out of many. The extended family, the church, and civic and social groups all can and do play major roles in preserving our culture.

If properly guided, each institution can influence our daughters and helps provide some practical ways to do so, little and big. The following two examples certainly fall under the category of "big." The blowback each effort faced shows just how determined the entertainment media are to resist any efforts to rein them in. Yet the cause is so just and the need so strong that persist we must.

Stand Up and Speak Out

Had President Obama followed the career of former vice president Dan Quayle, he may not have backed off as quickly as he did. The truth, he would have learned, outlasts the next election. In 1992, Quayle explained to a San Francisco audience the root causes of the devastating Rodney King riots in Los Angeles. He attributed the "lawless social anarchy" in no small part to "the breakdown of family structure, personal responsibility and social order in too many areas of our society."

Had Quayle stopped there, the media would likely have ignored him. But he chose to implicate his own baby-boomer generation in the moral breakdown. As Charles Murray has pointed out, it is very nearly taboo in the apocryphal "Belmont" to say what Quayle was about to say. "I know it is not fashionable to talk about moral values, but we need to do it," said Quayle. Already on thin ice, he ventured out even further. "It doesn't help matters," he added, "when prime time TV has Murphy Brown—a character who supposedly epitomizes today's intelligent, highly paid, professional woman—mocking the importance of fathers, by bearing a child alone, and calling it just another 'lifestyle choice.'"[7]

Murphy Brown was a character played by Candice Bergen on a popular sitcom of the same name. On the show, the fortysomething Brown worked as an investigative reporter for a fictional TV show called *FYI*. The story line had her impregnated by her ex-husband, who chose not to abandon his "lifestyle" to help raise the baby. The Brown character played the pregnancy for politicized laughs. "Several people don't want me to have the baby," she said at one point, "Pat Robertson, Phyllis Schlafly, half of Utah." In another episode, several real TV journalists—Katie Couric among them—showed up at the show's baby shower.

Quayle's Murphy Brown allusion set off a classic media firestorm. Here is how the *Washington Post* summarized the brouhaha at the time:

> The statement drew an incredible amount of mocking from the news and entertainment media—even a full episode of Murphy Brown devoted to poking fun at the vice president was aired. In the end, this frenzy left the GOP's family values platform somewhat tainted and kept Quayle the anointed prince of gaffes.[8]

Even the fictional cast of *FYI* got into the act. In the season premiere of the 1992–93 season, "You Say Potatoe, I Say Potato," a direct rebuttal of Quayle's remarks, the *FYI* crew produced a special show celebrating the new "diversity" of the American family.

Months later, however, with Democrat Bill Clinton safely elected president, the liberal *Atlantic* magazine published a thoughtful cover story headlined "Dan Quayle Was Right." In the article, Barbara Dafoe Whitehead cited a "growing body of social-scientific evidence" to affirm Quayle's thesis. Yes, children in single-parent families were six times as likely to be poor. They stayed poor longer. They were at least twice as likely to have behavioral problems and much more likely to drop out of school, get pregnant, abuse drugs, go to jail, and be sexually abused.[9]

In 2010, *USA Today* ran an article with the headline "Was Dan Quayle (gasp!) Right?" Writer Jim McKairnes made the semi-accurate point that the media frenzy had less to do with what was said than with who said it. Yes, Quayle caught more heat than others would have, but anyone would have caught some. It was the message that unnerved Hollywood, many of whose denizens have never even seen a functioning nuclear family. "Yet the simple fact is," said McKairnes, "that TV can and often does get it wrong. And looking at it 18 years later, it seems *Murphy Brown* whiffed."[10]

In May 2012, Isabel Sawhill drove the same point home on the pages of the *Washington Post*. "Twenty years later," she wrote, "Quayle's words seem less controversial than prophetic." Sawhill went on to point out that for women under the age of thirty, more than half of their babies are born out of wedlock. "A lifestyle once associated with poverty has become mainstream," she added. "The only group of parents for whom marriage continues to be the norm is the college-educated."[11]

Pay Attention to the Culture

One did not have to be Republican to provoke the scorn of the media-entertainment complex. In the mid-1980s, Tipper Gore, the then wife of then US Senator Al Gore, was asked by Pam Howar, Sally Nevius, and Susan Baker to join the Parents Music Resource Center (PMRC) in its fight against the music industry and its promotion of highly offensive, misogynistic rock music, especially its hip-hop and rap mutations.

These conservative women were well connected. Pam was married to powerful real estate entrepreneur and developer Raymond Howar; Sally to Washington City Council chairman John Nevius; and Susan to Jim Baker, then Secretary of the Treasury. They knew that this issue was too important to be defined by party lines, a sentiment I shared with regard to our mission with the Best Friends program.

They believed, as I do, that the saving of our culture is too critical to be politicized. Tipper, as the mother of teenagers, understood how the music industry was changing. Growing numbers of preteens and teenagers were listening and dancing to music with themes that no rational parent would possibly allow in her home.

With the advent of MTV a few years earlier, parents were coming face-to-face with the increasingly violent and sexualized lyrics of popular music. According to one study, music videos portray more than ninety sexual situations per hour, including ten or more that flirt with hard-core sex. Music had come a long way from the song lyrics of our baby-boomer adolescence, like Sam Cooke's line "I find myself wanting to marry you and take you home" in the song "You Send Me," or the Dixie Cups' "Goin' to the chapel and we're gonna get married." Just how far it had come Tipper realized when she and her daughter Karenna heard the song "Darling Nikki" by the superstar known as Prince, a track that played on the soundtrack of his popular movie, *Purple Rain*. The song begins by introducing listeners to a girl named Nikki. "I met her in a hotel lobby/ Masturbating with a magazine," the song continues.[12] The lyrics go downhill from there.

What troubled Tipper, Pam, Sally, and Susan was that parents were buying this kind of music for their children without any awareness of its content. Movies, at least, had ratings that theaters were obliged to honor. Record stores had no such restrictions. When the PMRC managed to get a Senate hearing on this subject, the music industry attacked Tipper, a senator's wife, as a prude, a cultural dinosaur, and a champion of censorship. Called to testify about the PMRC's interpretation of his lyrics, Dee Snider of Twisted Sister said, "I can't help it if Tipper Gore has a dirty mind."[13] At the time, this seemed to be the consensus opinion, and much worse was said about Tipper than that. Even John Denver testified in protest against the proposed guidelines.

An even more dedicated foe of music industry corruption was the late and much missed C. Delores Tucker. Once the highest-ranking African American woman in Pennsylvania state government, Tucker risked her status in the community and her personal security to fight what she called the "pornographic filth" of gangsta rap, then in its ascendancy. She argued the inescapable point that the music demeans the black women whose dignity she had been fighting for all her life.

A longtime civil rights activist, Tucker went to battle in 1994 when the NAACP, on whose board she sat, chose to give one of its Image Awards to rapper Tupac Shakur. Shakur acknowledged her resistance by rhyming her name with the obvious obscenity in a retaliatory song. Several other rappers joined in the ritual defamation of this courageous lady.

Enlisting as allies my husband, Bill, and Senator Joseph Lieberman, Tucker eventually succeeded in persuading Time Warner to sell its interest in the Interscope label, a source of much of the worst of the music. When Tucker died in 2005, RapMusic.com reflected the vileness of the whole genre by headlining its story "The Wicked Witch Is Dead: C. Delores Tucker Passes."[14]

Twenty-five years later, however, several of the rockers themselves have come to wonder whether they had gone too far. In 1985, Blackie Lawless was front man of the metal band W.A.S.P., one of whose songs made the PMRC's "Filthy Fifteen" list. "Words are indeed powerful," says Lawless, now a born-again Christian. "They are either tools or they are weapons." He now understands the PMRC's logic: "I honestly believe anything that gives parents a heads up with what is going on in the lives of their children has to be helpful."[15]

Cyndi Lauper, whose song "She Bop" also made the Filthy Fifteen, now confesses to being troubled by the songs her young son listens to: "It's one thing to make that kind of stuff," she says. "But if they're going to play it on the radio, that's another story, isn't it? They're selling sex because sex sells."[16]

In the end, the Recording Industry Association of America agreed to put labels on its albums, and some stores, most notably Walmart, restricted sales of problematic albums. In the final analysis, however, not enough citizens proved willing to keep the pressure on the music industry. The brutalization of people like Tipper Gore and C. Delores Tucker scared a lot of people off. It is hard to claim victory, after all, when the industry continues to produce megahits like the recent one by Cee Lo Green, "F__ You," a song, the ads tell us, that can be sent as a ringtone to your cell phone.

Create Positive Alternatives

Despite the efforts of the Parents Music Resource Center and Tucker's National Congress of Black Women, the entertainment media have continued to feed our daughters music that strips them of their dignity. As I read the lyrics of the songs on this week's top ten hip-hop and R & B charts, I am reminded of that. The Prince song that prompted Pam Howar to found PMRC and Tipper Gore to join the cause would seem positively tame by comparison.

With one or two exceptions, the songs that topped the charts on, say, March 24, 2012, thoroughly degrade our daughters and demean our sons. In every case, the singer is African American, and in nine out of ten cases, the singer is male. The one female is Beyoncé Knowles, whose number one song, "Love on Top," despite the innuendo of the title, does not offend.[17] The rest do.

The number two song on that day, "The Motto," by Drake featuring Lil Wayne, does not have a two-sentence stretch of lyrics that is fit to print. No racial or sexual slur escaped the lyricist's pen. No racial or sexual stereotype went unmined. The song's literal motto is "You only live once." For the songwriter, that means playing with guns, wearing jewelry, doing drugs, and, most of all, exploiting women.

The number three song, Chris Brown's "Strip," is well titled. Throughout the song, the singer encourages his women to take their clothes off. "I wanna peel them clothes off your body like a banana."[18] That is one of the more printable lyrics. The one song on the top ten that would seem to hold any promise was Trey Songz's "Sex Ain't

Better Than Love." Although the song's title complements the messages our girls hear at Best Friends, its lyrics do not fulfill its promise. In the song, the singer cajoles his girlfriend to his bed so they can make a baby together, out of wedlock, of course.

One would think that those who profess to care about urban culture—the civic leaders who extol its virtue, the firebrands who defend it, the politicians whose careers hinge on its votes—would step up and say, "Enough!" But for a variety of reasons, none of them good, they remain silent. No one responsible for these lyrics—from the studio to the executive suites—would dare read them to their children.

To fight this kind of cultural degradation, it helps to have something to fight back with. With the help of grants from the Department of Education, Department of Health and Human Services, and the Department of Justice, Best Friends created the program "Make Music, Not Madness." In fact, it was Delores Tucker, that gracious and beautiful woman, who inspired me to introduce this successful and captivating program to students in the DC Public Schools. At our first such assembly, we presented the "C. Delores Tucker Excellence in Music Award" to a former Diamond Girl and Diamond Girl choir director, Robin Williams, a talented vocalist who performs locally in the Washington, DC, metropolitan area. It was gratifying all around to see that the legacy of Delores Tucker endures.

As to the production itself, I developed "Make Music, Not Madness" with input from our excellent choreographer and fitness program manager, Rita Burns. The lyrics for the program's theme song were written and arranged by the gifted Lori Williams, Best Friends jazz choir director at the time, and now the vocal ensemble director at Wilson High School in Washington, DC, and a professional vocalist. Knowing that the music young people listen to affects their behavior, we created productions that enriched, inspired, and uplifted, and provided an alternative to the "madness" entertainment that degrades, depresses, and leads to danger. We spelled out our intentions in the lyrics of our theme song, "Make Music Not Madness":

Make Music, not madness
Make music . . . music
Make music, not madness
Make music . . . music

Best Friends
They want you to know
Choosin' positive music is the way to go
No matter what the style you happen to love
Make the right choices and let others know to . . .

Make Music, not madness
Make music . . . music
Make music, not madness
The music you listen to reflect who you are
Lyrics tell the story
You've got to raise the bar
Choose the higher road—Leave the madness behind
Just . . .
Make Music, not madness
Make music . . . music
Make music, not madness

Best Friends produced eight of these interactive and compelling assemblies. In their evaluations, 98 percent of the students rated the production as very worthwhile.

Ironically, one of the songs we interpreted through dance in our seminar "Stop the Silence. Prevent the Violence" was a song by Eminem and Rihanna called "Love the Way You Lie." I say "ironic" because Rihanna, as explained earlier, would become a very public victim of dating violence. Personally, I was greatly disappointed that in our latest assembly we had little support from the private and parochial schools in the Washington, DC, area, even though it was without cost. We had designed an imaginative way to showcase the dangers of dating violence, through an excellent production featuring "The Yellow Dress" by Deana's Educational Theater, but the suburban administrators were apparently not ready for it, or just not interested.

Music is too valuable a source of inspiration, uplift, and sheer energy to ignore. That is one reason why Best Friends and Best Men celebrate positive music and constructive choices. We remind our young people that life is full of choices, and music is one of them. Whether they listen to rock, pop, gospel, country, jazz, classical, or even hip-hop, they can begin to redefine themselves by choosing music that speaks to who they are and who they want to be.

Pick the Right Battle

Given that neither Dan Quayle nor Tipper Gore fully succeeded in their efforts to resist the spread of cultural decline, the ordinary citizen may be tempted to think the battle is not worth fighting. I would recommend otherwise. By picking the right battle, one that can be won on a local basis, a small group of people can make a big difference.

A few years back, the young women at Spelman College did just that. The rapper Nelly had been scheduled to make a campus appearance at this historically black college in Atlanta. At the time, a video of his, called "Tip Drill," was making the rounds on the music video stations. The video shows images of men throwing money between women's legs, women simulating sex with each other, and Nelly swiping a credit card through a woman's backside.

The women of Spelman, not known to be prudish, had had enough. More than three hundred of them showed up for a protest meeting. "It's very harsh. This is something we have to see and listen to on a daily basis," said senior Shanequa Yates of the rap videos in general. Zenobia Hikes, vice president for student affairs, put the issue in a larger context. "Black entertainers have become the new myth makers, showing gangsters and bikini-clad women with hyperactive libidos," she said. "For non-black children, it creates a gross misrepresentation of the black experience." Nelly got the message and canceled. "Nelly just didn't want to come here and face the criticism for the choices he's made," said Yates.[19]

The Spelman women wanted to take their protest to the next level, specifically to Black Entertainment Television, which features Nelly videos and much worse, but they did not deceive themselves about their capabilities. A win is a win. As with the Parent Music Resource Center, the critics were quick to cry, "Censorship!" But there is a huge difference between refusing to sponsor a given entertainer and urging the government to silence him or her.

Start Small

Early in 2012, a Facebook page was launched called Protecting Young Women. Like many such launches, this one is imperfect and uneven, but the person who launched it has done a good job of collecting in one place a variety of other small efforts to address the very real threats that young women face.

"I found this heartbreaking website made by a brave woman who told her story to help other survivors," says the host of a website titled The Story of a Rape Victim. The host posts another link to a book titled *The Other Side of Silence: Women Tell About Their Experiences with Date Rape* by Christine Carter. Another link takes the viewer to a short video made on date rape that won first place in the Guelph, Ontario, Police Service video contest.

Not all the posts are about rape. The host posts a memoir by Victor Frankl titled *Man's Search for Meaning*. Published in 1946, the book recounts Frankl's experience as the inmate of a Nazi death camp and documents his will to live. "I recommend this reading for anyone that has experienced a traumatic event in their life," the host wrote generously. "It teaches one how to live and make the world a better place rather than seeking revenge for past wrongs." These efforts may seem small, but the date rape video, for instance, has already been viewed nearly 1 million times. If the website spares one young woman the heartbreak of rape, it has been worth the effort.

Don't Accept the Status Quo

There has been much talk, some of it accurate, some of it overheated, about a feminist takeover of the Girl Scouts of America (GSUSA). Girl Scouts was an important and much valued part of my life growing up. I am proud of my achievement of the Curved Bar, which is now the Gold Award (comparable to the Boy Scouts Eagle Scout award). I take the organization at its word that it is "neutral" on issues such as abortion and that it avoids "advocacy or promotion of any social or religious perspective."[20] The fact that many GSUSA chapters have partnered with Planned Parenthood is testament to the organization's moral relativism.

Rather than complain about the evolving neutral values of the Girl Scouts, a group of parents in West Chester, Ohio, decided to start their own organization, American Heritage Girls. "We realized in 1995 that we weren't going to be able to change much with our local council, much less with our national council, so it was time to start something new," said founder Patti Garibay. To succeed, Garibay understood that they would have to work actively to counter the culture with "a Judeo-Christian focused" agenda.[21] This they have done, proof of which is that in the seventeen years of AHG's existence, the organization has expanded to forty-five states with nearly twenty thousand members.

Stick Up for Our Daughters

Many young celebrities have withered under the spotlights over the years, but in the cable/Internet era, the media have turned these meltdowns into a spectator sport. The death of pop singer Whitney Houston in early 2012 showed just how tragically these spectacles can end.

A highly successful model while still an adolescent, Houston achieved breakout success with her debut album *Whitney Houston* as a twenty-one-year-old. It is hard to pinpoint when exactly her life began to unravel—her family blames her marriage to R & B star Bobby Brown—but by her midthirties Houston had fallen into the classic rock star downward spiral: drugs, alcohol, missed performances, crumbling marriage, all of this emblazoned across the supermarket tabloids and cable entertainment networks.

It shocked no one who knew her well when Houston was found dead in her bathtub from what appeared to be a toxic combination of prescription drugs and alcohol. "Told you she was a gutter bucket of pills and booze," said an all-too-typical blog respondent. "Have no idea why the truth puts you all in a tizzy." A more sympathetic and astute observer commented, "Losing a loved one is hard enough but to have the blow by blow publicized by every media outlet on the planet has to be devastating."[22] As in the case of Yeardley Love, everyone watched, and no one intervened successfully.

Indeed, the morbid interest of the presumed fans keeps the paparazzi and their media outlets in business. The attention they provide only hastens the decline. Britney Spears had been performing publicly since she was three. At eighteen, her debut album, *Baby One More Time*, entered the pop charts in the number one spot. That same year, *Rolling Stone* magazine featured Spears on its cover, lying seductively on a bed, with her top open. The next year, while performing at the MTV Video Music Awards, Britney ripped off her black suit to reveal a flesh-colored bodysuit. The media applauded her provocative new image.

The headlines tell the rest of the story: "Britney Spears Files for

Divorce";[23] "Bald and Broken: Inside Britney's Shaved Head";[24] "Spears Will Lose Custody of Children."[25] In 2008, Britney's bizarre behavior led to her being placed under the control of a "conservator."[26] At the same time, despite the occasional misfire, her career continued to soar. All the twisted publicity seemed to help. Britney would blame the paparazzi for her meltdown, but they helped make her the best-selling female artist of the decade.

At decade's end, the collapsing young star Lindsay Lohan would replace Spears at the center of this perverse media universe. Like Spears, Lohan began her show business career at age three. By the age of ten, she was a regular on a soap opera. By twelve, she was making her first movie. By nineteen, she was hospitalized for being "overheated." By the end of that same year, she was attending Alcoholics Anonymous, and by the next year she was in rehab. Lohan got her first DUI before her twenty-first birthday and her second trip to rehab as a result of the DUI. At twenty-four, she went to prison for the first time and then more rehab. At twenty-five, she went to prison again. Although insurance companies are reluctant to bond her, all of this crazed exposure has only enhanced her name identification and her career.

It remains to be seen whether Spears and Lohan can turn their lives around before they slip into the same fatal skid that claimed Whitney Houston's life. If they fail, there will be far too many people to blame, including those of us who bought the magazines and watched the tabloid TV shows that egged these young women on. A single voice raised in protest may accomplish nothing at all, but we never know when those individual voices will swell to a chorus of protest.

Be Sober, Be Strong

Trevor Tierney, son of former Princeton coach Bill Tierney who a few years back was national goaltender of the year at Princeton University, does not blame the game of lacrosse for the death of Yeardley Love, but neither does he excuse the game and its backers of all responsibility. While at Princeton, Tierney fell into what he calls "the party culture of our sport." NCAA studies back up his claim to lacrosse's unfortunate distinction in this regard. The sport has the highest rate of alcohol and drug abuse in college athletics. Added Tierney, the game's culture "completely dragged me down as a person." It took him six years to dry out, and now he looks at the game with a knowing eye.

As Tierney relates, one of the more chilling bits of evidence introduced in the George Huguely trial was a letter that Huguely had written to Love shortly before killing her. "Alcohol is ruining my life," he wrote all too prophetically. "I'm scared to know that I can get that drunk to the point where I cannot control . . . how I act." And yet for all of Huguely's troubling behavior—for all of Love's, for that matter—no one said or did anything to stop them. "Just the fact alone that a guy like Huguely can thrive in our culture," says Tierney, "and not get called out on behaving in manners that are completely unacceptable, shows that our entire lacrosse world is skewed in some way." As Tierney sees it, he and his colleagues are all "enablers." He explains: "We simply look the other way as these problems continue to persist."

Tierney has had enough. "Everyone in our game first has to look themselves in the mirror and decide what they need to change in their own lives," he says, adding, "Big changes start with small steps." For his own part, Tierney has started a Facebook group and Twitter hash tag labeled "#BESOBERBESTRONG"—that is, "be sober, be strong."[27]

Look Around You

"Everywhere girls are encouraged to sacrifice their true selves," wrote Mary Pipher in *Reviving Ophelia*. "Their parents may fight to protect them, but their parents have limited power." With good cause, Pipher blames "the culture" for causing girls to abandon their true selves and adopt "false selves."[28]

The false self is the one that a girl contrives, the one she thinks her peers want to see, the one that is shaped consciously or otherwise by the demands of the media, the one that insists she be both "cool" emotionally and "hot" physically. As Pipher has documented in one case after another, it is the false self that leads girls prematurely into sex and a host of other situations they are too young to handle. If Whitney and Britney and Lindsay have had to endure the culture at its most crushing, our daughters are bearing more than they should have to. They need help. We parents can provide just so much of it. Every one of us has the responsibility to intervene when we have the opportunity—whether the girl in question is a student, friend, relative, neighbor, or a daughter of a friend. We cannot blame Whitney Houston's friends and family for letting her die if we do no better for the girls in our lives.

Leigh Anne and Sean Tuohy, the couple that adopted Michael Oher, call their strategy "popcorn giving." By this they mean that when a situation pops up in front of you, you address it. In their case, they instinctively provided Oher with the thing he needed most in life, a welcoming home. "If you grew up with a loving and supportive family, think about what they gave you," he wrote. "And what they gave you," Oher added, "be good enough to give to others."[29]

Take the Initiative

There was a story floating around the Internet that Mitt Romney, when head of Bain Capital, just about shut his business down and directed all company resources to find the missing daughter of a partner. Since the story sounded too good to be true, the various political fact-checking sites were deluged with inquiries.

PolitiFact.com, a left-leaning service, put its sleuths to work and concluded, "We can't speak to what this episode says about Romney's deeper character, but we can verify the facts of the episode."[30] In fact, the episode says a great deal about Romney's character.

As PolitiFact reported, in 1996 the fourteen-year-old girl told her parents she was going to play tennis and snuck away to a rave party in New York. There she took Ecstasy and promptly disappeared. Once alerted that she was missing, Romney set up a command center in New York to start searching. "I don't care how long it takes," he told his partner, "we're going to find her."

Romney directed his fifty employees to hit the streets, recruit other volunteers, and search for the missing girl, posting fliers as they went. Their efforts generated a 911 call, with the caller asking for a reward, but he hung up after he was put on hold. The call was traced to a home in New Jersey. The girl was found, near death, in the basement of the home. Five days after she disappeared, the girl was reunited with her parents. Obviously, not everyone has the resources to do what Romney did, but when it comes to saving our daughters, we have the responsibility to do as much as we can.

Measure Your Results

Too many programs, especially government ones, do no more good for the salaried administrators than for the intended beneficiaries. Some even do harm. Working through Best Friends, I have learned that it pays to quantify results.

According to the Department of Justice, more than 60 percent of children surveyed are exposed to violence in a given year. Some 30 percent of all children either bully or are bullied. Roughly 10 percent of all high school students have been a victim of dating violence, and 80 percent of the girls abused in those relationships continue to date their abusers. As the DOJ confirms, children who are exposed to physical or emotional violence may undergo lasting physical, mental, and emotional harm. They may be more prone to dating violence, sexual activity, substance abuse, delinquency, and further victimization.[31]

Our Best Friends and Best Men, despite the fact that many live in challenging environments, do considerably better than their peers who are not exposed to comparable training. Consider the following data from 2008 to 2009:

- 80 percent of Best Friends and 70 percent of Best Men students did not miss days of school because they felt unsafe. Many students skip school because of fear of violence.
- 91 percent of Diamond Girls and 76 percent of Best Men Leadership students did not miss days of school because they felt unsafe.
- 82 percent of Best Friends and 79 percent of Best Men did not drink alcohol.
- 80 percent of Diamond Girls and 75 percent of Best Men Leadership did not drink alcohol.
- 14 percent of Diamond Girls and 14 percent of Best Men Leadership students reported that they had been physically violent toward someone during the school year—a 13 percent decrease for Diamond Girls and a 7 percent decrease for Best Men Leadership since joining the program.
- 94 percent of Best Friends and 87 percent of Best Men are not in gangs.
- None of the Diamond Girls Leadership students are in gangs.
- 100 percent of Diamond Girl and Best Men Leadership students graduate from high school.

Acknowledge Reality

All the best initiatives, however well executed and well measured, will prove fruitless if we do not acknowledge one basic reality: our daughters are vulnerable in ways that our sons are not. The case of Morgan Harrington, the young woman who was murdered after being turned away from a Metallica concert on the University of Virginia campus, speaks directly to this problem. Denied reentry to the concert and clearly disoriented from drugs or alcohol, Morgan interacted with any number of men outside the arena, including several players on the university's basketball team. Although none of them exploited or abused her, none saw fit to help her either.[32]

For too many years, the culture has been telling our children that men and women are the same and ought to be treated as such. But sexual predators have not gotten that memo. While the culture is refusing to acknowledge the unique vulnerability of women alone, predators are taking advantage of that vulnerability. Our sons and our daughters need to know what they can do to help themselves and to help each other, and all of us are responsible for informing them.

What an Aware Young Woman Should Know

Ultimately, no one can save our daughters better than our daughters themselves. Ideally, young girls will know enough to see trouble coming and avoid it, but wisdom is a hard-earned commodity. Few of us earn enough of it as adolescents to avoid the temptations that adolescence brings.

Our daughters need help. They will not only welcome it but also embrace it when offered by caring adults in an organized peer-support program. I founded the Best Friends program upon realizing that so many young women had little real help in their lives, and what support they did have was unstructured and insubstantial. Aristotle once wrote that there are three kinds of friendship—those of utility, pleasure, and virtue. The highest form of friendship is based on virtue, that of a person wishing the best for friends, regardless of utility or pleasure. This is the truest of friends.

Our credo at the Best Friends Foundation is "The best friend to have is the one who makes you a better person." Appropriately, the curriculum begins with the unit called "Friendship." Friendship matters as much to boys as it does to girls, and it is the theme that unites our program.

I believe that the surest step a girl can take to protect herself when she is away from home is to have at least one good friend on whom she can rely. The curriculum units within the Best Friends program contain vital information for the protection of our girls. In the program, in order to make the girls their own first line of defense, we focus on a series of related assumptions.

- Friends respect each other while they pursue a common goal and help each other make the right decisions, and the best friend to have is that person who makes her friend a better person.
- Sex and love are not the same, sex is never a test of love, friendship precedes love, and abstinence until marriage is the best policy.
- In middle school and high school, it is better to have boyfriends who are the same age and certainly no more than two years older.
- Girls can earn self-respect through honesty, self-control, and accomplishment; self-respect begins with the assumption of responsibility for one's behavior.
- When girls accept responsibility for their decisions and make choices that show respect for themselves and for others, they will succeed.
- Alcohol impairs their decision making, erodes their health, clouds their judgment about sex, and should be avoided, especially since so many people today have a predisposition to alcoholism. We also make it clear that it is illegal to drink alcohol until age twenty-one.
- Drugs cause all the problems that alcohol does and, in addition, can lead to addiction, imprisonment, and death. In the vast majority of states it is illegal to use marijuana and other addictive drugs.
- Fitness requires proper nutrition, regular exercise, and self-discipline. Being fit provides the rewards of good health and self-respect.

- The only sure protection against HIV/AIDS and sexually transmitted diseases is abstinence from intravenous drug use and abstinence from sexual activity until both partners are in a monogamous marriage.

As timeless as these lessons are, as rich as they are in common sense, our girls must do constant battle with a culture that mocks and diminishes virtues and these practices. At the end of the day, each of our daughters must face not just one Goliath, but many. Although each daughter must ultimately stand alone, there is much we can do to arm her.

Know Yourself

"You never find yourself until you face the truth," said the great singer Pearl Bailey, and this is a bit of wisdom that never changes.[2] As the popularity of Jane Austen books suggests, there is a timeless quality to truth seeking.

One reason young readers have embraced Austen is that they can identify with one or more of her female characters. Indeed, Jennifer Marshall has a subchapter in her book titled, "Everybody Loves Lizzy," in reference to Elizabeth Bennett, the protagonist of *Pride and Prejudice*. They love her, Jennifer suggests, because she seems so modern—"witty, sharp, engaging, and an intellectual sparring partner." More specifically, men like Lizzy because she is extremely feminine and irrepressibly joyful. Women like her because she is strong, responsible, and highly confident despite her lack of family wealth or even great beauty, and this in a book written almost exactly two hundred years ago.[3]

In *The Jane Austen Guide to Happily Ever After*, Elizabeth Kantor pulls any number of useful life lessons from the Austen characters, especially Elizabeth Bennett. Here are just a few of them:

"Don't neglect the job every happy Jane Austen heroine undertakes: Discerning the 'real character' of the man you're interested in."

Don't "confuse true love with rebellion against your parents, rejection of convention, or selfishness."

"Acquire the forgotten skill Jane Austen heroines possess: the ability to discern his intentions."

Know the difference between "finding the right man and finding yourself."[4]

Not every woman can be an Elizabeth Bennett. Certainly none of the other four Bennett girls were. And yet the advice Austen dispensed remains timeless. In her book *Unhooked: How Young Women Pursue Sex, Delay Love and Lose at Both*, Laura Sessions Stepp offers comparable advice to today's young women under the heading "A guy can make you feel valuable, but it's not the guy who makes you valuable":

It's okay to feel ordinary right now. You are still figuring you out— your purpose, your principles, what and who will help you get where you want to go. Take advantage of the choices you have that build inner confidence, and not just the choices in the college catalogue. Learn to scuba dive. Teach a child to read. Invest in good friendships. Explore intimacy within relationships. Avoid hookups. They'll make you feel more ordinary than you already feel—and look more ordinary to the guy you set your sights on. He will seek to win you over only if he thinks you're a prize.

The more confident you become, independent of love, the more confident you will be in love.[5]

Eleanor Roosevelt, the wife of President Franklin Roosevelt and a liberal icon in her own right, willed herself to a stature she could never have achieved through looks. She said, wisely, "Nobody can make you inferior without your consent."[6]

Respect Yourself

In her 2007 book, *Prude: How the Sex-Obsessed Culture Damages Girls*, Carol Platt Liebau acknowledged that "scarlet letters still exist in American life. But ironically it's now the chaste who must wear them." This is a reality girls must face. And yet, as Liebau argued persuasively, chastity ought to be seen not as a deprivation, nor as a way to avoid pregnancy, social disease, and emotional distress, but rather as a gift to oneself.[7]

Liebau continued,

> Being a virgin means being truly in control of oneself: body, heart, and soul. It's a way of determining which boys care about a girl for herself, rather than simply for her body. And although it's no guarantee against heartbreak, virginity *does* ensure that a girl will never know the bitter regret of having given part of herself to someone who was unworthy of the gift.[8]

In the Best Friends program we make certain that girls understand that true friendship means encouraging friends to resist males who pressure them for sex. We know that a supportive peer group is the key to an adolescent's ability to avoid sexual activity as well as drug and alcohol use. Our program model and research data were cited in the book *Smart and Good High Schools*, by Thomas Lickona, one of the most recognized and respected authorities on character education.

Lickona commends the Best Friends program for its distinctive success in teaching sexual values and encouraging peer group support, the keys to changing behavior. "The program set out to do what many educators thought impossible," he wrote, "get inner-city girls not to have sex with their boyfriends despite strong pressure from their peer culture that encouraged early sexual activity and childbearing."[9]

I was also honored to see Carol Liebau cite the Best Friends program as the kind of support system that works. "Each year," she wrote, "culminates in an Annual Family and School Recognition Ceremony honoring Best Friends girls, Diamond Girls, mentors, and parents."[10] I have always felt that if we ask our girls *not* to do something, we have to replace that with something worthy *to do.*

Have Courage

Occasionally, very occasionally, Hollywood produces a movie that shows a young girl doing the right thing, even the courageous thing, the kind of behavior that we would encourage in Best Friends. In 2010, it produced two such movies—*True Grit* and *Winter's Bone*—and they were both justifiably nominated for an Academy Award.

True Grit, based closely on Charles Portis's 1968 novel of the same name, is set on America's frontier in the post–Civil War era. The story opens with the murder of Frank Ross by a wayward hired hand, Tom Chaney. When Chaney flees with seeming impunity into Indian country, Ross's fourteen-year-old daughter, Mattie, sets out to seek justice. Perplexed, the sheriff asks Mattie why the responsibility is hers. Mattie replies, "Nobody here knew my father and I am afraid nothing much is going to be done about Chaney except I do it. My brother is a child and my mother is indecisive and hobbled by grief."[11]

Much as in the *Wizard of Oz*, Mattie undertakes her travels with avuncular men as guides, the marshal Rooster Cogburn and the Texas Ranger LeBoeuf. For the contemporary viewer, the plot is as fanciful as the *Wizard of Oz*, but the message is much the same. To accomplish a goal and return home safely takes confidence, cooperation with others, self-respect, sound decision making, and, of course, true grit. For Mattie, it also takes a deep and abiding faith in the Lord. Not by coincidence, the movie begins and ends with the nineteenth-century spiritual "Leaning on the Everlasting Arms":

> *What have I to dread, what have I to fear,*
> *Leaning on the everlasting arms?*
> *I have blessed peace with my Lord so near,*
> *Leaning on the everlasting arms.*[12]

Accept Responsibility

Winter's Bone, a book and movie set in the present-day Ozarks, serves up one of the most heroic roles for young females in a generation. Although seventeen-year-old Ree Dolly's life is more harrowing than that of most adolescents—her meth dealer father often leaves the family to its own devices—the fundamental conflict in her life is one that every girl faces. It is the same one that a Jane Austen or a Louisa May Alcott character would inevitably face. That conflict is timeless: namely, whether to satisfy her own desires first or to accept the responsibility that life has thrust upon her.

With her mother mentally incapacitated and barely functional, Ree has chosen to assume responsibility for the mother's care, as well as that of her two younger siblings. She cooks for them. She cleans. She hunts. She teaches the boys (in the movie, a boy and a girl) to handle guns responsibly. She works at humanizing them to ensure they will "not be dead to wonder by age twelve, dulled to life, empty of kindness, boiling with mean," like so many other children in her rough part of the world.[13]

Evaluate Decisions

As the book and movie begin, Ree's father has gone missing after having posted the family home as part of the bond for a recent arrest. To save the house, Ree has to find him. While her high school peers are busy with things like ROTC and the Family, Consumer, and Career Leaders of Forsyth, Missouri, Ree sets out bravely to get the truth from people who have no interest in sharing it. "Ain't you got no men could do this?" an observer asks her. Says Ree, "No, Ma'am, I don't."

As did Mattie Ross, Ree undertakes a greater risk than anyone's daughter should have to, but does so because no one else will. Neither character undertakes it casually. In both cases, Ree's most obviously, the girls weigh the risk against the reward—in Ree's case saving her home and keeping her family together. What is troubling about the risk so many young women run today is that it is gratuitous, pointless, and without any lasting benefit, indeed without any real benefit at all. Not to spoil the films, but both Ree and Mattie succeed in their respective quests, though not without some bruising along the way. If their environments are rough, the girls' virtues—courage, compassion, resourcefulness—work in any environment; the rougher the environment, the more necessary the virtue.

Curiously, the actress who plays Ree Dolly, Jennifer Lawrence, plays a nearly identical role in the adolescent-oriented, sci-fi megahit *Hunger Games*. Her character, Katniss Everdeen, watches out for her younger sister and feckless mother, and she proves to be as resourceful, responsible, and brave as the Ree Dolly character.

Sad to say, but there are girls in our Best Friends program whose lives do not vary that much from Ree Dolly's and who have survived by making many of the same choices. Consider the following excerpts from an essay entered into our national competition by Holly Saylor of Clay County, Kentucky, the poorest county in the country, and part of the world not unlike Ree's southern Missouri:

Throughout my life, I have experienced deaths in the family because of drugs. I lost my cousin because of a drug overdose. On August 13th, it will be two years that my dad has been gone. He was declared dead on the scene. The thing that hurts the most is that the person that killed my dad is still running free on the streets because it was a hit and run.

I love the Best Friends program. I plan to stay in the Best Friends program as long as I can. Thanks to this outstanding program I think I am prepared for what life has in store for me. I hope this program stays so all little girls can be involved and become more mature young ladies like me.[14]

Never Give Up

The real world can be as frightening as fiction. This Julia Holcomb can surely tell you. If readers can learn anything from Julia's story, it is that no matter the circumstances, redemption is *always* possible.

Julia grew up about as hard as a middle-class girl can. Her father, a rogue and gambler, saddled her schoolteacher mother with debts she could not hope to pay. When her mom discovered she was pregnant with Julia, some family members urged her to seek an abortion even though abortions were then still illegal. Julia's mom toughed it out. "Thankfully she gave birth to me and later to my younger brother," says Julia, "and was a loving mother."[15]

When creditors garnished her salary to pay her husband's gambling debts, Julia's mom sought a divorce. Even after the divorce, stressed as she was by work and constricted circumstances, she remained caring and supportive of Julia. At the time, the family still prayed together and went to church regularly.

The mom's second marriage to an alcoholic began to erode the fabric of the family. A tragic auto accident pulled it apart. The accident killed Julia's little brother and her stalwart grandfather and badly injured Julia, her older sister, and her grandmother, who lost a leg.

After the accident, Julia's mother suffered an emotional meltdown. Julia's stepfather did not fare much better, and this marriage also ended in divorce.

With all of this going on, Julia and her sister were sent to live with an uncle and an aunt. When they were able to return home, they came back to a mother who was still too wounded by the death of her son and the subsequent stress to sustain a harmonious home life. The family ceased to go to church, ceased even to function as a family. "After we stopped living our faith in an active way," Julia told me, "I was shocked at how quickly my life degraded."

When the mom took up with a new man, Julia and her sister felt abandoned and estranged. They had almost no guidance as they moved into their teenage years, turbulent under the best of circumstances. At fifteen, Julia fell under the sway of a twenty-four-year-old friend who knew her way around the backstage of rock concerts. If the culture lays a claim on girls from stable homes, imagine its pull on girls as vulnerable and unstable as Julia. The friend taught her to act and dress provocatively to attract the attention of rock stars, and Julia did exactly that. Just after turning sixteen, she went backstage to a rock concert for the first time and met lead Aerosmith singer Steven Tyler, now also a judge on the popular TV show *American Idol.* "So much to be dealt with when you fall," wrote Tyler in his memoir, *Does the Noise in My Head Bother You?* "And I fell hard. And I fell heavy. And I fell so in love."[16]

Wanting the sixteen-year-old to travel around the country with him, Tyler somehow persuaded Julia's mom to sign guardianship of Julia over to him. Despite what Tyler has said, there was no money exchanged. So began their three-year relationship. "In Steven's world it was sex, drugs, and rock and roll," says Julia, "but it seemed no less chaotic than the world I left behind. I didn't know it yet, but I would barely make it out alive."

When the couple first lived together, Julia was taking birth control pills. She remembers Tyler throwing her pills off the balcony of a hotel where they were staying as a way of announcing his intention to have a baby with her. She was overjoyed. Julia became pregnant within a year, and Tyler was pleased to hear the news. Although Tyler would later spread rumors otherwise, his was her first pregnancy. He asked Julia to marry him and took her up to New Hampshire to meet his parents and grandmother. In something of a classic double standard, the parents were not thrilled that their son would marry a woman who was living the kind of lifestyle he was, such a young woman at that. They would not give their blessing, and Tyler would not proceed without it.

Devoid of almost all sense of her real self, Julia depended on Tyler for her very identity, and it was quickly unraveling. She began to doubt him and question the trust she had placed in him. He, in turn, began to doubt her.

Left alone in a Boston apartment while Tyler traveled, Julia almost died in an apartment fire. She woke up in a hospital. Although the unborn baby of five months survived the fire in good health, Tyler threatened to abandon Julia if she did not proceed with an abortion. "I was traumatized by the experience," she says. "My baby had one defender in life; me, and I caved in to pressure because of fear of rejection and the unknown future."[17]

The experience devastated Tyler as well. In *Walk This Way*, an oral history of Aerosmith, Tyler's friend Ray Tabano admitted that the abortion "really messed Steven up because it was a boy."[18] Despite the abortion, the baby was born alive. Tyler witnessed it. "You go to the doctor and they put the needle in her belly and they squeeze the stuff in and you watch," said a regretful Tyler. "And it comes out dead. I was pretty devastated. In my mind, I'm going, Jesus, what have I done?"[19] Good question!

Seek Forgiveness and Give It

After the abortion, nothing was the same. Although the relationship meandered on, Julia could never look at Tyler again as the protector she once thought him to be. More than three years after they first met, seemingly powerless and all but uneducated, Julia returned home to her mother, a broken spirit.

By this time, her mother's life had stabilized. Her mother and her third husband had a handsome, happy little boy. Julia returned to church. At a weeklong church retreat with young adults her own age, Julia began to take pleasure anew in the simple things. "I left there with a renewed sense of hope that God existed," she says. "He loved me in spite of my sins, and I could find forgiveness and a measure of real happiness within a family of my own if I began to rebuild my life." She was soon baptized.

With her mother's help, Julia got her GED and gained the confidence to start college. There she met her "true hero," the man who would become her husband and the father of their six sons. Along the way, the couple joined the Catholic Church because of its consistent teaching on the subject of life.

Although her husband knew about her relationship with Tyler, Julia stayed publicly quiet about it for years. When Tyler became a judge on the popular mainstream TV show *American Idol*, the media began to dig up nuggets about his past, many of them inaccurate. Tyler compounded the problem by telling the story in his book. It was then that Julia came forward and shared the truth with her grown sons. It was not easy.

Today she has a very succinct message to those who are stewards of our nation's daughters: "Supervise your daughters; love them; pray with them; be a part of their lives."

As Julia looks around, she sees a culture more universally precarious than when she was a girl. If situations like hers were unusually risky, today—minus the rock star—they are almost commonplace. She warns us not to let our daughters, especially those like her who have suffered trauma and abuse, be used as sexual playthings. It pains her to see the girls' male partners toss their unborn children aside like unwanted objects, all as a way to dodge responsibility for them.

"Marriage and the family are the building blocks of all virtuous societies," says an older and wiser Julia. "I learned this lesson in a trial by fire that taught me to trust God's plan no matter what occurs." She remains hopeful for the future of the nation. "If a single individual can rebuild her life, a family can, and so can a whole society.[20]

Embrace the Spiritual

Julia turned her life around when she recognized that she needed help and had to find it. The road to redemption began at home for Julia and wound its way through her experiences in church. Indeed, for the last two thousand years and more, millions have found solace and structure in faith groups.

Christianity offers the wonderful example of Mary Magdalene. Although there is some dispute about the details of her life, Mary was a sinner who was cleansed by Jesus and became his most prominent female disciple. Indeed, in the Orthodox Church she is called "Equal to the Apostles." She was present at the crucifixion and at the resurrection and has since been canonized. In the Christian tradition, Mary embodies the potential of redemption even for those whom society scorns. As with Mary Magdalene, girls should never rule faith out as a way to regain control of one's life.

Have a Sense of the Situation

As a three-hundred-pound left tackle for the Baltimore Ravens (the 2013 Super Bowl Champions), Michael Oher might seem an unlikely expert on the subject of manners, but as a lifelong observer, he has learned a thing or two and is not hesitant to share what he has learned. "It is so important to have a basic working understanding of etiquette," he wrote unabashedly.[21] He cited one case of a young girl applying for an office job. He admonished her not to walk into an interview wearing a short skirt and low-cut blouse or laughing loudly on her cell phone or using profanity.

"It is so important to have a sense of the situation and what kind of behavior it requires," he noted. "It's not a matter of snobbery; it's a matter of understanding how the world works and showing your smarts by picking up on the difference of each setting."[22]

On a lighter note, when a reporter interviewed one of our younger girls at our annual recognition luncheon, she asked, "What did you learn?" This bright-eyed, eager young girl replied with a happy smile, "At Best Friends we learned about sex and fine dining."

As I turned myself away to suppress my laughter, I thought, *Well, yes, but not necessarily in that order!* This little girl had recently taken part in an etiquette class we had provided prior to our Annual Family and School Recognition Luncheon. Our young girls were intrigued with becoming young ladies and knowing good manners. Her darling way of expressing in a nutshell what she had learned is a story that warms my soul whenever I tell it.

Feel God's Pleasure

At Best Friends, we have found that when we ask children not to do something that is potentially harmful to their health, we must give them something positive to do in its place. Adolescents need activity. If we do not give them positive activities, the opportunity to find negative activities will greatly increase. Unfortunately, it seems that many programs that encourage activity for fun and enjoyment have disappeared. For many, the only outlet for activity is competitive sports. As much as I support competitive sports—they were certainly beneficial for my sons, especially when the coaches were good role models—they do not do enough to keep our daughters healthy and wholesome.

This is why we developed a "Health Is Happiness" program as a part of the Best Friends curriculum. The program takes place on Saturdays. This enables our middle school Best Friends to come to school for a full day of fun activity and good, spirited games. The day concludes with our theme song and step drill team competition.

There is a need for activities that are intrinsically fun and stress team building. Girls do not need to have great skills to enjoy themselves. Many of our girls do not, but it is wonderful to see them—sixth, seventh, and eighth graders—laughing as they are involved in tugs-of-war, relay races, and fitness drills involving music. Physical health and activity are vital to emotional health. As the Eric Liddell character said in *Chariots of Fire*, "When I run, I feel God's pleasure."[23] That is a beautiful statement. One does not have to be a gifted athlete to feel that pleasure.

Seek Support

We applaud the other programs throughout the nation that do many of the things that we do, but after twenty-five years, we know our program works. Allow me to share a few other testimonials from our girls.

What Tyheria Brown of Holly Springs, Mississippi, learned in Best Friends reminds me of what Julia Holcomb learned through her faith group and what Marianne Dashwood learned from her sister, Elinor, in Jane Austen's *Sense and Sensibility*:

> People should have self-control because this makes us better people. Having self-control makes you feel better about yourself. In Best Friends, friendship is really important because you get to know other people and their cultures. We learn that we have a lot of things in common. Friendship is one of the most important things in the world. Friendship makes you happy when you have another person to trust and talk to. Self-respect gives you pride. Having respect for yourself makes you an important person in everything you do. Respecting yourself makes you a person that others admire.[24]

Dajana Durica absorbed some very useful and timeless wisdom as well:

> I learned to stay away from drugs and alcohol, help friends if they had problems, not to have sex until I am married, and to make the right decisions! Best Friends helped me become a young, smart lady with a wonderful life that is ahead of me. It also helped me understand these people that are going through these things. It helped me make right decisions in life and stay safe and healthy.[25]

Without meaning to, these girls are echoing the sentiments of Helen Keller, the blind and deaf woman whose astonishing story of self-actualization continues to inspire. Said she on the subject of mutual support: "My friends have made the story of my life. In a thousand ways they have turned my limitations into beautiful privileges, and enabled me to walk serene and happy in the shadow cast by my deprivation."[26]

Learn from Others

Our culture grinds up some of our daughters and spits them out with stunning indifference. The closer one is to the center of that culture, the greater the risk of being destroyed. Each year it seems the bestseller list is topped by a former child star who has suffered terribly and finally found the strength and courage to tell her story. I think here of Drew Barrymore's *Little Girl Lost*, Tatum O'Neal's *A Paper Life*, and Mackenzie Phillips's *High on Arrival*, one book more horrific than the other.

In her still unfinished story, O'Neal wrote poignantly:

> I've overcome neglect and deprivation.
> I've overcome abandonment and abuse.

I've overcome physical and mental brutality—and fought back.

I've triumphed over addiction.

I've stood my ground in life, alone, even against overwhelming forces with the might and money to crush me. I've purged myself of bitterness and anger and remained open to love. I've kept my moral compass intact and aimed at true north.

I have survived and won.[27]

As much as I admire Tatum's resilience, I am forced to ask myself upon tracking her life or Drew's or McKenzie's, why do we put our daughters through such madness? Why don't we learn from their experience? Why don't we do more to help them avoid these horrible trails?

What Lies Ahead for Our Daughters

In my review of the feminists' philosophy, I sense that much of their motivation flows from unhappiness. Almost inevitably, they trace this unhappiness to an external force: namely, men. "We are taught you must blame your father, your sisters, your brothers, the school, the teachers—you can blame anyone, but never blame yourself," actress Katharine Hepburn shrewdly observed. "It's never your fault. But it's always your fault, because if you wanted to change, you're the one who has got to change. It's as simple as that, isn't it?"[1]

Reality is never simple, but it is inevitable. While certainly there are men who can cause women great unhappiness—always have been, always will be—our daughters need to get beyond blaming others. They need to know they are responsible for their own decisions, and those decisions, wisely or unwisely made, will shape their future.

Some of the young women about whom I have written chose very unwisely. In a few cases, their decisions led to their being attacked or even killed. Some, like Eve Carson, were brilliant and innocent spirits who did nothing at all to deserve their fates. Some of the women about whom I have written came back from the depths of despair. Some have not. All the women I have mentioned have faced major obstacles on the road to health and happiness, the best and brightest on America's college campuses not excluded by a long shot.

As I have documented, these young women must make their way through a labyrinth of everyday corruption, often without a guidebook. The siren song of alcohol, drugs, and casual sex lured many of them from their chosen path, if they had chosen a path to begin with. So many of the twists and turns they faced are so new that even the best parents and the wisest educators are hard-pressed to guide them. Some of our daughters set out with no guidance at all.

Although a few will not survive this soul-searing hookup culture, almost all will. Many of these, however, will bear the emotional scars and even the physical ills that they acquired during what was supposed to be the time of their lives. There is not a parent who would want his or her daughter to experience the hard edge of this culture. There is not a mother who would want her son to marry a girl who had.

Too many of our sons are unsteady partners in the relationships that emerge in this culture. The messages they have received from the feminist establishment are so twisted and the diversions from achieving adulthood are so tempting that it is a wonder any of them successfully marry. In a very real way, our daughters are setting our sons up for failure. If they have been rejected or abandoned by a man, either a father or a previous lover, their ability to trust in a future relationship is greatly diminished. Some of our daughters have been so hurt that the possibility of their having successful marriages is slight.

Our daughters have been taught, too, that their careers are of equal importance to a husband's and a necessary prerequisite before having children. They have been instructed by the progressive feminist culture that they can have it all, and too often they end up having nothing of consequence.

So, how do we save our daughters from an empty adulthood? How do we give our future daughters-in-law a responsible, caring husband in the home? We have to begin a conversation, a serious one, free from accusations of sexism or racism or ageism or homophobia. Too much is at stake not to.

For starters, we must tell our daughters to treasure their futures, take care of them, nurture them, and make them count. We must remind them that their youth is a wonderful gift that the wealthiest people cannot buy. We must caution them not to waste it on behaviors that will fill them with shame the next morning and regret for many mornings to come.

We must remind our daughters to keep their heads, even while others about them are losing theirs. We must encourage them to keep open minds, but not so open that drug fumes can seep in or their brains fall out.

We must exhort our daughters to find passion for what they know and like and pursue it. We must urge them to forget short-term "happiness" and focus instead on the things that keep us happy over the long haul—honor, truth, decency, faith, family, country. As one of my eleven-year-old students said to me, "What we do in Best Friends is bring my joy up."

We must instruct our daughters that the road is hard, but not so hard that those who have already traveled it don't envy them. We must remind them how complex life is but how simple are its basic truths.

We must confront them when they need confrontation and befriend them when they need a friend, not when we do. We must give them boundaries and enforce them.

I will never forget the mother of a Best Friends girl who came to me with tears in her eyes and said, "Please talk to my daughter. I love her too much to be rational." That I did. As the years went by, I came to see that it was often easier for me to talk to the girls than it was for their mothers. Having no daughters of my own, I had less trouble maintaining perspective and keeping an objective stance. This process will help me as well to become, God willing, a better mother-in-law and a better grandmother.

At the end of the program, our survey data showed that 98 percent of our girls understood the difference between love and sex. Fewer than half did before the program started. This is a critical understanding, but our daughters will not come to it if no one talks to them, if no one gives them guidance in making good decisions, if no one helps them understand the consequences of their behavior, if no one reaches out and loves them. Even with girls who are not our own daughters, it seems that many women can offer help and caring to girls who need this.

To the daughters who may one day marry my sons, I would tell them what we tell our Diamond Girls: "A diamond is the strongest, brightest gem. When tested by fire and stress, the diamond becomes even stronger, if cared for."

If our girls can become the kind of women good men will want to care for and protect, everything else will start to make sense.

If we give our daughters our best, they will respond with their best. But it is almost certain that if we do not, our daughters will be in danger.

Best Friends Foundation
Violence and Abuse Protocol

Best Friends Foundation Mission Statement

The Best Friends Foundation strives to provide a nationwide network of programs that is dedicated to the physical and emotional well-being of adolescents. It provides scientifically researched and developmentally sound curriculum designed for high school students. The Foundation promotes self-respect through self-control and gives participants the skills, guidance, and support needed to avoid risky behavior that is destructive to relationships. In the spirit of true friendship, the Best Friends Foundation fosters positive peer groups for adolescents and creates an environment that raises aspirations and promotes achievement.

Purpose of the Protocol

The dating violence protocol was developed to ensure that the Best Friends Foundation will address dating violence in a comprehensive and appropriate manner. In 2005, the Teen Health survey "Am

I in a Healthy Relationship" found that 20 percent of American girls reported having been hit, slapped, or forced into sexual activity by their partners. Young men also experience violence, but they were much less likely to report it to the authorities. And 40 percent of all teens said they knew someone at school who experienced dating violence.

Definition of Dating Violence

Dating violence is any intentional sexual, physical, or psychological attack on one partner by the other in a dating relationship.

Identifying and Responding to Dating Violence Issues

We ask that all Best Friends Foundation replication sites coordinators and instructors be alert for the following signs that a teen may be involved in a relationship that is or has the potential to become abusive. When these changes happen suddenly, or without explanation, there may be cause for concern.

- Does the individual have unexplained bruises, scratches, or injuries?
- Do you see signs that the individual is afraid of his/her boyfriend or girlfriend?
- Does the boyfriend or girlfriend lash out, or insult the individual?
- Has the individual's appearance or behavior suddenly changed?
- Has the individual stopped spending time with friends and family?
- Has the individual recently started using alcohol or drugs?
- Have you seen the boyfriend or girlfriend become abusive toward other people or things?

- Does the individual seem to have lost interest or to be giving up things that were once important? Has he/she lost interest in school or other activities?
- Does the boyfriend or girlfriend seem to try to control the individual's behavior, making all the decisions, checking up on his/her behavior, demanding to know who the individual has been with, and acting jealous and possessive?
- Does the individual apologize for the boyfriend or girlfriend's behavior to you and others? Has the individual casually mentioned the boyfriend or girlfriend's temper or violent behavior, but then laughed it off as a joke?
- Have you seen sudden changes in the individual's mood or personality? Is the individual becoming anxious or depressed, acting out, or being secretive? Is the individual avoiding eye contact, having "crying jags" or getting "hysterical"?

Protocol

1. When the Diamond Girl/ Best Men Leadership School Coordinator is informed by or suspects that a student has experienced abuse or violence in the home or dating relationship from a boyfriend or a girlfriend, ask the student about his/her relationship.
   a. Be specific about why you are concerned. (i.e. "I saw a boy push you hard. Is he your boyfriend? Why did he do that?")
   b. If the student *does not* want to discuss this, encourage him/her to talk to a trusted adult (i.e. parent, school guidance counselor, Diamond Girl Leadership Coordinator/ Mentor, or Best Men Leadership Coordinator/Mentor).
   c. Give the student the National Teen Dating Abuse Helpline number 1-866-331-9474 and the website www.LoveIsRespect.org; the National Domestic Violence

Hotline number—1-800-799-SAFE; or the Rape, Abuse, & Incest National Network (RAINN) hotline 1.800.656.HOPE and the website http://rainn.org/get-involved for immediate and confidential advice and referrals.

    d. If the student *does* want to talk, do not criticize or attack the abuser. Ask, "What can I do to help?"

    e. The school coordinator must report the conversation to the school guidance counselor immediately. (Refer to step 2.)

2. The Diamond Girl/ Best Men School Coordinator immediately reports abuse and violence to the school guidance counselor and the school principal as it is their legal obligation as defined by the DC Law 2-22 (Child Abuse Act). The law states the following: School employees are directed not to try to resolve or investigate a suspected case of student abuse, violence, or neglect. Rather, an employee's legal obligation is to orally report such knowledge or suspicion to either the Metropolitan Police Department ("MPD") Youth Division, 202-576-6763; MPD non emergency, 202-727-1010; or, if a crime is in progress, 911, or the Child Protective Services Division of the Department of Human Services ("CPSD") 202-727-0995. A written report is required if requested from MPD or CPSD, or if the abuse involves drug related activity.

[The law provided that any employee who willfully fails to make a report when he or she suspects student abuse, violence, or neglect shall be fined or imprisoned for not more than thirty days, or both.]

Note: Best Friends Foundation replication sites follow the abuse and violence protocol as determined and adopted by the respective school systems in the replication sites.

Notes

Preface

1. Robert Lerner, "Can Abstinence Work? An Analysis of the Best Friends Program," *Adolescent & Family Health* 3, no. 4 (2004): 185–92.
2. John B. Jemmott III, PhD; Loretta Sweet Jemmott, PhD, RN, FAAN; Geoffrey T. Fong, PhD, "Abstinence and Safer Sex HIV Risk-reduction Interventions for African American Adolescents: A Randomized Controlled Trial," *Journal of the American Medical Association* 279, no. 19 (1998): 1529–1536.
3. Bill Albert, *With One Voice 2012: America's Adults and Teens Sound Off About Teen Pregnancy* (Washington DC: The National Campaign to Prevent Teen and Unplanned Pregnancy), 8. This report is available for download at http://www.thenationalcampaign.org/resources/pdf/pubs/WOV_2012.pdf.
4. David Brown, "A Sweeping Survey of Americans' Sexual Behavior," *Washington Post,* March 4, 2011.
5. Ibid.

Chapter 1: Life in the Fast Lane

1. Cosmo Lee, review of "Get Thrashed: The Story of Thrash Metal," directed by Rick Ernst, *Stylus,* April 7, 2007, http://www.stylusmagazine.com/articles/movie_review/get-thrashed-the-story-of-thrash-metal.htm.
2. Although their edgy, aggressive, often druggy nihilism is indicative of the "culture" we are resisting, Metallica has offered a $50,000 reward for information leading to the killer's arrest. UPI, "Metallica

Aids in Search for Suspect," June 13, 2012, http://www.upi.com/ Top_News/US/2012/06/13/Metallica-aids-in-search-for-suspect/ UPI-26651339633485/.

3. Amber Hunt, *All-American Murder* (New York: St. Martin's Paperbacks, 2011), 31.

4. Leonard Sax, *Girls on the Edge: The Four Factors Driving the New Crisis for Girls* (New York: Basic Books, 2010), 169.

5. Hunt, *All-American Murder,* 198.

6. Emilie Surrusco, "Yeardley Love's Story—and Mine," *Washington Post,* February 10, 2012, http://articles.washingtonpost.com/2012-02-10/ opinions/35442418_1_dorm-room-bright-futures-sexual-abuse.

7. Hunt, *All-American Murder,* 76.

8. "The police would later report "lots of yelling and screaming" but no physical violence

9. Tucker Max, *I Hope They Serve Beer in Hell* (New York: Citadel Press, 2009), 52.

10. Dave Itzkoff, "Rude, Crude and Coming to a Theater Near You," *New York Times,* September 4, 2009, http://www.nytimes.com/2009/ 09/05/movies/05tucker.html?_r=1.

11. Juliet Macur, "Lacrosse Player Admitted Shaking Woman," *New York Times,* May 4, 2010, http://www.nytimes.com/2010/05/05/ sports/05lacrosse.html.

12. Jenna Johnson and Mary Pat Flaherty, "George Huguely and Yeardley Love Had Volatile Relationship, Say Lawyers and Witnesses," *Washington Post,* February 9, 2012.

13. William Congreve, *The Mourning Bride,* act 3, scene 8.

14. Alexandra Petri, "The Tragedy of George Huguely," *Washington Post,* February 22, 2012, http://www.washingtonpost.com/blogs/compost/ post/the-tragedy-of-george-huguely/2012/02/15/gIQAwOQBUR_ blog.html.

15. Donna St. George, "Text Messages Become a Growing Weapon in Dating Violence," *Washington Post,* June 21, 2010, http://www .washingtonpost.com/wp-dyn/content/article/2010/06/20/ AR2010062003331.html.

16. Mary Pat Flaherty, "George Huguely Trial Evidence to Be Shown," *Washington Post,* May 14, 2012, http://www.washingtonpost.com/ local/crime/george-huguely-trial-evidence-to-be-shown/2012/ 05/14/gIQAJLQKPU_story.html.

17. Petri, "The Tragedy of George Huguely."

18. www.amethystinitiative.org. According to a notice from GoDaddy.

com that displays when Amethyst's URL is accessed, their domain name expired in June 2012. For another source that cites this initiative's aim, see next note.

19. Sarah, "Choose Responsibility Launches Amethyst Initiative," *Middblog*: Middlebury College's Alternative News Source, August 19, 2008, http://midd-blog.com/2008/08/19/ choose-responsibility-launches-amethyst-initiative/.

20. "Cops: Lacrosse Player Admits Deadly Beating," *Today*, aired May 5, 2010, http://video.today.msnbc.msn.com/ today/36958656#36958656.

21. Notre Dame Preparatory School, https://www.notredameprep.com/ service_and_justice/index.aspx (page discontinued).

22. "Q&A with Yeardley Love," VirginiaSports.com (University of Virginia), March 18, 2009, http://www.virginiasports.com/ ViewArticle.dbml?DB_OEM_ID=17800&ATCLID=3695494.

23. Edmund Burke, "A Letter to a Member of the National Assembly," (1791; Paris: J. Dodsley, no date given), 69.

24. Liz Seccuro, *Crash into Me: A Survivor's Search for Justice* (New York: Bloomsbury USA, 2011), 47.

25. Ibid., 61.

26. Ibid., 71.

27. Ibid., 241.

28. Max, *I Hope They Serve Beer in Hell*, 299.

29. *Saturday Night: Untold Stories of Sexual Assault at Duke*, www .duke.edu/web/saturdaynight.

30. "The comprehensive 2007 Campus Sexual Assault study reported that 19 percent of female undergraduates on America's campuses had experienced an assault, either attempted or completed"

31. *Saturday Night: Untold Stories of Sexual Assault at Duke*, "About," http://www.duke.edu/web/saturdaynight/about.html.

32. Mary Eberstadt, *Adam and Eve After the Pill: Paradoxes of the Sexual Revolution* (San Francisco: Ignatius Press, 2012), 78.

33. Ibid., 93.

34. Sax, *Girls on the Edge*, 110.

35. Joseph A. Califano Jr., "Substance Abuse: The Feminine Mystique," *America*, May 19, 2003, http://www.americamagazine.org/content/ article.cfm?article_id=2975.

36. CASA: The National Center on Addiction and Substance Abuse at Columbia University, *The Formative Years: Pathways to Substance Abuse Among Girls and Young Women Ages 8–22* (New York: CASA,

2003), ii, http://www.casacolumbia.org/articlefiles/380-Formative_
Years_Pathways_to_Substance_Abuse.pdf.

37. Koren Zailckas, *Smashed: Story of a Drunken Girlhood* (New York:
Penguin, 2005), xiv.

38. Karen Owen, "Karen Owen's Duke List Powerpoint," http://www
.youtube.com/watch?v=hahYUHkw9KY.

39. Caitlin Flanagan, "The Hazards of Duke," *Atlantic Monthly*,
January/February 2011, http://www.theatlantic.com/magazine/
archive/2011/01/the-hazards-of-duke/308328/.

40. Ibid.

41. Petri, "The Tragedy of George Huguely."

42. Seccuro, *Crash into Me*, 241.

43. Crimesider Staff, "Alexandra Kogut Murder: Boyfriend Charged in
Beating Death of SUNY Brockport College Student," October 1, 2012,
http://www.cbsnews.com/8301-504083_162-57523353-504083/
alexandra-kogut-murder-boyfriend-charged-in-beating-death
-of-suny-brockport-college-student/.

Chapter 2: In Loco Parentis

1. Eve Carson, "Eve Welcome Back to UNC!" www.youtube.com/
watch?v=5sOJT9_Jzbo.

2. Matthew Price, "Carson Goes to Bat for Students," *Daily Tarheel*,
February 25, 2008 (upd. March 10, 2011), http://www.dailytarheel
.com/index.php/article/2008/02/carson_goes_to_bat_for_students.

3. Beth Velliquette, "Carson Asked Lovette to Pray with
Her," *Herald-Sun* (Durham, NC), December 13, 2011,
http://heraldsun.com/view/full_story/16772147/
article-Carson-asked-Lovette-to-pray-with-her-.

4. Troy Shelton, "2 Murders Bring Repeat Offenders into Spotlight,"
The Chronicle, March 19, 2008, http://www.dukechronicle.com/
article/2-murders-bring-repeat-offenders-spotlight.

5. Anne Blythe, "Lovette Guilty of Murdering Carson; Gets Life
Sentence," Newsobserver.com, December 21, 2011, http://www
.newsobserver.com/2011/12/21/1724323/lovette-guilty-of
-murdering-carson.html.

6. "Good Samaritan Talks of Abduction Rescue," ABC Eyewitness News,
WTVD-TV Raleigh-Durham NC, May 13, 2010, http://abclocal.go
.com/wtvd/story?section=news/local&id=7440097.

7. "Office of Student Conduct," Liberty University, http://www.liberty
.edu/index.cfm?PID=24102.

8. Ibid., "About Liberty: Doctrinal Statement," http://www.liberty.edu/index.cfm?PID=6907.

9. The Honor Committee, *On My Honor* (video), University of Virginia, http://www.virginia.edu/OnMyHonor/.

10. Liz Seccuro, *Crash into Me: A Survivor's Search for Justice* (New York: Bloomsbury USA, 2011), 75.

11. Christina Ng, "Yeardley Love's Mother Sues Lacrosse Coach over Daughter's Death," ABC News, May 4, 2012, http://abcnews.go.com/US/yeardley-loves-mother-sue-lacross-coaches-daughters-death/story?id=16279118; *Sharon D. Love v. The Commonwealth of Virginia*, May 3, 2012, http://www2.timesdispatch.com/mgmedia/file/693/lawsuit-love-family-vs-uva-lacrosse-coaches/.

12. Petri, "The Tragedy of George Huguely." (See chap. 1, n. 13.)

13. Albert Bandura, *Social Foundations of Thought and Action: A Social Cognitive Theory* (Englewood Cliffs, NJ: Prentice-Hall, 1985), 1986.

14. Daniel R. Weinberger, Brita Elvevåg, and Jay N. Giedd, *The Adolescent Brain: A Work in Progress* (Washington, DC: The National Campaign to Prevent Teen Pregnancy, June 2005), 26, http://www.thenationalcampaign.org/resources/pdf/BRAIN.pdf.

15. Ibid., 2.

16. Ibid., 29.

17. Arthur Miller, *Death of a Salesman* (1949; New York: Dramatists Play Service, 1980), 40.

Chapter 3: The Feminist Misdirection

1. Miriam Grossman, *Unprotected: A Campus Psychiatrist Reveals How Political Correctness in Her Profession Endangers Every Student* (New York: Sentinel, 2007), xxi.

2. Jennifer Marshall, *Now and Not Yet: Making Sense of Single Life in the Twenty-First Century* (Colorado Springs: Multnomah Books, 2007), 2.

3. Hanna Rosin, "Sexual Freedom and Women's Success," *Wall Street Journal*, March 23, 2012, http://online.wsj.com/article/SB10001424052702304724404577299391480959420.html.

4. Mary Pipher, *Reviving Ophelia: Saving the Selves of Adolescent Girls* (New York: Riverhead Books, 1994), 27.

5. JoAnn Deak, *Girls Will Be Girls: Raising Confident and Courageous Daughters* (New York: Hyperion, 2002), 13.

6. Gloria Steinem, Letter to the Editor, *Time* magazine, October 16, 2000, http://www.phrases.org.uk/meanings/414150.html.

7. David Kennedy, *Birth Control in America: The Career of Margaret Sanger* (Yale University Press, 1970), 1, 22.

8. Margaret Sanger, *The Autobiography of Margaret Sanger* (Mineola, NY: Dover Publications, 2004), 69.

9. Ibid., 86–87.

10. Margaret Sanger, *The Pivot of Civilization* (New York: Brentano's, 1922), 16.

11. Ibid., 24.

12. Ibid., 82.

13. Ibid., 263.

14. Ibid., 108.

15. Ibid., 123, 99.

16. Ibid., 175.

17. Ibid., 25.

18. Progressive icon Oliver Wendell Holmes delivered the opinion of the Court. See *"Buck v. Bell,"* Legal Information Institute, Cornell University Law School, http://www.law.cornell.edu/supct/html/historics/USSC_CR_0274_0200_ZO.html.

19. "Margaret Sanger Is Dead at 82; Led Campaign for Birth Control" (Obituary), special to the *New York Times,* September 7, 1966, http://www.nytimes.com/learning/general/onthisday/bday/0914.html.

20. Meredith Melnick, "Margaret Sanger," in "The 25 Most Powerful Women of the Past Century," *Time Specials,* November 18, 2010, http://www.time.com/time/specials/packages/article/0,28804,2029774_2029776_2031825,00.html.

21. Betty Friedan, *Life So Far: A Memoir* (New York: Simon & Schuster, 2000), 15.

22. Anne Frank, *Diary of a Young Girl* (1947; New York: Doubleday, 2010), 209.

23. Friedan, *Life So Far,* 18.

24. Ibid., 31.

25. Ibid., 224.

26. Steinem, Letter to the Editor, *Time,* October 16, 2000.

27. Nancy Hass, "Gloria Steinem Still Wants More," *Newsweek,* August 7, 2011.

28. Patricia Marcello, *Gloria Steinem: A Biography* (Westport, CT: Greenwood Press, 2004), 3–32.

29. Sarah Hepola, "Gloria Steinem, a Woman Like No Other," *New York Times,* March 16, 2012, http://www.nytimes.com/2012/03/18/fashion/in-the-womans-movement-who-will-replace-gloria-steinem.html?pagewanted=all&_r=0.

30. Susan Dominus, "30th Anniversary Issue/Gloria Steinem: First Feminist," *New York*, April 6, 1998, http://nymag.com/nymetro/news/people/features/2438/.

31. *Anderson Cooper 360*, CNN, April 11, 2012, http://ac360.blogs.cnn.com/2012/04/11/the-candidates-war-for-women/.

32. Ezra Klein, "Komen Vice President Karen Handel Resigns," *Washington Post*, February 7, 2012, http://www.washingtonpost.com/blogs/wonkblog/post/komen-vice-president-karen-handel-resigns/2012/02/07/gIQAYP0WwQ_blog.html.

33. Rick Klein, "Palin Slams Letterman's 'Sexually Perverted' Joke," *ABC News*, June 11, 2009.

34. David Savage and Alan Miller, "Clinton Allegations Dividing Feminists," *Los Angeles Times*, March 23, 1998.

35. Mary Eberstadt, "Has the Sexual Revolution Been Good for Women? No," *Wall Street Journal*, March 30, 2012, http://online.wsj.com/article/SB10001424052702304724404577297422171909202.html.

36. Ibid.

Chapter 4: The New Sexual Regime

1. Germaine Greer, *The Female Eunuch* (New York: Harper Perennial, 2008), 23.

2. Ibid., 358.

3. Ibid., 211.

4. Betty Friedan, *The Feminine Mystique* (New York: W. W. Norton, 2001), 393.

5. Greer, *Female Eunuch*, 200.

6. Germaine Greer, "Writing Politics," Q&A, *ABC Television*, August 14, 2008, http://www.enotes.com/topic/Germaine_Greer.

7. Kerry Cohen, *Loose Girl: A Memoir of Promiscuity* (New York: Hyperion, 2008), 7, 64–65, 115, 146–48, 181–82.

8. Ibid., 92.

9. Jennifer Marshall, *Now and Not Yet: Making Sense of Single Life in the Twenty-First Century* (Colorado Springs: Multnomah Books, 2007), 49.

10. Karen Owen, "Karen Owen's Duke List Powerpoint," http://www.youtube.com/watch?v=hahYUHkw9KY.

11. Greer, *Female Eunuch*, 217.

12. Caitlin Flanagan, "The Hazards of Duke," *Atlantic Monthly*, January/February 2011, http://www.theatlantic.com/magazine/archive/2011/01/the-hazards-of-duke/308328/.

13. Mary Eberstadt, "Has the Sexual Revolution Been Good for Women?

No," *Wall Street Journal*, March 30, 2012, http://online.wsj.com/article/SB10001424052702304724404577297422171909202.html.

14. Ellen Willis, "Lust Horizons," *The Village Voice*, October 18, 2005, http://www.villagevoice.com/2005-10-18/specials/lust-horizons.

15. George Gilder, "Freedom from Welfare Dependency," *Religion & Liberty*, March–April 1994, http://www.acton.org/pub/religion-liberty/volume-4-number-2/freedom-welfare-dependency.

16. "Mark Zuckerberg's Online Diary," http://www.scribd.com/doc/538697/Mark-Zuckerbergs-Online-Diary. See also Claire Hoffman, "The Battle for Facebook," *Rolling Stone*, September 15, 2010, http://www.rollingstone.com/culture/news/the-battle-for-facebook-20100915?page=2.

17. Greer, *The Female Eunuch*, 300.

18. Pope Paul VI, "*Humanae Vitae*: On Human Life" (encyclical letter), Helpers of God's Precious Infants, July 25, 1968, www.helpersny.org/hv9.htm.

19. "Sexually Transmitted Diseases," Centers for Disease Control and Prevention, http://www.cdc.gov/std/.

20. Miriam Grossman, *Unprotected: A Campus Psychiatrist Reveals How Political Correctness in Her Profession Endangers Every Student* (New York: Sentinel, 2007), 23.

21. "STD Trends in the United States," Centers for Disease Control and Prevention, www.cdc.gov/std/stats10/trends.htm.

22. Grossman, *Unprotected*, 16.

23. Cohen, *Loose Girl*, 153.

24. Ibid., 153–54.

25. Ibid., 153.

26. Grossman, *Unprotected*, 18.

27. "Trends in Reportable Sexually Transmitted Diseases in the United States," Centers for Disease Control and Prevention, January 13, 2009.

28. Miriam Grossman, *Unprotected*, Nook ed. (New York: Sentinel, 2006), 12. (Unless identified as the Nook edition, all references to *Unprotected* are from the print edition.)

29. Grossman, *Unprotected*, xv.

30. Ibid., xvi.

31. Cohen, *Loose Girl*, 168.

Chapter 5: Coming Apart

1. Charles Murray, "The New American Divide," *Wall Street Journal*,

January 21, 2012, http://online.wsj.com/article/SB100014240529702
04301404577170733817181646.html.

2. James R. Wetzel, "American Families: 75 Years of Change," *Monthly Labor Review*, March 1990, http://www.bls.gov/mlr/1990/03/art1full.pdf.

3. Kay Hymowitz, "An Enduring Crisis for the Black Family," *Washington Post*, December 6, 2008, http://www.washingtonpost.com/wp-dyn/content/article/2008/12/05/AR2008120503088.html.

4. Murray, "The New American Divide."

5. Ibid.

6. Hanna Rosin, "Sexual Freedom and Women's Success," *Wall Street Journal*, March 23, 2012, http://online.wsj.com/article/SB10001424052702304724404577299391480959420.html.

7. Ibid.

8. Lyndon Johnson, as quoted in Diane Ravitch, ed., *The American Reader* (New York: Harper Collins, 2000), 596.

9. Hymowitz, "An Enduring Crisis for the Black Family."

10. Kathleen Kingsbury, "Pregnancy Boom at Gloucester High," *Time*, June 18, 2008, http://www.time.com/time/magazine/article/0,9171,1816486,00.html.

11. Ibid.

12. "Stories on Gloucester Pact to Become Pregnant with Fathers," Berkshire Fatherhood, June 23, 2008, http://www.berkshirefatherhood.com/index.php?mact=News,cntnt01,print,0&cntnt01articleid=643&cntnt01showtemplate=false&cntnt01returnid=77.

13. Kingsbury, "Pregnancy Boom at Gloucester High."

14. J. Munn, "Distributing Contraceptives No Answer to Complex Problems," *Gloucester Daily Times*, August 4, 2008.

15. Kingsbury, "Pregnancy Boom at Gloucester High."

16. *The O'Reilly Factor*, Fox News, November 9, 2007.

17. Beth Warren, "Mayors Join Superintendent to Confront Teen Pregnancy Problem in Memphis," *Commercial Appeal*, January 18, 2011, http://www.commercialappeal.com/news/2011/jan/18/mayors-join-superintendent-confront-teen-pregnancy/.

18. Heather Mac Donald, "Hispanic Family Values?" *City Journal*, Autumn 2006, http://www.city-journal.org/html/16_4_hispanic_family_values.html.

19. Michael Oher with Don Yaeger, *I Beat the Odds: From Homelessness, to the Blind Side, and Beyond* (New York: Gotham Books, 2011), 3.

20. Mac Donald, "Hispanic Family Values?"

21. Andrea Dworkin, *Pornography: Men Possessing Women* (New York: E. F. Dutton, 1989), 19.

22. Ibid., 59.

23. Susan Brownmiller, *Against Our Will: Men, Women and Rape* (New York: Ballantine, 1975), 15. Emphasis original.

24. Mary Cantwell, "The American Woman," *Mademoiselle*, June 1976.

25. Linda Gordon, as quoted in Leslie Barbara Tanner, ed., *Voices from Women's Liberation* (New York: New American Library, 1971), 187.

26. Robin Morgan, ed., *Sisterhood Is Powerful: An Anthology of Writings from the Women's Liberation Movement* (New York: Random House, 1970), 537.

27. Bonnie Goldstein, "Thinking of Having a Baby Solo? Don't," *Washington Post,* February 20, 2012, http://www.washingtonpost.com/blogs/she -the-people/post/thinking-of-having-a-baby-solo-dont/2012/02/19/ gIQADJ7WPR_blog.html.

Chapter 6: Suffering the Consequences

1. Charles Murray, "The New American Divide," *Wall Street Journal*, January 21, 2012, http://online.wsj.com/article/SB100014240529702 0430140457717073381718164 6.html.

2. Ibid.

3. Ibid.

4. "The Fatherless Generation," IDS 302 Project, April 23, 2010.

5. Amanda Terkel, "Rick Santorum's Two-Step Plan to End Poverty," *Huffington Post,* December 28, 2011, http://www.huffingtonpost .com/2011/12/28/rick-santorums-poverty_n_1173307.html.

6. Ibid.

7. Ibid.

8. Ibid.

9. Ibid.

10. Murray, "The New American Divide."

11. Jill Goldman and Marsha K. Salus, et. al, "A Coordinated Response to Child Abuse and Neglect: The Foundation for Practice," Office on Child Abuse and Neglect, 2003, https://www.childwelfare.gov/pubs/ usermanuals/foundation/foundation.pdf, .

12. "Domestic Violence Statistics," http://domesticviolencestatistics. org/domestic-violence-statistics/.

13. *Stop the Silence. Prevent the Violence* (booklet of the Best Friends Dating Violence Seminar) (Washington, DC: Best Friends Foundation, 2011), http://www.bestfriendsfoundation.org/images/ BFFDatingViolenceSeminarProgramFeb2011.pdf.

Chapter 7: Beyond Abuse

1. Mindelle Jacobs, "Barbaric and Unwanted," *Edmonton Sun*, June 18, 2010, http://www.edmontonsun.com/comment/columnists/mindelle_jacobs/2010/06/17/14429711.html.

2. Robert Spencer, "Honor Killing in Texas," *Human Events*, January 1, 2008, http://www.humanevents.com/2008/01/08/honor-killing-in-texas/.

3. Ibid.

4. Ibid.

5. Nina Shea, "States That Abuse Women," *National Review*, March 5, 2012, http://www.nationalreview.com/corner/292649/states-abuse-women-nina-shea.

6. In one well-documented case, as reported by the Asian Human Rights Commission and the British Pakistani Christian Association, a twelve-year-old Christian girl was kidnapped, raped, and forcibly converted to Islam.

7. Kay Hymowitz, "Why Feminism Is AWOL on Islam," *City Journal*, Winter 2003, http://www.city-journal.org/html/13_1_why_feminism.html.

8. Ibid.

9. Ibid.

10. Ibid.

11. Ibid.

12. Gil Kaufman, "Chris Brown Police Report Provides Details of Altercation," MTV.com, March 6, 2009, http://www.mtv.com/news/articles/1606481/chris-brown-police-report-provides-details-altercation.jhtml.

13. Josh Grossberg and Whitney English, "Chris Brown Sentenced to Probation, Must Keep Clear of Rihanna Till 2014," E! Online, August 25, 2009, http://www.eonline.com/news/141103/chris-brown-sentenced-to-probation-must-keep-clear-of-rihanna-till-2014.

14. Michael Cragg, "Rihanna and Chris Brown Release Two New Remixes That Feature Each Other," *Guardian*, February 21, 2012, http://www.guardian.co.uk/music/2012/feb/21/rihanna-chris-brown-remixes-brit-awards?newsfeed=true.

15. Ibid., in a comment posted the same day in response to the article.

16. Matt Stopera, "25 Extremely Upsetting Reactions to Chris Brown at the Grammys," BuzzFeed, http://www.buzzfeed.com/mjs538/horrible-reactions-to-chris-brown-at-the-grammys.

17. Bonnie Fuller, "Tina Turner to Rihanna: Leave Chris Brown Now!" *Huffington Post*, February 20, 2009, http://www.huffingtonpost .com/bonnie-fuller/tina-turner-to-rihanna-le_b_168736.html.

18. Maria La Ganga, "Mirkarimi Trial Is a Real-Life Soap Opera in San Francisco," *Los Angeles Times*, March 4, 2012, http://articles.latimes .com/2012/mar/04/local/la-me-mirkarimi-trial-20120304, 1.

19. Heather Knight, "Why Domestic Abuse Victims Often Refuse to Leave," *SFGate*, January 19, 2012, http://www.sfgate.com/crime/article/Why -domestic-abuse-victims-often-refuse-to-leave-2613260.php.

20. Arthur Santana and Sylvia Moreno, "'Just Totally Senseless,'" *Washington Post*, February 10, 2000, http://www.washingtonpost .com/wp-srv/WPcap/2000-02/10/100r-021000-idx.html.

21. Bill Clinton, "The President's News Conference," February 16, 2000, http://bulk.resource.org/gpo.gov/papers/2000/2000_vol1_257.pdf.

22. "Two Promising Seniors—Gone," *Washington Post*, January 11, 2000. Article available for view at http://www.highbeam.com/ doc/1P2-508526.html.

23. Neely Tucker, "Defense in Wilson Case Alleges Web of Affairs; Jealousy Led to Killings, Attorneys Say," *Washington Post*, February 3, 2001.

24. Ibid.

25. William Shakespeare, *Romeo and Juliet*, act 3.

26. Neely Tucker and Petula Dvorak, "Guilty Verdicts in Killing of 2 Teens," *Washington Post*, February 24, 2001.

27. Santana and Moreno, "'Just Totally Senseless.'"

28. Arthur Santana, "4 Years in Wilson High Slayings; Judge Calls Couple's Killing After Brawl at D.C. School 'Senseless,'" *Washington Post*, June 30, 2001.

29. Christina Hoff Sommers, "The New Mythology," *National Review*, June 27, 1994.

30. Ibid.

31. Ken Ringle, "Debunking the 'Day of Dread' for Women," *Washington Post*, January 31, 1993.

32. Bob Hohler, "Super Bowl Gaffe," *Boston Globe*, February 2, 1993, 1.

33. PR Newswire, "NFL Must Tackle Super Bowl Abuse Myth," February 24, 2011, http://www.prnewswire.com/news-releases/ nfl-must-tackle-super-bowl-abuse-myth-115274079.html.

34. Ibid.

Chapter 8: Blaming Boys

1. Leonard Sax, *Boys Adrift: The Five Factors Driving the Growing*

Epidemic of Unmotivated Boys and Underachieving Young Men (New York: Basic Books, 2007), 24.

2. Tucker Max, *I Hope They Serve Beer in Hell* (New York: Citadel Press, 2009), 25.

3. Sax, *Boys Adrift*, 15–22.

4. Ibid., 204.

5. Ibid.

6. Missy Howard, *25 Years of Success in Student Achievement: Thanks for the Memories: 1987–2012* (Washington, D.C.: Best Friends Foundation, 2012), http://www.bestfriendsfoundation.org/images/2012BFFNews Lttr32pg.4.12.12.pdf, 9.

7. Ibid.

8. "Boy Scout Oath," US Scouting Service Project, http://www.usscouts .org/advance/boyscout/bsoath.asp.

9. Max, *I Hope They Serve Beer in Hell*, 104.

10. Michael Ellsberg, "Tucker Max Gives Up the Game: What Happens When a Bestselling Player Stops Playing?" *Forbes*, January 18, 2012, http://www.forbes.com/sites/michaelellsberg/2012/01/18/ tucker-max-gives-up-the-game/2/.

11. Sax, *Boys Adrift*, 84.

12. *Dumbo*, directed by Sam Armstrong, et al., (1941; Walt Disney Studios).

13. Sax, *Boys Adrift*, 85.

14. Montgomery County Public Libraries, "High School: MCPL Enjoyable Reads Summer 2011," http://www6.montgomerycountymd.gov/ content/libraries/summerreading/2011booklistHS.pdf.

15. The National Secular Society, http://www.secularism.org.uk.

16. Fantastic Fiction, "Misfit," http://www.fantasticfiction.co.uk/s/ jon-skovron/misfit.htm.

17. Website of Jon Skovron, http://www.jonskovron.com/books/misfit/.

18. Sax, *Boys Adrift*, 157.

19. Ibid., 63.

20. Max, *I Hope They Serve Beer in Hell*, 87.

21. Sax, *Boys Adrift*, 132.

22. Ben Shapiro, *Porn Generation: How Social Liberalism Is Corrupting Our Generation* (Washington, D.C.: Regnery Publishing, 2005), 162.

23. Sax, *Boys Adrift*, 132.

24. Ibid., 133.

25. Max, *I Hope They Serve Beer in Hell*, 158.

26. Kerry Cohen, *Loose Girl: A Memoir of Promiscuity* (New York: Hyperion, 2008), 102.

27. William Bennett, "Hookup Culture Debases Women," *CNN Opinion*, April 4, 2012, http://www.cnn.com/2012/04/04/opinion/bennett -modern-women/index.html.

28. Sax, *Boys Adrift*, 165.

29. The best source on this story is Bernard Lefkowitz, *Our Guys* (New York: Vintage Books, 1998).

30. Mary Pipher, *Reviving Ophelia: Saving the Selves of Adolescent Girls* (New York: Riverhead Books, 1994), 70.

31. Unless otherwise noted, all quotations from this interview are from "Last Interview with Ted Bundy, on the Influence of Violent Porn," *The Critical I*, August 14, 2011, http://eyeresist.wordpress.com/2011/08/14/ last-interview-with-ted-bundy-on-the-influence-of-violent-porn/.

32. Ted Bundy, as quoted in Victor B. Cline, PhD, "Pornography's Effects on Adults and Children," Catholic News Agency, http://www .catholicnewsagency.com/resources/life-and-family/pornography/ pornographys-effects-on-adults-and-children/.

33. Jerry Bergman, "Kinsey, Darwin and the Sexual Revolution," Creation.com, December 2006, http://creation.com/kinsey -darwin-and-the-sexual-revolution#txtRef7.

34. Robert H. Knight, "How Alfred C. Kinsey's Sex Studies Have Harmed Women and Children," Concerned Women for America, http://www.cwfa.org/images/content/kinsey-women_11_03.pdf.

35. Dr. Judith Reisman (website), "Playboy Lost to Reisman! Reisman Child Porn Study Defeats Playboy's Dutch Libel Suit," http://www .drjudithreisman.com/reisman_won_playboy_libel_suit.html.

36. Matt Barber, "Obama's HHS 'Grooming' Children for Sex," *WND Commentary*, October 26, 2012, http://www.wnd.com/2012/10/ obamas-hhs-grooming-children-for-sex/.

37. The comments by Judith A. Reisman were taken from an interview with the author.

38. Sax, *Boys Adrift*, 117.

39. Quotes for Tripp (Character) from *Failure to Launch* (2006), International Movie Database, http://www.imdb.com/character/ ch0016261/quotes.

40. Ibid.

41. Robin Marantz Henig, "What Is It About 20-Somethings?" *New York Times*, August 18, 2010, http://www.nytimes.com/2010/08/22/ magazine/22Adulthood-t.html?pagewanted=all.

42. Louis Uchitelle and David Leonhardt, "It's a Trend: Men with No Jobs or Ambition," *New York Times*, July 31, 2006, http://www

.nytimes.com/2006/07/31/world/americas/31iht-men.2342788
.html?pagewanted=all&_r=0.

43. Sax, *Boys Adrift*, 142.

44. Ibid.

Chapter 9: Why the Home Matters

1. *"The Wizard of Oz*—Movie Script," transcribed by Paul Rudoff and available for viewing at http://www.wendyswizardofoz.com/printablescript.htm. (Script copyright © 1939 Metro-Goldwyn-Meyer.)

2. Ibid.

3. Michael Oher with Don Yaeger, *I Beat the Odds: From Homelessness, to the Blind Side, and Beyond* (New York: Gotham Books, 2011), Nook ed., 102.

4. Ibid., 143.

5. Meg Meeker, *Your Kids at Risk: How Teen Sex Threatens Our Sons and Daughters* (Washington, D.C.: Regnery, 2007), 212.

6. Judith Wallerstein, Julia Lewis, and Sandra Blakeslee, *The Unexpected Legacy of Divorce: The 25 Year Landmark Study* (New York: Hyperion, 2000), 199–200.

7. As quoted in Cynthia Dailard, "Recent Findings from the 'Add Health' Survey: Teens and Sexual Activity," *The Guttmacher Report on Public Policy* 4, no. 4, August 2001, http://www.guttmacher.org/pubs/tgr/04/4/gr040401.pdf, 3.

8. Meeker, *Your Kids at Risk*, 202.

9. Dailard, "Recent Findings from the 'Add Health' Survey," 3.

10. Ibid.

11. Wanda Mallette, Bob Morrison and Patti Ryan, "Looking for Love," recorded by Johnny Lee in 1980 at Full Moon Records.

12. Clea McNeely and Jayne Blanchard, *The Teen Years Explained: A Guide to Healthy Adolescent Development* (Center for Adolescent Health at Johns Hopkins Bloomberg School of Public Health, 2009), http://www.jhsph.edu/sebin/s/e/Interactive%20Guide.pdf.

13. *Rebel Without a Cause*, directed by Nicholas Ray (1955; Warner Bros. Studios). Screenwriter Stewart Stern's script available at http://www.dailyscript.com/scripts/Rebel_Without_A_Cause.html.

14. Meeker, *Your Kids at Risk*, 205.

15. Ibid., 208.

16. McNeely and Blanchard, *The Teen Years Explained*, 24.

17. "Obesity: Nutrition and Exercise," *The Teen Years Explained*, http://www.jhsph.edu/research/centers-and-institutes/center-for

-adolescent-health/_includes/Obesity_Standalone.pdf, 3; McNeely and Blanchard, *The Teen Years Explained*, 19.

18. Gail Parent, *A Sign of the Eighties* (New York: Berkley Publishing Group, 1988), 30.

19. Marge Piercy Quotes, BrainyQuote, http://www.brainyquote.com/quotes/authors/m/marge_piercy.html.

20. Meeker, *Your Kids at Risk*, 203.

21. Ibid., 204–5.

22. Ibid., 205.

23. JoAnn Deak, *Girls Will Be Girls: Raising Confident and Courageous Daughters* (New York: Hyperion, 2002), 18.

24. Ibid., 31–32.

25. Ibid., 28.

26. McNeely and Blanchard, *The Teen Years Explained*, 25.

27. Mary Pipher, *Reviving Ophelia: Saving the Selves of Adolescent Girls*, Nook ed., (New York: Riverhead Books, 1994), 94.

28. Barbara Costikyan, quoted by Simran Khurana, "Mom Quotes: Mom's the Word," http://quotations.about.com/od/happymothersday/a/mom.htm.

29. Kerry Cohen, *Loose Girl: A Memoir of Promiscuity* (New York: Hyperion, 2008), 42.

30. Meeker, *Your Kids at Risk*, 211.

31. Margaret Thatcher Quotes, as quoted in John Blundell, *Margaret Thatcher: A Portrait of the Iron Lady* (New York: Algora, 2008), 25.

32. McNeely and Blanchard, *The Teen Years Explained*, 35.

33. Naeesa Aziz, "UVA Omega Psi Phi Under Investigation for Hazing: University Police Are Looking into an Alleged Hazing Incident That Left a Pledge with Fractured Ribs," BET.com, August 30, 2012, http://www.bet.com/news/national/2012/08/30/uva-omega-psi-phi-under-investigation-for-hazing.html.

34. Michael Ellsberg, "Tucker Max Gives Up the Game: What Happens When a Bestselling Player Stops Playing?" *Forbes*, January 18, 2012, http://www.forbes.com/sites/michaelellsberg/2012/01/18/tucker-max-gives-up-the-game/2/.

35. Ibid.

36. Diane Sawyer, as quoted in Ramesh Deonaraine, *The Book of Wisdom for Students* (Lincoln: Writers Club Press, 2002), 34.

37. Pipher, *Reviving Ophelia*, 85–88.

38. Ibid.

39. Ibid.

40. Meeker, *Your Kids at Risk*, 212.

41. Leonard Sax, *Girls on the Edge: The Four Factors Driving the New Crisis for Girls* (New York: Basic Books, 2010), 35.

42. Cynthia Dailard, "Recent Findings from the 'Add Health' Survey: Teens and Sexual Activity," *The Guttmacher Report on Public Policy* 4, no. 4, August 2001, http://www.guttmacher.org/pubs/tgr/04/4/gr040401.pdf, 3.

43. Meeker, *Your Kids at Risk*, 213.

44. Shirley MacLaine, as quoted in O Magazine Editors, *Words that Matter* (New York: HarperCollins, 2010), 36.

45. Dailard, "Recent Findings from the 'Add Health' Survey," 2.

46. Kathleen Kingsbury, "Pregnancy Boom at Gloucester High," *Time*, June 18, 2008, http://www.time.com/time/magazine/article/0,9171,1816486,00.html.

47. CDC Fact Sheet, "HIV-Related Risk Among U.S. High School Students: Trends from the National Youth Risk Behavior Survey since 1991" (Washington: US Department of Health and Human Services, Centers for Disease Control and Prevention, July 2012), http://www.cdc.gov/nchhstp/newsroom/docs/2012/YRBS-Fact-Sheet-072312-508.pdf, 2.

48. Ibid., 3.

49. Lena H. Sun, "More Black Teenagers Practicing Safe Sex," *Daily Herald*, July 30, 2012, http://www.dailyherald.com/article/20120730/entlife/707309971.

50. National Women's Health Network, "Securing Sexual & Reproductive Health and Autonomy," http://nwhn.org/securing-sexual-reproductive-health-and-autonomy.

51. Offered as an aside, from "2011 Class Day Remarks." For prepared text, see http://www.princeton.edu/main/news/archive/S30/67/81I02/index.xml.

52. Phil McGraw, "Monitor Your Child's Cell Phone and Internet Activity," www.drphil.com/articles/article/603.

53. Ibid.

Chapter 10: What Mothers and Sisters Can Do

1. JoAnn Deak, *Girls Will Be Girls: Raising Confident and Courageous Daughters* (New York: Hyperion, 2002), 62.

2. Julie Bosman, "Suddenly, Kids Only Have Eyes for e-books," *New York Times*, March 6, 2011.

3. Louisa May Alcott, *Little Women* (Rockville, MD: Serenity Publishers, 2009), 7.

4. Ibid., 71.

5. Ibid.

6. "What Parents Give Their Children," Parent Communication Network, http://www.sfpcn.org/Quotes%20Give.htm.

7. Helen Hayes, as quoted in Christy L. Dmetrakis, *Faith to Conquer Fear* (Bloomington: iUniverse, 2010), 79.

8. Alcott, *Little Women*, 255.

9. Ibid., 122.

10. Ibid., 222.

11. Ibid., 358.

12. Ibid., 397.

13. Ibid., 84.

14. Lynn Neary, "Jo March, Everyone's Favorite Little Woman," *NPR Books*, June 9, 2008, http://www.npr.org/templates/story/story .php?storyId=91245378.

15. *Studies in Women & Gender Spring 2012 Course Offering Booklet*, University of Virginia, www.virginia.edu/womenstudies/ . . . / SPRING2012.doc, 4–7.

16. Jane Austen, *Sense and Sensibility* (London: Richard Bentley, 1833), 4.

17. Ibid., 40.

18. Ibid., 287.

19. Ibid., 301.

Chapter 11: What Fathers and Brothers Can Do

1. All Chris Rock quotes in this chapter are from the HBO comedy special "Never Scared," aired July 4, 2009.

2. Leonard Sax, *Girls on the Edge: The Four Factors Driving the New Crisis for Girls* (New York: Basic Books, 2010), 22.

3. Michael Ellsberg, "Tucker Max Gives Up the Game: What Happens When a Bestselling Player Stops Playing?" *Forbes*, January 18, 2012, http://www.forbes.com/sites/michaelellsberg/2012/01/18/ tucker-max-gives-up-the-game/2/.

4. Meg Meeker, *Strong Fathers, Strong Daughters: 10 Secrets Every Father Should Know* (New York: Ballantine Books, 2007), 7.

5. Ibid., 23.

6. Ibid., 24.

7. Ibid., 77.

8. s.v. "humility," Thesaurus.com, http://thesaurus.com/browse/ humility?s=t.

9. Meeker, *Strong Fathers, Strong Daughers*, 77.

10. Ibid., 78.

11. Ibid., 83.

12. Louisa May Alcott, *Little Women* (Rockville, MD: Serenity Publishers, 2009), 186.

13. Kerry Cohen, *Loose Girl: A Memoir of Promiscuity* (New York: Hyperion, 2008), 62.

14. Ibid., 67.

15. Ibid.

16. Brenda Hunter, *From Santa to Sexting: Keeping Kids Safe, Strong, and Secure in Middle School* (Abilene, TX: Abilene Christian University Press, 2012), 239.

17. Cohen, *Loose Girl*, 27–28.

18. The dialogue that follows is taken from *The Sound of Music* (1965), *Database of Movie Dialogs*.

19. Michael Sliney, LC, and Matt Williams, "Tips for Men on How to Be Great Dads," *Regnum Christi*, June 21, 2009, http://www.legionariesofchrist.org/eng/articulos/articulo2.phtml?se=239&ca=651&te=475&id=26561&csearch=651&width=1600&height=1200&width=.

20. Meeker, *Strong Fathers, Strong Daughters*, 80.

21. *Thirteen*, directed by Catherine Hardwicke (20th Century Fox, 2003). The script is available for view at www.script-o-rama.com.

22. Cohen, *Loose Girl*, 78.

23. Meeker, *Strong Fathers, Strong Daughters*, 202.

24. Lane DeGregory, "One Teen Boy, Two Teen Girls, and Homicide," *Tampa Bay Times*, July 18, 2010, http://www.tampabay.com/features/humaninterest/article1109362.ece.

25. Emma Brown, "Joy Keo, Paralyzed After Being Shot by Boyfriend in 1982, Dies of Respiratory Illness at 45," *Washington Post*, December 15, 2010, http://www.washingtonpost.com/wp-dyn/content/article/2010/12/15/AR2010121506798.html?hpid=moreheadlines.

26. Ibid.

27. "Shut up, b——," William Beebe snarled at Liz Seccuro just before raping her.

28. Tucker Max, *I Hope They Serve Beer in Hell* (New York: Citadel Press, 2009), 273.

29. Mark Gado, "A Killing in Central Park: The Preppy Murder Case," *Crime Library*, upd. October 2007, http://www.trutv.com/library/crime/notorious_murders/not_guilty/park/4.html.

30. Cohen, *Loose Girl*, 61.

31. *Cosmopolitan*, November 2009.

32. Michael Roberts, "[Profane] Tweets and More Help CU Land Top 100 Recruit Yuri Wright," Denver *Westword*, January 26, 2012, http://blogs.westword.com/latestword/2012/01/yuri_wright_pussy_tweets_colorado_cu.php.

33. Associated Press, "Abuses Detailed in Colorado Football Program," *New York Times*, March 2, 2005, http://www.nytimes.com/2005/03/02/sports/ncaafootball/02colorado.html?_r=0.

34. Guy Andrews, *Lost in Austen* (television miniseries) (UK), directed by Dan Zeff; original run dates September 3–24, 2008.

35. Harper Lee, *To Kill a Mockingbird* (New York: HarperCollins, 2006), 152.

36. Meeker, *Strong Fathers, Strong Daughters*, 219.

37. Lee, *To Kill a Mockingbird*, 25.

38. Author interview; the subject's name has been changed to protect his identity.

Chapter 12: Why Healthy Relationships Matter

1. "Secrets of a Successful Marriage," *The Simpsons*, Season 5, first aired May 19, 1994.

2. Rachel Clark, "A Connection Between Parental Divorce and Death?" *Psychology Today*, May 5, 2011, http://www.psychologytoday.com/blog/marry-divorce-reconcile/201105/connection-between-parental-divorce-and-death.

3. "Children and Watching Television," "Facts for Families" (fact sheet of the American Academy of Child & Adolescent Psychiatry) no. 54: December 2011, http://www.aacap.org/cs/root/facts_for_families/children_and_watching_tv.

4. David McCullough, *Truman* (New York: Simon & Schuster, 1992), 179.

5. "End of a Love Story," *BBC News*, June 5, 2004, http://news.bbc.co.uk/2/hi/americas/265714.stm.

6. Emilie Raymond, *From My Cold, Dead Hands: Charlton Heston and American Politics* (Lexington: University of Kentucky Press, 2006), 12.

7. Quotes About the Marriage of Lydia and Charlton Heston, http://marriage.about.com/od/entertainmen1/a/charltonheston_2.htm.

8. *Complex Mag*, "Hey Ma: The 10 Hottest Celebrity Single Mothers," December 17, 2009, http://www.complex.com/girls/2009/12/hey-ma-the-10-hottest-celebrity-single-mothers.

9. William J. Bennett, *The Broken Hearth: Reversing the Moral Collapse of the American Family* (2001; repr., New York: Doubleday, 2003), 186.

10. George Eliot, *The Sad Fortunes of the Rev. Amos Barton* (New York: Harper & Brothers, Publishers, 1887), 79.

11. Bennett, *The Broken Hearth*, 186.

12. Ibid., 186–87.

13. Ibid., 187.

14. Ibid.

15. The Respect Life Office for the Archdiocese of New York nicely defines marriage as a "vocation" and a "great adventure," one in which the couple "will establish a new family, grow in love with each other, and encounter Christ."

16. General Social Survey, *The Phora*, June 4, 2009.

17. "God's Plan for a Joy-Filled Marriage," http://joyfilledmarriage.com.

18. Michael Reagan, *Twice Adopted: An Important Social Commentator Speaks to the Cultural Ailments Threatening America Today* (Nashville: Broadman & Holman Publishers, 2004), 44.

19. "Marriage and Divorce," Centers for Disease Control and Prevention, http://www.cdc.gov/nchs/fastats/divorce.htm.

20. Reagan, *Twice Adopted*, 37.

21. Kerry Cohen, *Loose Girl: A Memoir of Promiscuity* (New York: Hyperion, 2008), 7.

22. Ibid., 165, 95.

23. Ibid., 184, 158, 160.

24. Judith Wallerstein, Julia Lewis, and Sandra Blakeslee, *The Unexpected Legacy of Divorce: The 25 Year Landmark Study* (New York: Hyperion, 2000), 39–46.

25. Cohen, *Loose Girl*, 70.

26. David Popenoe, "Cohabitation, Marriage, and Child Wellbeing," *Society* 46, no. 5 (September 2009): 429–36.

27. "Live Longer and Prosper by Doing the Opposite of What You've Heard," *Neuroscience News*, March 11, 2011, http://neurosciencenews.com/live-longer-prosper-myths-longevity-research-ucr/.

28. National Center for Health Statistics, "Health, United States, 2008," Centers for Disease Control and Prevention, http://www.cdc.gov/nchs/data/hus/hus08.pdf.

29. Mike and Harriett McManus, *Living Together: Myths, Risks & Answers* (New York: Howard Books, 2008), 208.

30. Meg T. McDonnell, "The Marriage Gap in the Women's Vote," *Crisis Magazine*, December 3, 2012, http://www.crisismagazine.com/2012/the-marriage-gap-in-the-womens-vote.

31. Elayne Bennett, "Conflicted Messages," in *Rethinking Responsibility:*

Reflections on Sex and Accountability (Washington, D.C.: National Campaign to Prevent Teen and Unplanned Pregnancy, 2009), 4.

32. Ibid., 3.
33. Commonsense Media, "Media & Child and Adolescent Health: A Systematic Review," November 2008, http://ipsdweb.ipsd.org/ uploads/IPPC/CSM%20Media%20Health%20Report.pdf.
34. L. Brent Bozell, "TV's Contempt for Marriage," *Washington Post*, August 27, 2008.
35. Douglas Kirby, *Emerging Answers 2007: Research Findings on Programs to Reduce Teen Pregnancy and Sexually Transmitted Diseases* (Washington, DC: National Campaign to Prevent Teen and Unplanned Pregnancy, 2007), 12.

Chapter 13: What Schools Can Do

1. Associated Press, "Three Aruba Suspects Going to Prison," Fox News, June 18, 2005, http://www.foxnews.com/story/0,2933, 159970,00.html.
2. Bryan Burrough, "Missing White Female," *Vanity Fair*, January 2006, http://www.vanityfair.com/culture/features/2006/01/ natalee200601.
3. "Transcript: Holloway Chaperone Speaks Out," Fox News, February 24, 2006, http://www.foxnews.com/story/0,2933,186017,00.html.
4. Portola Middle School brochure, http://www.portolams.org/about_ us/brochure.jsp.
5. This video, viewable at http://www.youtube.com/watch?v=v3aB8Q PTGOg, is one of a number of YouTube videos about a "Portola Middle School." There are several schools with that name in California, and this is one of many disturbing videos. The most disturbing is "FIGHT!!! White Teacher vs Black Students," set in El Cerrito and viewable at http://www.youtube.com/watch?v=FFjDLcjBL8M.
6. Vincent Ianelli, "When Should Puberty Start?" March 26, 2005, http://pediatrics.about.com/cs/conditions/a/early_puberty.htm.
7. Mary Pipher, *Reviving Ophelia: Saving the Selves of Adolescent Girls* (New York: Riverhead Books, 1994), 11.
8. Student Assignment/Transportation Review, "Overview," Boston Public Schools, http://www.bostonpublicschools.org/zones.
9. Portola Middle School brochure, par. 2.
10. Portola Middle School Student Dress Code, http://www.portolams .org/about_us/dress_code.jsp.

11. President William Jefferson Clinton, State of the Union Address, January 23, 1996.
12. Google Groups Forum, School Uniforms and Sexism, https://groups.google.com/forum/?fromgroups#!topic/soc.feminism/Lp8v2lPzUzU.
13. Bret Stephens, "Attention graduates: Tone down your egos, shape up your minds," *Wall Street Journal*, May 7, 2012, http://online.wsj.com/article/SB10001424052702304451104577389750993890854.html.
14. Leonard Sax, *Girls on the Edge: The Four Factors Driving the New Crisis for Girls* (New York: Basic Books, 2010), 130.
15. Ibid., 134.
16. "Principal Forced Out over 9-Year-Old's 'Sexual Harassment' suspension," MSNBC.com, December 7, 2011, http://usnews.nbcnews.com/_news/2011/12/07/9277654-principal-forced-out-over-9-year-olds-sexual-harassment-suspension?lite.
17. Jake Jones, "Boston School Claims 7 Year Old's Self Defense Was 'Sexual Harassment'!" examiner.com, December 3, 2011, http://www.examiner.com/article/boston-school-claims-7-year-olds-self-defense-was-sexual-harassmentv.
18. JoAnn Deak, *Girls Will Be Girls: Raising Confident and Courageous Daughters* (New York: Hyperion, 2002), 88.
19. Padre Pio Academy, Philosophy of Education, http://www.padrepioacademy.org/philosophy/.
20. Katie Moisse, "New York City to Mandate Sex Education in Public Schools," ABC News, April 10, 2011, http://abcnews.go.com/Health/Wellness/york-city-mandate-sex-education-public-schools/story?id=14271854.
21. Claudia Wallis, "The Evolution Wars," *Time* magazine, August 7, 2005, http://www.time.com/time/magazine/article/0,9171,1090909,00.html.
22. Barbara Bradley Hagerty, "Lawsuit Challenges Abstinence Education Program," NPR, May 17, 2005, http://www.npr.org/2005/05/17/4654638/lawsuit-challenges-abstinence-education-program.
23. "Sex Education in Americ: An NPR/ Kaiser/Kennedy School Poll," NPR, February 24, 2004, http://www.npr.org/templates/story/story.php?storyId=1622610.
24. Susan Edelman, "Parent Furor at Bawdy Sex Ed," *New York Post*, October 22, 2011, http://www.nypost.com/p/news/local/parent_furor_at_bawdy_sex_ed_hdtJZVpYrFFtTZeVKMbGvN.

25. Miriam Grossman, *Unprotected: A Campus Psychiatrist Reveals How Political Correctness in Her Profession Endangers Every Student* (New York: Sentinel, 2007), xiv.

26. "Go Ask Alice," http://goaskalice.columbia.edu.

27. Grossman, *Unprotected*, xii.

28. Ibid., 10.

29. Brian Ray, "Homeschool Population Size and Growth," National Home Education Research Institute, December 23, 2008, http://www.nheri.org/research/nheri-news/us-homeschool-population-size-and-growth-comments.html.

30. "Home Schooling," *Education Week*, updated July 13, 2011, http://www.edweek.org/ew/issues/home-schooling/.

31. Missy Howard, *25 Years of Success in Student Achievement: Thanks for the Memories: 1987–2012* (Washington, D.C.: Best Friends Foundation, 2012), http://www.bestfriendsfoundation.org/images/2012BFFNewsLttr32pg.4.12.12.pdf, 9.

32. Ibid.

33. Mary McLeod Bethune, as quoted in Deborah F. Atwater, *African American Women's Rhetoric* (Lanham, MD: Lexington Books, 2009), 65.

34. Jack Cashill, *What's the Matter with California?* (New York: Simon & Schuster, 2007), 253–56.

35. Ibid., 256.

36. Ibid.

37. Ibid.

Chapter 14: What Universities Can Do

1. Tom Wolfe, *I Am Charlotte Simmons* (New York: Farrar, Straus, and Giroux, 2004), 127.

2. Miriam Grossman, *Unprotected: A Campus Psychiatrist Reveals How Political Correctness in Her Profession Endangers Every Student* (New York: Sentinel, 2007), 149.

3. Ibid., 26.

4. Mary Eberstadt, "Bacchanalia Unbound: The Toxic Forces of Sex, Alcohol, and Drugs in College Life," *First Things*, November 2010, www.firstthings.com/article/2010/10/bacchanalia-unbound.

5. Grossman, *Unprotected*, 26.

6. University of Virginia, "Sexual Harassment," http://www.sexualassault.virginia.edu/harassment_intro.htm.

7. "Frequently Asked Questions," Tucker Max's website, http://www.tuckermax.com/about/faq/.

8. University of Virginia, "Sexual Assault," sexualassault.virginia.edu/sa_intro.htm.

9. University of Virginia, "Your Legal Rights," http://www.sexualassault.virginia.edu/legal_rights.htm.

10. E. Fuller Torrey, OpEd in New York Post, April 23, 2007, Article accessed on http://www.treatmentadvocacycenter.org/resources/consequences-of-lack-of-treatment/violence/249-help-the-ill-before-they-kill.

11. Matt Apuzzo, "Gunman's Video Assaults Campus Again," Associated Press, April 19, 2007, http://www.washingtonpost.com/wp-dyn/content/article/2007/04/18/AR2007041800340.html.

12. The Trustees of Princeton University, "Sexual Misconduct," http://www.princeton.edu/diversity/policy/sexual-misconduct/. Princeton's full Sexual Misconduct Policy can be viewed at http://www.princeton.edu/pub/rrr/part1/#compSexualMisconduct, or by following the link on the previous page.

13. Davidson College, "Alcohol Policy," http://www3.davidson.edu/cms/x8897.xml.

14. Matt Zapotosky, "Using Live Video From Phones, U-Md. Plans to Offer Virtual Safety Escorts to Students," *Washington Post*, May 27, 2012, http://articles.washingtonpost.com/2012-05-27/local/35455572_1_mobile-phone-iphone-version-apps.

15. Grossman, *Unprotected*, xxii.

16. Ibid., 8.

17. Ibid., 91.

18. Ibid., 148.

19. Ibid., 146.

20. Ibid., 144.

21. Ibid., 150.

22. Richard Arum and Josipa Roksa, *Academically Adrift: Limited Learning on College Campuses* (Chicago: University of Chicago Press, 2011), 34.

23. Scott Jaschik, "Academically Adrift," *Inside Higher Ed*, January 18, 2011, http://www.insidehighered.com/news/2011/01/18/study_finds_large_numbers_of_college_students_don_t_learn_much.

24. Dom Starsia Lacrosse Camps, www.starsialax.com.

25. "Huguely Evidence Casts UVA Students in an Unattractive Light," Snook & Haughey, P.C., February 9, 2012, http://www.snookandhaughey.com/news/huguely-evidence-casts-uva-students-in-an-unattractive-light/.

26. Emily Friedman, "UVA Lacrosse Teams to Honor Yeardley Love at NCAA Tournament," *ABC Good Morning America*, May 11, 2010,

http://abcnews.go.com/GMA/university-virginia-lacrosse-teams
-honor-yeardley-love-ncaa/story?id=10609683.

27. William J. Bennett, *The Book of Man: Readings on the Path to Manhood* (Nashville: Thomas Nelson, 2011), 222–24.

28. Ibid., 116.

29. Alexandra Petri, "The Tragedy of George Huguely," *Washington Post*, February 22, 2012, http://www.washingtonpost.com/blogs/compost/post/the-tragedy-of-george-huguely/2012/02/15/gIQAwOQBUR_blog.html.

30. Wolfe, *I Am Charlotte Simmons*, 238, 237, 482.

31. Grossman, *Unprotected*, 145.

32. Michael Geer, "Penn State Falls into a Pit," Capitol Watch, July 12, 2012, http://thecapitolwatch.com/2012/07/penn-state-falls-into-a-pit/.

33. "High School Soccer Captain Makes Mission Trips to Haiti," WISTV.com, June 2, 2011, http://www.wistv.com/Global/story.asp?S=14700676.

34. Elizabeth Barrett Browning, "My Kate," stanza 4.

35. Gabriel Debenedetti, "The Nude Olympics: 10 Years After the Ban," *The Daily Princetonian*, November 10, 2009, http://www.dailyprincetonian.com/2009/11/10/24366/.

36. "Sexual Assualt and Relationship Violence Training and Education Task Force- SARVTAE," Campus Health Services, University of North Carolina, http://campushealth.unc.edu/ipv/sarvtae.html.

37. "HAVEN Training," Safe @ UNC, University of North Carolina, http://safe.unc.edu/get-involved/haven-training/.

38. "Safe Ride," Police Department of the University of Virginia, October 29, 2012, http://www.virginia.edu/uvapolice/saferide.html.

39. "Resources," Police Department of the University of Virginia, http://www.virginia.edu/uvapolice/resources.html.

40. John Garvey, "Why We're Going Back to Single-Sex Dorms," *Wall Street Journal*, Opinion, June 13, 2011, http://online.wsj.com/article/SB10001424052702304432304576369843592242356.html.

41. Ibid.

42. Ibid.

Chapter 15: What Peer Groups Can Do

1. Jet Song Lyrics from *West Side Story*, available for view at STlyrics.com, http://www.stlyrics.com/songs/w/westsidestory7630/jetsong273780.html.

2. Cynthia Dailard, "Recent Findings from the 'Add Health' Survey: Teens and Sexual Activity," *The Guttmacher Report on Public Policy*

4, no. 4, August 2001, http://www.guttmacher.org/pubs/tgr/04/4/gr040401.pdf, 3.

3. William Shakespeare, *Romeo and Juliet*, act 3, scene 1.

4. *West Side Story*, directed by Robert Wise and Jerome Robbins; produced by Robert Wise, 1961.

5. Melinda Henneberger, "Yeardley Love's Home Team," *Washington Post*, February 9, 2012, http://www.washingtonpost.com/blogs/she-the-people/post/yeardley-loves-home-team/2012/02/09/gIQAToWr2Q_blog.html.

6. Alexandra Petri, "The Tragedy of George Huguely," *Washington Post*, February 22, 2012, http://www.washingtonpost.com/blogs/compost/post/the-tragedy-of-george-huguely/2012/02/15/gIQAwOQBUR_blog.html.

7. Ibid.

8. "Let's Get Grounded," www.virginia.edu/getgrounded/about.html.

9. "Calendar of Events," Let's Get Grounded, http://www.virginia.edu/getgrounded/calendar.html.

10. "Step Up!" http://www.virginia.edu/getgrounded/stepup.html.

11. "Best Friends Foundation Student Abuse & Violence Protocol," in *Best Friends Diamond Girl Leadership Program Guide*, 4th ed. (Washington, D.C.: Best Friends Foundation, 2009), 10.56, http://www.bestfriendsfoundation.org/images/DGLProgramGuideHealthyRelationships.pdf.

12. Wanda Franz, "Adolescent Cognitive Abilities and Implications for Sexual Decision-Making," paper presented at the Annual Eastern Symposium on Building Family Strengths, University Park, PA, March 23–25, 1987.

13. Michael Oher with Don Yaeger, *I Beat the Odds: From Homelessness, to the Blind Side, and Beyond*, Nook ed. (New York: Gotham Books, 2011), 126. (See chap. 5, n. 16.)

14. Miriam Grossman, *Unprotected: A Campus Psychiatrist Reveals How Political Correctness in Her Profession Endangers Every Student* (New York: Sentinel, 2007), 32–33.

15. Clea McNeely and Jayne Blanchard, *The Teen Years Explained: A Guide to Healthy Adolescent Development* (Center for Adolescent Health at Johns Hopkins Bloomberg School of Public Health, 2009), http://www.jhsph.edu/sebin/s/e/Interactive%20Guide.pdf., 73.

16. Sharon Scales Rostosky et al., "Coital Debut: The Role of Religiosity and Sex Attitudes in the Add Health Survey," *Journal of Sex Research* 40, no. 4, (November 2003): 358–67.

17. Grossman, *Unprotected*, 34.
18. Ibid., 43. "Believing in God Is Good for You" is also the chapter's subtitle.
19. Ibid., 45.
20. "Scout Decision Appealed to U.S. Supreme Court," wnd.com, July 11, 2006, http://www.wnd.com/2006/07/36980/.
21. Nancy Gibbs, "The Gospel of *Glee*: Is It Anti-Christian?" *Time*, December 7, 2009, http://www.time.com/time/magazine/article/0,9171,1942957,00.html.
22. Mary Pipher, *Reviving Ophelia: Saving the Selves of Adolescent Girls* (New York: Riverhead Books, 1994), 66.
23. Gayle Trotter, "*GCB*: Good Christian Hypocrites," *Washington Post*, March 9, 2012, http://www.washingtonpost.com/blogs/guest-voices/post/gcb-good-christian-hypocrites/2012/03/09/gIQAuLP80R_blog.html.
24. Oher, *I Beat the Odds*, 154.
25. McNeely and Blanchard, *The Teen Years Explained*, 2–3.
26. Pipher, *Reviving Ophelia*, 28.
27. Ibid., 68.
28. Adam Taxin, "Mob of 50 Black Teenage Girls Attacks Police in Staten Island," examiner.com, December 7, 2011, http://www.examiner.com/article/mob-of-50-black-teenage-girls-attacks-police-staten-island.
29. Pipher, *Reviving Ophelia*, 68.
30. Craig Mackenzie, "Heartbreak for Family at Funeral of 15-Year-Old Who Killed Herself Because of Bullying—and Are Still Bombarded with Hate Messages on Facebook Tribute Page," *MailOnline*, January 7, 2012, http://www.dailymail.co.uk/news/article-2083504/Amanda-Cummings-suicide-Hate-messages-Facebook-tribute-page.html.
31. Ibid.
32. McNeely and Blanchard, *The Teen Years Explained*, 41.
33. Sax, *Girls on the Edge*, 137–40.
34. Patricia Neal, as quoted in Kevin Ryan and James Michael Cooper, *Those Who Can, Teach* (Boston: Houghton Mifflin, 2007), 161.
35. "TV Reporter Goes Back in Front of Cameras to Tell of Underage Drinking," msnbc.com, February 15, 2012, http://usnews.nbcnews.com/_news/2012/02/15/10419928-tv-reporter-goes-back-in-front-of-cameras-to-tell-of-underage-drinking?lite.
36. "Child Obesity," the Obesity Prevention Source, Harvard School of Public Health, 2012, http://www.hsph.harvard.edu/obesity-prevention-source/obesity-trends/global-obesity-trends-in-children/index.html.

37. Sarah O'Meara, "Obesity Leads to Early Puberty in Young Girls," *Huffpost Lifestyle*, June 15, 2012, http://www.huffingtonpost.co.uk/2012/06/15/health-obesity-speeds-up-puberty_n_1599284.html.

38. Tara Parker-Pope, "The Fat Trap," *New York Times*, December 28, 2011, http://www.nytimes.com/2012/01/01/magazine/tara-parker-pope-fat-trap.html?pagewanted=all.

39. Not her real name.

40. Mikael Elinder and Oscar Erixson, *Every Man for Himself: Gender, Norms and Survival in Maritime Disasters*, April 10, 2012, http://www.nek.uu.se/Pdf/wp20128.pdf.

41. As remembered by the author.

42. Oher, *I Beat the Odds*, 149.

43. *Stop the Silence. Prevent the Violence* (booklet of the Best Friends Dating Violence Seminar) (Washington, D.C.: Best Friends Foundation, 2011), http://www.bestfriendsfoundation.org/images/BFFDatingViolenceSeminarProgramFeb2011.pdf, ii, 17.

44. "20 Ways to Fight Peer Pressure" by Sharon Scott, taken from the *Best Friends Foundation 2008 Best Friends Program Guide*, "Friendship," 1.4–1.5.

Chapter 16: What the Rest of Us Can Do

1. "Obama's Father's Day Speech," CNN Politics, June 27, 2008, http://articles.cnn.com/2008-06-27/politics/obama.fathers.ay_1_foundation-black-children-rock/2?_s=PM:POLITICS.

2. Jesse Washington, "Blacks Struggle with 72 Percent Unwed Mothers Rate," NBCNews.com, November 7, 2010, http://www.msnbc.msn.com/id/39993685/ns/health-womens_health/t/blacks-struggle-percent-unwed-mothers-rate/.

3. Patrick McCain, "Jesse Jackson Obama Comments (Video)" RightPundits.com, July 11, 2008, http://www.rightpundits.com/?p=1704. (See embedded video to hear the comments.)

4. Ebony Jones, "Jesse Jackson Attempts to Grab Obama with His Crab Claw," Urbanswirl.com, July 9, 2008, http://www.urbanswirl.com/news/politics/884-jesse-jackson-attempts-to-grab-obama-with-his-crab-claw.html.

5. "Obama Accepts Jesse Jackson's Apology," NBCNews.com, July 10, 2008, http://www.msnbc.msn.com/id/25611808/ns/politics-decision_08/t/obama-accepts-jesse-jacksons-apology/.

6. Karen Herzog, "Milwaukee's Teen Birthrate Plunges for Second Straight Year," *Journal Sentinel* (Milwaukee), October 12, 2011, http://

www.jsonline.com/features/health/milwaukees-teen-birthrate
-plunges-for-second-straight-year-131566918.html.

7. Dan Quayle, "Address to the Commonwealth Club of California,"
   May 19, 1992, http://www.vicepresidentdanquayle.com/speeches_
   StandingFirm_CCC_1.html.

8. "Dan Quayle v. Murphy Brown—1992," Clinton Accused Special
   Report, *Washington Post*, 1998, http://www.washingtonpost.com/
   wp-srv/politics/special/clinton/frenzy/quayle2.htm.

9. Barbara DaFoe Whitehead, "Dan Quayle Was Right," *Atlantic*, April
   1993, http://www.theatlantic.com/magazine/archive/1993/04/
   dan-quayle-was-right/307015/.

10. Jim McKairnes, "Was Dan Quayle (gasp!) Right?" *USA Today*, May 17,
    2010, http://usatoday30.usatoday.com/news/opinion/forum/
    2010-05-18-column18_ST_N.htm.

11. Isabel Sawhill, "20 Years Later, it Turns Out Dan Quayle Was Right
    about Murphy Brown and Unmarried Moms," *Washington Post*,
    May 25, 2012, http://articles.washingtonpost.com/2012-05-25/
    opinions/35457123_1_father-moves-marriage-biological-parents.

12. Prince, "Darling Nikki," *Purple Rain* (Warner Bros., 1984).

13. Melanie Falina, "Still Hungry but Not Dangerous: An Interview with
    Dee Snider of Twisted Sister," examiner.com, June 29, 2009, http://
    www.examiner.com/article/still-hungry-but-not-dangerous-an
    -interview-with-dee-snider-of-twisted-sister.

14. Kelvin McSnoogin, "The Wicked Witch Is Dead: C. Delores Tucker
    Passes," RapMusic.com, October 13, 2005, http://board.rapmusic.
    com/hip-hop-central/936027-wicked-witch-dead-c-delores-tucker
    -passes.html.

15. Bryan Reesman, "25 Years After Tipper Gore's PMRC Hearings, the
    Opposing Sides Aren't So Far Apart," Vulture.com, September 20,
    2010, http://www.vulture.com/2010/09/pmrc_25_anniversary.html.

16. Ibid.

17. "R&B/ Hip-Hop Songs," Billboard.com, March 24, 2012, http://www.
    billboard.com/charts/r-b-hip-hop-songs?chartDate=2012-03-24#/
    charts/r-b-hip-hop-songs?chartDate=2012-03-24.

18. Chris Brown, "Strip," *Fortune* (RCA Records, 2011).

19. "Spelman College Swipes Back at Nelly Video," Associated
    Press, April 24, 2004, http://www.sptimes.com/2004/04/24/
    Worldandnation/Spelman_College_swipe.shtml.

20. "Girl Scouts," Snopes.com, February 23, 2012, http://www.snopes
    .com/politics/sexuality/girlscouts.asp.

21. Jason Pierce, "Conservative Alternative to Girl Scouts Builds Membership," CNSNews.com, May 4, 2002, http://archive.newsmax .com/archives/articles/2002/5/3/202745.shtml.

22. "Whitney Houston: Family Told She Died from Rx Not Drowning," *TMZ*, February 13, 2012, http://www.tmz.com/2012/02/13/whitney -houston-cause-of-death-prescription-drugs-drowning-atlanta/.

23. "Britney Spears Files for Divorce".

24. "Inside Britney's Shaved Head".

25. "Spears will lose custody of chilcren".

26. Britney's bizarre behavior led her to being place under the control of a "conservator".

27. Trevor Tierney, "Huguely Trial Shows It's Time For Lacrosse to Grow Up," *Inside Lacrosse*, February 24, 2012, http://insidelacrosse.com/news/2012/02/24/ trevor-tierney-huguely-trial-shows-its-time-lacrosse-grow.

28. Mary Pipher, *Reviving Ophelia: Saving the Selves of Adolescent Girls* (New York: Riverhead Books, 1994), 44.

29. Michael Oher with Don Yaeger, *I Beat the Odds: From Homelessness, to the Blind Side, and Beyond*, Nook ed. (New York: Gotham Books, 2011), 165.

30. "Viral Internet story says Mitt Romney helped locate missing teen daughter of Bain Capital partner," Politifact.com, http://www .politifact.com/truth-o-meter/statements/2012/jan/30/chain-email/ viral-internet-story-says-mitt-romney-helped-locat/.

31. "Associate Attorney General Tom Perrelli Speaks at the Department of Education's Bullying Summit," US Department of Justice, August 12, 2010, http://www.justice.gov/asg/speeches/2010/asg-speech-100812.html.

32. "Local Search Intensifies as Morgan Harrington's Remains Are Found," *C-Ville Weekly*, February 2, 2010, http://www.c-ville.com/ Local_search_intensifies_as_Morgan_Harringtons_remains_are_ found_with_video/#.UP3xRWeS-So.

Chapter 17: What an Aware Young Woman Should Know

1. Adapted from *Best Friends Program Guide* (Washington DC: Best Friends Foundation), messages provided at the beginning of curriculum units, Topics 1–8.

2. Pearl Bailey, as quoted in Ashton Applewhite, *And I Quote, Revised Edition* (New York: Thomas Dunne Books, 2003), 114.

3. Jennifer Marshall, *Now and Not Yet: Making Sense of Single Life in the Twenty-First Century* (Colorado Springs: Multnomah Books, 2007), 79.

4. Elizabeth Kantor, *The Jane Austen Guide to Happily Ever After* (Washington: Regnery, 2011), 128, 24, 23, 160, 24 respectively.

5. Laura Sessions Stepp, *Unhooked: How Young Women Pursue Sex, Delay Love and Lose at Both* (New York: Riverhead Books, 2007), 261.

6. Eleanor Roosevelt, as quoted in Lucile Davis, *Eleanor Roosevelt* (Mankato: Capstone, 1998), 22. Tumblr, http://www.tumblr.com/tagged/eleanor+roosevelt.

7. Carol Platt Liebau, *Prude: How the Sex-Obsessed Culture Damages Girls* (New York: Hachette Book Group, 2007), 8.

8. Ibid.

9. Thomas Lickona and Matthew Davidson, *Smart & Good High Schools: Integrating Excellence and Ethics for Success in School, Work, and Beyond (A Report to the Nation)* (Cortland, NY: Center for the 4th and 5th Rs, 2005), 168.

10. Liebau, *Prude*.

11. *True Grit*, directed by Joel and Ethan Coen (Paramount Pictures, 2010). Script available for viewing at www.imsdb.com/scripts.

12. Elisha A. Hoffman (words), Anthony J. Showalter (music), "Leaning on the Everlasting Arms," (Dalton, Georgia: A.J. Showalter Company, 1887). Tune and lyrics available at http://www.cyberhymnal.org/htm/l/o/lotearms.htm.

13. All *Winter's Bone* quotes are from Daniel Woodrell, *Winter's Bone* (New York: Hachette Book Group, 2006).

14. Holly Saylor, Best Friends program material.

15. Unless otherwise specified, Holcomb information comes from March 2012 interviews with Julia and her husband, Brad Misley, as well as Kevin Burke's "Mother of Aerosmith Singer Steven Tyler's Aborted Baby Now Pro-Life," *LifeNews.com*, May 24, 2011, http://www.lifenews.com/2011/05/24/mother-of-aerosmith-singer-steven-tylers-aborted-baby-speaks-out/.

16. Steven Tyler with David Dalton, *Does the Noise in My Head Bother You?* (New York: Harper Collins, Nook version, 2011), 141.

17. Burke, "Mother of Aerosmith Singer Steven Tyler's Aborted Baby Now Pro-Life."

18. Stephen Davis, *Walk This Way: The Autobiography of Aerosmith* (New York: HarperCollins, 2009), 275.

19. Ibid.

20. Burke, "Mother of Aerosmith Singer Steven Tyler's Aborted Baby Now Pro-Life."

21. Michael Oher with Don Yaeger, *I Beat the Odds: From Homelessness, to the Blind Side, and Beyond*, Nook ed. (New York: Gotham Books, 2011), 110.

22. Ibid.

23. *Chariots of Fire*, directed by Hugh Hudson (1981; Burbank, CA: Warner Home Video, 1982), VHS.

24. Best Friends program material.

25. Ibid.

26. Hellen Keller, *The Story of My Life*, James Berger, ed. (New York: Modern Library, 2004), 111.

27. Tatum O'Neal, *A Paper Life* (New York: Harper Collins, 2004), 8.

Chapter 18: What Lies Ahead for Our Daughters

1. Katharine Hepburn, as quoted in James Robert Parish, *Katharine Hepburn: The Untold Story* (Advocate, 2005), 18.

Acknowledgments

I would like to acknowledge my husband Bill for his loving encouragement and sound advice, and our young adult sons, John and Joseph, for reading sensitive parts of this book and allowing me to write the truth even though it would be easier on them if I did not. They also advised me on what was better left unsaid. I am confident they will always be the kind of men who care for and protect the women in their lives.

I especially want to thank Craig Wiley for thinking I had something to offer and presenting a book proposal to Joel Miller at Thomas Nelson. I am very grateful to Joel that he believed I should and could do this book.

I also want to thank Jack Cashill for his excellent research and editing skills and for his personal commitment to protecting young women. Without his belief in my work, I may not have completed this book.

My appreciation goes to Martha Kendrick Kettmer for her careful reading of the manuscript and her wise, well-written edits and exemplary legal skills. She is not only a true professional, but she is a loving mother with a deep commitment to giving back to her community and church.

There are several men and women who read long and complex drafts of this book and still encouraged me to publish. Their support was greatly needed and appreciated. They include Dorothy Glover, my ninety-three years young mother, Rosemarie Peterkin , the essential program director in Newark, Liz Seccuro, Kay Weed Cheetham, Ginnie White, Pam Howar, Daina Mahar, Marty Devine, Ann Hingston, and Gayle Trotter.

Thomas Lickona, Bill Sbarra, and Father Michael Sliney, the good men who all read the entire draft, no small feat in itself, offered a valuable perspective to the manuscript.

Credit is also due to Annie Goldsmith and Pauline Hamlette who worked to make certain I did finally write this book and tell the story of Best Friends and its success. This success was largely due to Pauline Hamlette and certain other staff members throughout the years. These include Elliott Glover, my brother, Roberta Freer, Ann Hingston, Monte Monash, Rita Burns, Lori Williams, Robin Williams—one of the original Best Friends, Diamond Girls, and College Council members—Lesley Long, who shared that distinction as did Maria Bennett. I would also like to thank Grace Chen who graciously worked as a volunteer when our funds were depleted.

I would like to acknowledge the men who believed in the Best Men program and all the Best Men boys who will grow up to become men worthy of respect. Besides my husband Bill, the men who stepped up were George Sanker, Jon Carter, David Gill, Danny Flynn, Valentine Davies, Jimmy Kemp, Jeff Jones, and Tim Overcash.

In addition, there are those who came through with vital financial support for the Best Friends Foundation through thick and thin for many years, Diana Davis Spencer, Abby Moffett, Bill O'Reilly, Tom and Mary Firth, Marlene and Fred Malek, Mel and Suellen Estrin, and Angie and John Marriott.

I am forever grateful to Alma and Colin Powell for their early essential support and belief in the Best Friends and Best Men model for schools. Thanks, too, to Barbara Bush who encouraged me to keep pushing Best Friends early on and who presented heart pins to more than 500 Best Friends girls over several years.

Allow me also to express gratitude to the inspirational women in my life, some of whom have been my friends for many years. I wish to thank Joanne Kemp, Nancy Campbell, Ann Chalk, Cheri Murphy, Vicki Campbell, Pam Howar, Ceil Malphrus, and Janet Phillips. I also want to thank Noreen Burns for her perfectly timed assistance.

There are mothers of daughters from whose example I drew strength and confidence in proceeding with this book to help young women. These include Milah Lynn, Gina Rice, Cindi Henderson, Nonie Williams, Liz Seccuro and my sister Diane who embodies the best of a mother's love to her daughter Carson.

Also Ana Ramirez whose help made it possible for me to write this book and her daughter, my goddaughter Nathalie, whom I adore. And Stephanie Hale and her daughter, Kelsey. Ginnie White and her daughter Alison, Nancy Campbell and her daughter Lauren, Cheri Murphy and her daughters Bridget and Chatigny, Ann Chalk and her daughter Logan and granddaughter Harper.

And Nancy Glover the mother of my nieces Molly and Lily. And especially Vicki Gove who shared the memory of her daughter, the lovely Bridgette Gove.

Also to those who talked to me with helpful personal information and wish to remain unnamed.

And finally, to those daughters who left the world too soon; may their stories help other young women and their memories inspire us to action.

Index

Nagai, Althea, xvii
National Abortion Rights Action
League (NARAL), xviii
National Campaign to Prevent Teen and
Unplanned Pregnancy, xviii, xix, 158
National Center on Addiction and
Substance Abuse (CASA), 16
National Domestic Violence Hotline,
142, 262–263
National Healthy Marriage Resource
Center, 157
National Institutes of Health (NIH), xi
National Organization for Women
(NOW), xviii
National Survey of Family Growth, xix
National Teen Dating Abuse Helpline,
262
National Women's Health Network,
112–113
Nelson, Jill, 69
New York Times, 93
nihilism, 264n2
nonconformance to standards,
punishment for, 207
North Carolina, criminal justice
system, 22
Now and Not Yet (Marshall), 31
nuclear family, 58
nurturing environment, 168–169

O
Obama, Barack, 219
    Dreams from My Father, 145
Obama administration, xvii, 41
obesity, 210
The Odyssey, 95
Oher, Michael, 96, 199, 204, 214,
251–252
    adoptive parents, 235
    I Beat the Odds, 57
O'Neal, Tatum, A Paper Life, 254–255
oral contraceptives, 159. See also
contraceptives
O'Reilly, Bill, 55–56

organized charity, Sanger on, 34
The Other Side of Silence (Carter), 230
others, learning from, 254–255
overseas travel, dangers of, 162
Owen, Karen, 17–18, 44

P
Pakistan, 68
Palin, Sarah, 39–40
Palin, Willow, 40
A Paper Life (O'Neal), 254–255
parents. *See also* fathers; mothers
    changes in, 169
    decisions, xi
    as examples for teens, 97
    men living with, 92–94
    preparing for middle school,
    165–166
    role in sex education, 171, 172
Parents Music Resource Center
(PMRC), 223
parochial schools, 164–165
Parvez, Aqsa, 66
Paterno, Joe, 187
patriarchal authority, 119
Paul VI (pope), *Humanae Vitae*, 46
peer groups, 194–218
    creating positive, 204
    daughters roles in, 199–200
    decision making, 199
    emphasizing responsibility,
    211–212
    intervention by, 195–196
    resisting oppressors, 202–204
    search for working, 204–207
peer pressure, 113
Penn State University, 190
Perfect Chemistry (Elkeles), 84
Perot, Dan, 188
perseverance, 247
Peterkin, RoseMarie, 175
Petri, Alexandra, 7–8, 28, 190
Phillips, Mackenzie, *High on Arrival*,
254

About the Author

Elayne Bennett developed the Best Friends program in 1987, and due to the overwhelming demand for a boys' program, she launched Best Men in 2000. She earned her BA and MEd from the University of North Carolina at Chapel Hill. Mrs. Bennett serves as the president and founder of the Best Friends Foundation. In addition to teaching the Foundation's youth development curriculum and training educators throughout the country, Mrs. Bennett serves as a spokeswoman on issues of adolescent behavior and development.

Mrs. Bennett was honored with the prestigious Jefferson Award for National Public Service, the John Carroll Society Award, the William E. Simon Foundation Award for Social Entrepreneurship, and the St. Elizabeth Ann Seton Award. She is a member of the Ethics, Religion, and Public Policy task force of the National Campaign to Prevent Teen Pregnancy. She is the wife of William J. Bennett and the mother of two sons.